Java 9 High Performan __

Practical techniques and best practices for optimizing Java applications through concurrency, reactive programming, and more

Mayur Ramgir
Nick Samoylov

BIRMINGHAM - MUMBAI

Java 9 High Performance

First published: November 2017

Production reference: 1251017

Published by Packt Publishing Ltd.
Livery Place
35 Livery Street
Birmingham
B3 2PB, UK.

ISBN 978-1-78712-078-5

www.packtpub.com

Credits

Authors
Mayur Ramgir
Nick Samoylov

Copy Editors
Pranjali Chury
Karuna Narayanan
Laxmi Subramanian

Reviewer
Aristides Villarreal Bravo

Project Coordinator
Vaidehi Sawant

Commissioning Editor
Kunal Parikh

Proofreader
Safis Editing

Acquisition Editor
Denim Pinto

Indexer
Francy Puthiry

Content Development Editor
Rohit Kumar Singh

Graphics
Jason Monteiro

Technical Editor
Ruvika Rao

Production Coordinator
Shraddha Falebhai

About the Authors

Mayur Ramgir has more than 16 years of experience in the software industry, working at various levels. He is a Sun Certified Java Programmer and Oracle Certified SQL Database Expert. He completed an MS in computational science and engineering at Georgia Tech, USA (rank 7th in the world for computer science), and an M.Sc. in multimedia application and virtual environments at University of Sussex, UK. He has also attended various universities for other degrees and courses, such as MIT for applied software security, and University of Oxford for system and software security.

He is the CEO of a software company, Zonopact, Inc. headquartered in Boston, USA, which specializes in bringing innovative applications based on AI, robotics, big data, and more. He has single-handedly developed Zonopact's flagship product, Clintra (B2B-integrated AI-assisted business management software). He is also the inventor of two patent pending technologies, ZPOD (an automated cloud-based medical kiosk system) and ZPIC (an AI-enabled robotic in-car camera system). Apart from this, he is also a prolific business writer who has authored two international award-winning books, *Unbarred Innovation: A Pathway to Greatest Discoveries* and *Evolve Like a Butterfly: A Metamorphic Approach to Leadership*.

He was featured on the TV and in print media, including Fox News, NBC News, CBS News, Fox Business, Bloomberg International TV, Forbes, Inc. magazine, Daily Mirror, and The Huffington Post. He is also a contributing author of New York Daily Newspaper, the Software Development Times magazine, Newsmax Finance, AlleyWatch, Singapore's top entrepreneurship magazine *Young Upstarts*, and several more. He is frequently invited as a guest lecturer at various technical and management schools. He has also been invited as a judge at an international innovation challenge competition (Living Talent) in Dubai in December 2017.

Nick Samoylov was born in Moscow, raised in Ukraine, and lived in the Crimea. He graduated as an engineer-physicist from Moscow Institute of Physics and Technologies and has even worked as a theoretical physicist. He has learned programming as a tool for testing his mathematical models using FORTRAN and C++.

After the demise of the USSR, Nick created and successfully ran a software company, but was forced to close it under the pressure of governmental and criminal rackets. In 1999, with his wife, Luda, and two daughters, he emigrated to the USA and has been living in Colorado since then.

Nick adopted Java in 1997 and used it for his work as a software developer-contractor for a variety of companies, including BEA Systems, Warner Telecom, and Boeing. For Boeing, he and his wife, also a Java programmer, developed a system to load application data to an airplane via the internet.

Nick's current projects are related to machine learning and developing a highly scalable system of microservices using non-blocking reactive technologies, including Vert.x, RxJava, and RESTful webservices on Linux deployed in a cloud.

Nick and Luda have two daughters who graduated from Harvard and Tufts universities, respectively. One of their daughters has also received a doctoral degree from Brown University and now works as a professor in the University of California in Chico. Their other daughter is an executive director of the investment bank JPMorgan, in Madrid, Spain.

In his free time, Nick likes to read (mostly non-fiction), write (fiction novels and blogs), and hike the Rocky Mountains.

About the Reviewer

Aristides Villarreal Bravo is a Java developer, a member of the NetBeans Dream Team, Java User Groups, and a developer of the jMoordb framework. He lives in Panamá. He has organized and participated in various conferences and seminars related to Java JavaEE, NetBeans, NetBeans Platform, free software, and mobile devices, nationally and internationally. He is a CEO of Javscaz Software Developers.

He has done the technical reviews of the books, *Primefaces BluePrints*; *Apache Hive CookBook*; *Dart By Example*; *ExpressJS BluePrints*; *Java 9 CookBook*; *Angular UI Development with PrimeNG*; *Java EE Development with Eclipse, Second Edition*; *Mastering Google App Engine*; and *PrimeFaces Cookbook, Second Edition*; all published by Packt.

Thanks to Llelat for believing in dreams.

www.PacktPub.com

For support files and downloads related to your book, please visit www.PacktPub.com.

Did you know that Packt offers eBook versions of every book published, with PDF and ePub files available? You can upgrade to the eBook version at www.PacktPub.com and as a print book customer, you are entitled to a discount on the eBook copy. Get in touch with us at service@packtpub.com for more details.

At www.PacktPub.com, you can also read a collection of free technical articles, sign up for a range of free newsletters and receive exclusive discounts and offers on Packt books and eBooks.

https://www.packtpub.com/mapt

Get the most in-demand software skills with Mapt. Mapt gives you full access to all Packt books and video courses, as well as industry-leading tools to help you plan your personal development and advance your career.

Why subscribe?

- Fully searchable across every book published by Packt
- Copy and paste, print, and bookmark content
- On demand and accessible via a web browser

Customer Feedback

Thanks for purchasing this Packt book. At Packt, quality is at the heart of our editorial process. To help us improve, please leave us an honest review on this book's Amazon page at `https://www.amazon.com/dp/1787120783`.

If you'd like to join our team of regular reviewers, you can e-mail us at `customerreviews@packtpub.com`. We award our regular reviewers with free eBooks and videos in exchange for their valuable feedback. Help us be relentless in improving our products!

Table of Contents

Preface

With JDK 8 and JDK 9 enhancements, Java confirmed again its status among the major programming languages that address the issues faced by software developers working on the cutting edge of the industry. Streams, parallel and asynchronous processing, multithreading, JSON support, reactive programming, and microservices comprise the hallmark of modern programming and are now fully integrated into the JDK and described in this book too, along with a toolbox full of developer tools that help to create, test, and monitor highly loaded and easily distributed applications deployable in any environment, whether a private network or a cloud.

All the topics and their discussions are illustrated by well-thought-through examples, which can also be downloaded from the dedicated website. The step-by-step guide allows you to progress naturally from the introduction to the more complex solutions encountered by the authors in real life.

What this book covers

Chapter 1, *Learning Java 9's Underlying Performance Improvements*, highlights various performance improvements in Java 9. It focuses on modular development and its impact on an application's performance. The later part of chapter looks at the advancement in concurrency and various underlying compiler improvements, such as tiered attribution and **Ahead-of-Time** (**AOT**) compilation, security manager improvements, and enhancements in graphics rasterizers.

Chapter 2, *Identifying Performance Bottlenecks*, focuses on JVM, operating systems, and network infrastructures to try to understand performance bottlenecks. Later in the chapter, we will explore various strategies that we can implement to optimize our code for these infrastructures. We will look at CPU infrastructure, I/O operations, database operations, network utilization, and memory utilization.

Chapter 3, *Learning How to Troubleshoot Code*, explores various techniques to troubleshoot your code to identify the root causes of bugs. Troubleshooting involves identifying the problem and gathering as much information as possible to accurately decide what action will help resolve the issue.

Chapter 4, *Learning How to Use Profiling Tools*, explains the importance of using various profiling tools and how to use them to improve code quality. You will learn about various advantages and disadvantages of using a profiling tool. Then, you will learn about various profiling tools.

Chapter 5, *Understanding Garbage Collection and Making Use of It*, explains what a garbage collector is, its features, and its benefits and demerits. Later, we will explore various garbage collection methods, such as escape analysis and reference counting. We will also see various disadvantages of reference counting, such as space reduction, cycles, and atomic tasks. Then, we will cover Parallel GC and parallelism. At the end, we will focus on new G1 collector and its impact and compare the G1 collector and Parallel GC.

Chapter 6, *Optimizing Code with Microbenchmarking*, discusses the concept of microbenchmarking. It describes its benefits and presence in Java. This is followed up by a detailed discussion of the **Java Microbenchmark Harness** (**JMH**) toolkit. This excellent solution provides the Java community with everything that they need to improve their microbenchmarking in the new, JDK 9.

Chapter 7, *Speeding Up JSON Generation*, sheds light on the JSON generation controls that are available in the new package and discusses how JSON allows Java community members to create RESTful APIs. We will present various elements of the Java.util package, which include creating events, input and output streams, value trees, and JSON generators.

Chapter 8, *Tools for Higher Productivity and Faster Application*, introduces two new tools added in Java 9--JShell and **Ahead-of-Time** (**AOT**) compiler--which were expected for a long time. JShell helps increase the developer's productivity, while AOT improves an application's performance.

Chapter 9, *Multithreading and Reactive Programming*, describes another approach to support the high performance of an application by programmatically splitting the task between several workers and increasing the throughput using asynchronous programming, bringing all the discussion to the focal point of reactive programming as the most effective and resilient modern processing model.

Chapter 10, *Microservices*, describes the solution many leaders of the industry have adopted while addressing flexible scaling under the load. The building of microservices that comprise a reactive system is discussed and illustrated by step-by-step examples, including a discussion on three possible deployment models--container less, self-contained, and in-container.

Chapter 11, *Making Use of New APIs to Improve Your Code*, describes improvements in the programming tools, including stream filters, a stack-walking API, the new convenient static factory methods for creating immutable collections, a new powerful CompletableFuture class in support of asynchronous processing, and the JDK 9 stream API improvements.

What you need for this book

To run the code examples, you will need a computer with at least 2 GB RAM, 10 GB free disk space, and Windows or Linux OS. The following software/libraries are required:

- JDK 9 (for all chapters)
- javassist.jar (for Chapter 2, *Identifying Performance Bottlenecks*)
- log4j-core-2.9.1.jar (for Chapter 3, *Learning How to Troubleshoot Code*)
- commons-collections4-4.1.jar, commons-io-2.5.jar, jackson-annotations-2.9.2.jar, jackson-core-2.9.2.jar, jackson-databind-2.9.2.jar, javax.json-1.1.jar, poi-3.17.jar, poi-excelant-3.17.jar, poi-ooxml-3.17.jar, poi-ooxml-schemas-3.17.jar, xmlbeans-2.6.0.jar (for Chapter 7, *Speeding up JSON generation*)
- The rxjava-math-1.0.0.jar and rxjava2-interop-0.10.0.jar files (for Chapter 9, *Multithreading and Reactive Programming*)
- The vertx-core-3.4.1.jar, vertx-web-3.4.1.jar, vertx-rx-java-3.4.1.jar, and vertx-jdbc-client-3.4.1.jar files (for Chapter 10, *Microservices*)
- The commons-lang -2.6.jar file (for Chapter 11, *Making Use of New APIs to Improve Your Code*)

Who this book is for

This book will appeal to Java developers who would like to build reliable and high-performance applications. Prior Java programming knowledge is assumed.

Conventions

In this book, you will find a number of text styles that distinguish between different kinds of information. Here are some examples of these styles and an explanation of their meaning.

Code words in text, database table names, folder names, filenames, file extensions, pathnames, dummy URLs, user input, and Twitter handles are shown as follows: "This place is used for storing all the objects created by using the new operator."

A block of code is set as follows:

```
private static Long counter = 0l;
public HeapAndStack() {
    ++counter;
}
```

When we wish to draw your attention to a particular part of a code block, the relevant lines or items are set in bold:

```
senators.stream()
  .filter(s -> s.getParty() == "Party1" &&
                        s.getVoteYes()[3] == 1)
  .findFirst()
  .ifPresent(s -> System.out.println("First senator "
        "of Party1 found who voted Yes on issue 3: "
                        + s.getName())));
```

Any command-line input or output is written as follows:

```
java -server -verbose:gc -XX:+DoEscapeAnalysis EscapeAnalysisTest
```

New terms and important words are shown in bold. Words that you see on the screen, for example, in menus or dialog boxes, appear in the text like this: "Clicking the **Next** button moves you to the next screen."

Warnings or important notes appear in a box like this:

Tips and tricks appear like this.

Customer support

Now that you are the proud owner of a Packt book, we have a number of things to help you to get the most from your purchase.

Downloading the example code

You can download the example code files for this book from your account at http://www.packtpub.com. If you purchased this book elsewhere, you can visit http://www.packtpub.com/support and register to have the files e-mailed directly to you. You can download the code files by following these steps:

1. Log in or register to our website using your e-mail address and password.
2. Hover the mouse pointer on the **SUPPORT** tab at the top.
3. Click on **Code Downloads & Errata**.
4. Enter the name of the book in the **Search** box.
5. Select the book for which you're looking to download the code files.
6. Choose from the drop-down menu where you purchased this book from.
7. Click on **Code Download**.

Once the file is downloaded, please make sure that you unzip or extract the folder using the latest version of:

- WinRAR / 7-Zip for Windows
- Zipeg / iZip / UnRarX for Mac
- 7-Zip / PeaZip for Linux

The code bundle for the book is also hosted on GitHub at `https://github.com/PacktPublishing/Java-9-High-Performance`. We also have other code bundles from our rich catalog of books and videos available at `https://github.com/PacktPublishing/`. Check them out!

Downloading the color images of this book

We also provide you with a PDF file that has color images of the screenshots/diagrams used in this book. The color images will help you better understand the changes in the output. You can download this file from `https://www.packtpub.com/sites/default/files/downloads/Java9HighPerformance_ColorImages.pdf`.

Errata

Although we have taken every care to ensure the accuracy of our content, mistakes do happen. If you find a mistake in one of our books-maybe a mistake in the text or the code-we would be grateful if you could report this to us. By doing so, you can save other readers from frustration and help us improve subsequent versions of this book. If you find any errata, please report them by visiting `http://www.packtpub.com/submit-errata`, selecting your book, clicking on the **Errata Submission Form** link, and entering the details of your errata. Once your errata are verified, your submission will be accepted and the errata will be uploaded to our website or added to any list of existing errata under the Errata section of that title.

To view the previously submitted errata, go to `https://www.packtpub.com/books/content/support` and enter the name of the book in the search field. The required information will appear under the **Errata** section.

Piracy

Piracy of copyrighted material on the Internet is an ongoing problem across all media. At Packt, we take the protection of our copyright and licenses very seriously. If you come across any illegal copies of our works in any form on the Internet, please provide us with the location address or website name immediately so that we can pursue a remedy. Please contact us at `copyright@packtpub.com` with a link to the suspected pirated material. We appreciate your help in protecting our authors and our ability to bring you valuable content.

Questions

If you have a problem with any aspect of this book, you can contact us at `questions@packtpub.com`, and we will do our best to address the problem.

1
Learning Java 9 Underlying Performance Improvements

Just when you think you have a handle on lambdas and all the performance-related features of Java 8, along comes Java 9. What follows are several of the capabilities that made it into Java 9 that you can use to help improve the performance of your applications. These go beyond byte-level changes like for string storage or garbage collection changes, which you have little control over. Also, ignore implementation changes like those for faster object locking, since you don't have to do anything differently and you automatically get these improvements. Instead, there are new library features and completely new command-line tools that will help you create apps quickly.

In this chapter, we will cover the following topics:

- Modular development and it's impact on performance
- Various string-related performance improvements, including compact string and indify string concatenation
- Advancement in concurrency
- Various underlying compiler improvements, such as tiered attribution and **Ahead-of-Time** (**AOT**) compilation
- Security manager improvements
- Enhancements in graphics rasterizers

Introducing the new features of Java 9

In this chapter, we will explore many under the cover improvements to performance that you automatically get by just running your application in the new environment. Internally, string changes also drastically reduce memory footprint requirements for times when you don't need full-scale Unicode support in your character strings. If most of your strings can be encoded either as ISO-8859-1 or Latin-1 (1 byte per character), they'll be stored much more efficiently in Java 9. So, let's dive deep into the core libraries and learn the underlying performance improvements.

Modular development and its impact

In software engineering, modularity is an important concept. From the point of view of performance as well as maintainability, it is important to create autonomous units called *modules*. These modules can be tied together to make a complete system. The modules provides encapsulation where the implementation is hidden from other modules. Each module can expose distinct APIs that can act as connectors so that other modules can communicate with it. This type of design is useful as it promotes loose coupling, helps focus on singular functionality to make it cohesive, and enables testing it in isolation. It also reduces system complexity and optimizes application development process. Improving performance of each module helps improving overall application performance. Hence, modular development is a very important concept.

I know you may be thinking, wait a minute, isn't Java already modular? Isn't the object-oriented nature of Java already providing modular operation? Well, object-oriented certainly imposes uniqueness along with data encapsulation. It only recommends loose coupling but does not strictly enforce it. In addition, it fails to provide identity at the object level and also does not have any versioning provision for the interfaces. Now you may be asking, what about JAR files? Aren't they modular? Well, although JARs provide modularization to some extent, they don't have the uniqueness that is required for modularization. They do have a provision to specify the version number, but it is rarely used and also hidden in the JAR's manifest file.

So we need a different design from what we already have. In simple terms, we need a modular system in which each module can contain more than one package and offers robust encapsulation compared to the standard JAR files.

This is what Java 9's modular system offers. In addition to this, it also replaces the fallible classpath mechanism by declaring dependencies explicitly. These enhancements improve the overall application performance as developers can now optimize the individual self-contained unit without affecting the overall system.

This also makes the application more scalable and provides high integrity.

Let's look at some of the basics of the module system and how it is tied together. To start off with, you can run the following commands to see how the module system is structured:

```
$java --list-modules
```

```
mayur@mayur-VirtualBox:~$ java --list-modules
java.activation@9
java.base@9
java.compiler@9
java.corba@9
java.datatransfer@9
java.desktop@9
java.instrument@9
java.jnlp@9
java.logging@9
java.management@9
java.management.rmi@9
java.naming@9
java.prefs@9
java.rmi@9
java.scripting@9
java.se@9
java.se.ee@9
java.security.jgss@9
java.security.sasl@9
java.smartcardio@9
java.sql@9
java.sql.rowset@9
java.transaction@9
java.xml@9
java.xml.bind@9
java.xml.crypto@9
java.xml.ws@9
java.xml.ws.annotation@9
javafx.base@9
javafx.controls@9
javafx.deploy@9
javafx.fxml@9
javafx.graphics@9
javafx.media@9
javafx.swing@9
javafx.web@9
jdk.accessibility@9
jdk.aot@9
jdk.attach@9
jdk.charsets@9
jdk.compiler@9
jdk.crypto.cryptoki@9
jdk.crypto.ec@9
jdk.deploy@9
jdk.deploy.controlpanel@9
jdk.dynalink@9
jdk.editpad@9
jdk.hotspot.agent@9
jdk.httpserver@9
jdk.incubator.httpclient@9
jdk.internal.ed@9
jdk.internal.jvmstat@9
jdk.internal.le@9
jdk.internal.opt@9
jdk.internal.vm.ci@9
```

If you are interested in a particular module, you can simply add the module name at the end of the command, as shown in the following command:

```
$java --list-modules java.base
```

```
mayur@mayur-VirtualBox:~$ java --list-modules java.base
java.activation@9
java.base@9
java.compiler@9
java.corba@9
java.datatransfer@9
java.desktop@9
java.instrument@9
java.jnlp@9
java.logging@9
java.management@9
java.management.rmi@9
java.naming@9
java.prefs@9
java.rmi@9
java.scripting@9
java.se@9
java.se.ee@9
java.security.jgss@9
java.security.sasl@9
java.smartcardio@9
java.sql@9
java.sql.rowset@9
java.transaction@9
java.xml@9
java.xml.bind@9
java.xml.crypto@9
java.xml.ws@9
java.xml.ws.annotation@9
javafx.base@9
javafx.controls@9
javafx.deploy@9
javafx.fxml@9
javafx.graphics@9
javafx.media@9
javafx.swing@9
javafx.web@9
jdk.accessibility@9
jdk.aot@9
jdk.attach@9
jdk.charsets@9
jdk.compiler@9
jdk.crypto.cryptoki@9
jdk.crypto.ec@9
jdk.deploy@9
jdk.deploy.controlpanel@9
jdk.dynalink@9
jdk.editpad@9
jdk.hotspot.agent@9
jdk.httpserver@9
jdk.incubator.httpclient@9
jdk.internal.ed@9
jdk.internal.jvmstat@9
jdk.internal.le@9
jdk.internal.opt@9
jdk.internal.vm.ci@9
jdk.internal.vm.compiler@9
jdk.jartool@9
```

The earlier command will show all the exports in packages from the base module. Java base is the core of the system.

This will show all the graphical user interface packages. This will also show `requires` which are the dependencies:

```
$java --list-modules java.desktop
```

```
mayur@mayur-VirtualBox:~$ java --list-modules java.desktop
java.activation@9
java.base@9
java.compiler@9
java.corba@9
java.datatransfer@9
java.desktop@9
java.instrument@9
java.jnlp@9
java.logging@9
java.management@9
java.management.rmi@9
java.naming@9
java.prefs@9
java.rmi@9
java.scripting@9
java.se@9
java.se.ee@9
java.security.jgss@9
java.security.sasl@9
java.smartcardio@9
java.sql@9
java.sql.rowset@9
java.transaction@9
java.xml@9
java.xml.bind@9
java.xml.crypto@9
java.xml.ws@9
java.xml.ws.annotation@9
javafx.base@9
javafx.controls@9
javafx.deploy@9
javafx.fxml@9
javafx.graphics@9
javafx.media@9
javafx.swing@9
javafx.web@9
jdk.accessibility@9
jdk.aot@9
jdk.attach@9
jdk.charsets@9
jdk.compiler@9
jdk.crypto.cryptoki@9
jdk.crypto.ec@9
jdk.deploy@9
jdk.deploy.controlpanel@9
jdk.dynalink@9
jdk.editpad@9
jdk.hotspot.agent@9
jdk.httpserver@9
jdk.incubator.httpclient@9
jdk.internal.ed@9
jdk.internal.jvmstat@9
jdk.internal.le@9
jdk.internal.opt@9
jdk.internal.vm.ci@9
jdk.internal.vm.compiler@9
jdk.jartool@9
```

So far so good, right? Now you may be wondering, I got my modules developed but how to integrate them together? Let's look into that. Java 9's modular system comes with a tool called *JLink*. I know you can guess what I am going to say now. You are right, it links a set of modules and creates a runtime image. Now imagine the possibilities it can offer. You can create your own executable system with your own custom modules. Life is going to be a lot more fun for you, I hope! Oh, and on the other hand, you will be able to control the execution and remove unnecessary dependencies.

Let's see how to link modules together. Well, it's very simple. Just run the following command:

```
$jlink --module-path $JAVA_HOME/jmods:mlib --add-modules java.desktop --
output myawesomeimage
```

This linker command will link all the modules for you and create a runtime image. You need to provide a module path and then add the module that you want to generate a figure and give a name. Isn't it simple?

Now, let's check whether the previous command worked properly or not. Let's verify the modules from the figure:

```
$myawesomeimage/bin/java --list-modules
```

The output looks like this:

```
mayur@mayur-VirtualBox:~$ jlink --module-path $JAVA_HOME/jmods:mlib --add-modules java.desktop --output myawesomeimage
mayur@mayur-VirtualBox:~$ myawesomeimage/bin/java --list-modules
java.base@9
java.datatransfer@9
java.desktop@9
java.prefs@9
java.xml@9
mayur@mayur-VirtualBox:~$
```

With this, you will now be able to distribute a quick runtime with your application. It is awesome, isn't it? Now you can see how we moved from a somewhat monolithic design to a self-contained cohesive one. Each module contains its own exports and dependencies and JLink allows you to create your own runtime. With this, we got our modular platform.

Note that the aim of this section is to just introduce you to the modular system. There is a lot more to explore but that is beyond the scope of this book. In this book, we will focus on the performance enhancement areas.

Quick introduction to modules

I am sure that after reading about the modular platform, you must be excited to dive deep into the module architecture and see how to develop one. Hold your excitement please, I will soon take you on a journey to the exciting world of modules.

As you must have guessed, every module has a property `name` and is organized by packages. Each module acts as a self-contained unit and may have native code, configurations, commands, resources, and so on. A module's details are stored in a file named `module-info.java`, which resides in the root directory of the module source code. In that file, a module can be defined as follows:

```
module <name>{
 }
```

In order to understand it better, let's go through an example. Let's say, our module name is `PerformanceMonitor`. The purpose of this module is to monitor the application performance. The input connectors will accept method names and the required parameters for that method. This method will be called from our module to monitor the module's performance. The output connectors will provide performance feedback for the given module. Let's create a `module-info.java` file in the root directory of our performance application and insert the following section:

```
module com.java9highperformance.PerformanceMonitor{
 }
```

Awesome! You got your first module declaration. But wait a minute, it does not do anything yet. Don't worry, we have just created a skeleton for this. Let's put some flesh on the skeleton. Let's assume that our module needs to communicate with our other (magnificent) modules, which we have already created and named--`PerformanceBase`, `StringMonitor`, `PrimitiveMonitor`, `GenericsMonitor`, and so on. In other words, our module has an external dependency. You may be wondering, how would we define this relationship in our module declaration? Ok, be patient, this is what we will see now:

```
module com.java9highperformance.PerformanceMonitor{
    exports com.java9highperformance.StringMonitor;
    exports com.java9highperformance.PrimitiveMonitor;
    exports com.java9highperformance.GenericsMonitor;
    requires com.java9highperformance.PerformanceBase;
    requires com.java9highperformance.PerformanceStat;
    requires com.java9highperformance.PerformanceIO;
 }
```

Yes, I know you have spotted two clauses, that is, `exports` and `requires`. And I am sure you are curious to know what they mean and why we have them there. We'll first talk about these clauses and what they mean when used in the module declaration:

- `exports`: This clause is used when your module has a dependency on another module. It denotes that this module exposes only public types to other modules and none of the internal packages are visible. In our case, the module `com.java9highperformance.PerformanceMonitor` has a dependency on `com.java9highperformance.StringMonitor`, `com.java9highperformance.PrimitiveMonitor`, and `com.java9highperformance.GenericsMonitor`. These modules export their API packages `com.java9highperformance.StringMonitor`, `com.java9highperformance.PrimitiveMonitor`, and `com.java9highperformance.GenericsMonitor`, respectively.

- `requires`: This clause denotes that the module depends upon the declared module at both compile and runtime. In our case, `com.java9highperformance.PerformanceBase`, `com.java9highperformance.PerformanceStat`, and `com.java9highperformance.PerformanceIO` modules are required by our `com.java9highperformance.PerformanceMonitor` module. The module system then locates all the observable modules to resolve all the dependencies recursively. This transitive closure gives us a module graph which shows a directed edge between two dependent modules.

Note: Every module is dependent on `java.base` even without explicitly declaring it. As you already know, everything in Java is an object.

Now you know about the modules and their dependencies. So, let's draw a module representation to understand it better. The following figure shows the various packages that are dependent on `com.java9highperformance.PerformanceMonitor`.

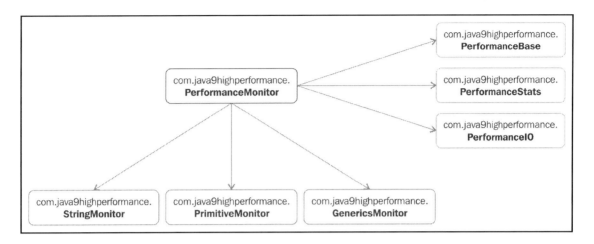

Modules at the bottom are `exports` modules and modules on the right are `requires` modules.

Now let's explore a concept called *readability relationship*. Readability relationship is a relationship between two modules where one module is dependent on another module. This readability relationship is a basis for reliable configuration. So in our example, we can say `com.java9highperformance.PerformanceMonitor` reads `com.java9highperformance.PerformanceStat`.

Let's look at `com.java9highperformance.PerformanceStat` module's description file `module-info.java`:

```
module com.java9highperformance.PerformanceStat{
    requires transitive java.lang;
}
```

This module depends on the `java.lang module`. Let's look at the `PerformanceStat` module in detail:

```
package com.java9highperformance.PerformanceStat;
import java.lang.*;

public Class StringProcessor{
    public String processString(){...}
}
```

In this case, com.java9highperformance.PerformanceMonitor only depends on com.java9highperformance.PerformanceStat but com.java9highperformance.PerformanceStat depends on java.lang. The com.java9highperformance.PerformanceMonitor module is not aware of the java.lang dependency from the com.java9highperformance.PerformanceStat module. This type of problem is taken care of by the module system. It has added a new modifier called *transitive*. If you look at com.java9highperformance.PerformanceStat, you will find it requires transitive java.lang. This means that any one depending on com.java9highperformance.PerformanceStat reads on java.lang. See the following graph which shows the readability graph:

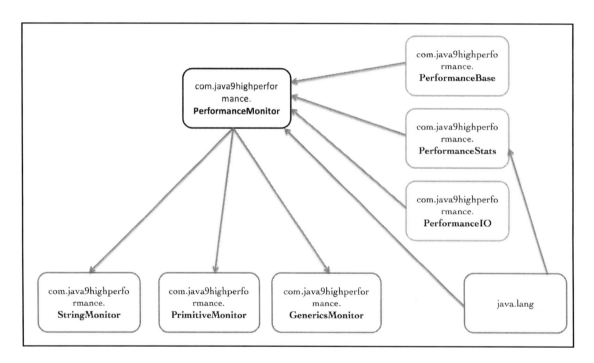

Now, in order to compile the com.java9highperformance.PerformanceMonitor module, the system must be able to resolve all the dependencies. These dependencies can be found from the module path. That's obvious, isn't that? However, don't misunderstand the classpath with the module path. It is a completely different breed. It doesn't have the issues that the packages have.

String operations performance

If you are not new to programming, string must be your best friend so far. In many cases, you may like it more than your spouse or partner. As we all know, you can't live without string, in fact, you can't even complete your application without a single use of string. OK, enough has been expressed about string and I am already feeling dizzy by the string usage just like JVM in the earlier versions. Jokes apart, let's talk about what has changed in Java 9 that will help your application perform better. Although this is an internal change, as an application developer, it is important to understand the concept so you know where to focus for performance improvements.

Java 9 has taken a step toward improving string performance. If you have ever come across JDK 6's failed attempt `UseCompressedStrings`, then you must be looking for ways to improve string performance. Since `UseCompressedStrings` was an experimental feature that was error prone and not designed very well, it was removed in JDK 7. Don't feel bad about it, I know it's terrible but as always the golden days eventually come. The JEP team has gone through immense pain to add a compact string feature that will reduce the footprint of string and its related classes.

Compact strings will improve the footprint of string and help in using memory space efficiently. It also preserves compatibility for all related Java and native interfaces. The second important feature is Indify String Concatenation, which will optimize a string at runtime.

In this section, we will take a closure look at these two features and their impact on overall application performance.

Compact string

Before we talk about this feature, it is important to understand why we even care about this. Let's dive deep into the underworld of JVM (or as any star wars fan would put it, the dark side of the Force). Let's first understand how JVM treats our beloved string and that will help us understand this new shiny compact string improvement. Let's enter into the magical world of heap. And as a matter of fact, no performance book is complete without a discussion of this mystical world.

The world of heap

Each time JVM starts, it gets some memory from the underlining operating system. It is separated into two distinct regions called *heap space* and *Permgen*. These are home to all your application's resources. And as always with all good things in life, this home is limited in size. This size is set during the JVM initialization; however, you can increase or decrease this by specifying the JVM parameters, -Xmx, and -XX:MaxPermSize.

The heap size is divided into two areas, the nursery or young space and the old space. As the name suggests, the young space is home to new objects. This all sounds great but every house needs a cleanup. Hence, JVM has the most efficient cleaner called *garbage collector* (most efficient? Well... let's not get into that just yet). As any productive cleaner would do, the garbage collector efficiently collects all the unused objects and reclaims memory. When this young space gets filled up with new objects, the garbage collector takes charge and moves any of those who have lived long enough in the young space to the old space. This way, there is always room for more objects in the young space.

And in the same way, if the old space becomes filled up, the garbage collector reclaims the memory used.

Why bother compressing strings?

Now you know a little bit about heap, let's look at the String class and how strings are represented on heap. If you dissect the heap of your application, you will notice that there are two objects, one is the Java language String object that references the second object char[] that actually handles the data. The char datatype is UTF-16 and hence takes up to 2 bytes. Let's look at the following example of how two different language strings look:

```
2 byte per char[]
Latin1 String : 1 byte per char[]
```

So you can see that Latin1 String only consumes 1 byte, and hence we are losing about 50% of the space here. There is an opportunity to represent it in a more dense form and improve the footprint, which will eventually help in speeding up garbage collection as well.

Now, before making any changes to this, it is important to understand its impact on real-life applications. It is essential to know whether applications use 1 byte per char[] strings or 2 bytes per char[] strings.

Learning Java 9 Underlying Performance Improvements

To get an answer to this, the JPM team analyzed a lot of heap dumps of real-world data. The result highlighted that a majority of heap dumps have around 18 percent to 30 percent of the entire heap consumed by `chars[]`, which come from string. Also, it was prominent that most strings were represented by a single byte per `char[]`. So, it is clear that if we try to improve the footprint for strings with a single byte, it will give significant performance boost to many real-life applications.

What did they do?

After having gone through a lot of different solutions, the JPM team has finally decided to come up with a strategy to compress string during its construction. First, optimistically try to compress in 1 byte and if it is not successful, copy it as 2 bytes. There are a few shortcuts possible, for example, the use of a special case encoder like ISO-8851-1, which will always spit 1 byte.

This implementation is a lot better than JDK 6's `UseCompressedStrings` implementation, which was only helpful to a handful of applications as it was compressing string by repacking and unpacking on every single instance. Hence the performance gain comes from the fact that it can now work on both the forms.

What is the escape route?

Even though it all sounds great, it may affect the performance of your application if it only uses 2 byte per `char[]` string. In that case, it make sense not to use the earlier mentioned, check, and directly store string as 2 bytes per `char[]`. Hence, the JPM team has provided a kill switch `--XX: -CompactStrings` using which you can disable this feature.

What is the performance gain?

The previous optimization affects the heap as we saw earlier that the string is represented in the heap. Hence, it is affecting the memory footprint of the application. In order to evaluate the performance, we really need to focus on the garbage collector. We will explore the garbage collection topic later, but for now, let's just focus on the run-time performance.

[19]

Indify String Concatenation

I am sure you must be thrilled by the concept of the compact string feature we just learned about. Now let's look at the most common usage of string, which is concatenation. Have you ever wondered what really happens when we try to concatenate two strings? Let's explore. Take the following example:

```
public static String getMyAwesomeString(){
    int javaVersion = 9;
    String myAwesomeString = "I love " + "Java " + javaVersion + " high
performance book by Mayur Ramgir";
    return myAwesomeString;
}
```

In the preceding example, we are trying to concatenate a few strings with the int value. The compiler will then take your awesome strings, initialize a new StringBuilder instance, and then append all these individuals strings. Take a look at the following bytecode generation by javac. I have used the *ByteCode Outline* plugin for *Eclipse* to visualize the disassembled bytecode of this method. You may download it from http://andrei.gmxhome.de/bytecode/index.html:

```
// access flags 0x9
public static getMyAwesomeString()Ljava/lang/String;
  L0
  LINENUMBER 10 L0
  BIPUSH 9
  ISTORE 0
  L1
  LINENUMBER 11 L1
  NEW java/lang/StringBuilder
  DUP
  LDC "I love Java "
  INVOKESPECIAL java/lang/StringBuilder.<init> (Ljava/lang/String;)V
  ILOAD 0
  INVOKEVIRTUAL java/lang/StringBuilder.append (I)Ljava/lang/StringBuilder;
  LDC " high performance book by Mayur Ramgir"
  INVOKEVIRTUAL java/lang/StringBuilder.append
(Ljava/lang/String;)Ljava/lang/StringBuilder;
  INVOKEVIRTUAL java/lang/StringBuilder.toString ()Ljava/lang/String;
  ASTORE 1
  L2
  LINENUMBER 12 L2
  ALOAD 1
  ARETURN
  L3
  LOCALVARIABLE javaVersion I L1 L3 0
```

```
LOCALVARIABLE myAwesomeString Ljava/lang/String; L2 L3 1
MAXSTACK = 3
MAXLOCALS = 2
```

Quick Note: How do we interpret this?

- **Invokestatic**: This is useful for invoking static methods
- **Invokevirtual**: This uses of dynamic dispatch for invoking public and protected non-static methods
- **Invokeinterface**: This is very similar to invokevirtual except that the method dispatch is based on an interface type
- **Invokespecial**: This is useful for invoking constructors, methods of a superclass, and private methods

However, at runtime, due to the inclusion of `-XX:+-OptimizeStringConcat` into the JIT compiler, it can now identify the append of `StringBuilder` and the `toString` chains. In case the match is identified, produce low-level code for optimum processing. Compute all the arguments' length, figure out the final capacity, allocate the storage, copy the strings, and do the in place conversion of primitives. After this, handover this array to the `String` instance without copying. It is a profitable optimization.

But this also has a few drawbacks in terms of concatenation. One example is that in case of a concatenating string with long or double, it will not optimize properly. This is because the compiler has to do `.getChar` first which adds overhead.

Also, if you are appending `int` to `String`, then it works great; however, if you have an incremental operator like `i++`, then it breaks. The reason behind this is that you need to rewind to the beginning of the expression and re-execute, so you are essentially doing `++` twice. And now the most important change in Java 9 compact string. The length spell like `value.length >> coder`; C2 cannot optimize it as it does not know about the IR.

Hence, to solve the problem of compiler optimization and runtime support, we need to control the bytecode, and we cannot expect `javac` to handle that.

We need to delay the decision of which concatenation can be done at runtime. So can we have just method `String.concat` which will do the magic. Well, don't rush into this yet as how would you design the method `concat`. Let's take a look. One way to go about this is to accept an array of the `String` instance:

```
public String concat(String... n){
    //do the concatenation
}
```

However, this approach will not work with primitives as you now need to convert each primitive to the `String` instance and also, as we saw earlier, the problem is that long and double string concatenation will not allow us to optimize it. I know, I can sense the glow on your face like you got a brilliant idea to solve this painful problem. You are thinking about using the `Object` instance instead of the `String` instance, right? As you know the `Object` instance is catch all. Let's look at your brilliant idea:

```
public String concat(Object... n){
    //do the concatenation
}
```

First, if you are using the `Object` instance, then the compiler needs to do autoboxing. Additionally, you are passing in the `varargs` array, so it will not perform optimally. So, are we stuck here? Does it mean we cannot use the preeminent compact string feature with string concatenation? Let's think a bit more; maybe instead of using the method `runtime`, let `javac` handle the concatenation and just give us the optimized bytecode. That sounds like a good idea. Well, wait a minute, I know you are thinking the same thing. What if JDK 10 optimizes this further? Does that mean, when I upgrade to the new JDK, I have to recompile my code again and deploy it again? In some cases, its not a problem, in other cases, it is a big problem. So, we are back to square one.

We need something that can be handled at runtime. Ok, so that means we need something which will dynamically invoke the methods. Well, that rings a bell. If we go back in our time machine, at the dawn of the era of JDK 7 it gave us `invokedynamic`. I know you can see the solution, I can sense the sparkle in your eyes. Yes, you are right, `invokedynamic` can help us here. If you are not aware of `invokedyanmic`, let's spend some time to understand it. For those who have already mastered the topic, you could skip it, but I would recommend you go through this again.

Invokedynamic

The `invokedynamic` feature is the most notable feature in the history of Java. Rather than having a limit to JVM bytecode, we now can define our own way for operations to work. So what is `inovkedynamic`? In simple terms, it is the user-definable bytecode. This bytecode (instead of JVM) determines the execution and optimization strategies. It offers various method pointers and adapters which are in the form of method handling APIs. The JVM then work on the pointers given in the bytecode and use reflection-like method pointers to optimize it. This way, you, as a developer, can get full control over the execution and optimization of code.

It is essentially a mix of user-defined bytecode (which is known as *bytecode + bootstrap*) and method handles. I know you are also wondering about the method handles--what are they and how to use them? Ok, I heard you, let's talk about method handles.

Method handles provide various pointers, including field, array, and method, to pass data and get results back. With this, you can do argument manipulation and flow control. From JVM's point of view, these are native instructions that it can optimize as if it were bytecode. However, you have the option to programmatically generate this bytecode.

Let's zoom in to the method handles and see how it all ties up together. The main package's name is `java.lang.invoke`, which has `MethodHandle`, `MethodType`, and `MethodHandles`. `MethodHandle` is the pointer that will be used to invoke the function. `MethodType` is a representation of a set of arguments and return value coming from the method. The utility class `MethodHandles` will act as a pointer to a method which will get an instance of `MethodHandle` and map the arguments.

We won't be going in deep for this section, as the aim was just to make you aware of what the `invokedynamic` feature is and how it works so you will understand the string concatenation solution. So, this is where we get back to our discussion on string concatenation. I know, you were enjoying the `invokedynamic` discussion, but I guess I was able to give you just enough insight to make you understand the core idea of Indify String Concatenation.

Let's get back on the concatenation part where we were looking for a solution to concatenate our awesome compact strings. For concatenating the compact strings, we need to take care of types and the number of types of methods and this is what the `invokedynamic` gives us.

So let's use `invokedynamic` for `concat`. Well, not so quick, my friend. There is a fundamental problem with this approach. We can not just use `invokedyanmic` as it is to solve this problem. Why? Because there is a circular reference. The `concat` function needs `java.lang.invoke`, which uses `concat`. This continues, and eventually you will get `StackOverflowError`.

Take a look at the following code:

```
String concat(int i, long l, String s){
    return s + i + l
}
```

So if we were to use `inovkedynamic` here, the `invokedynamic` call would look like this:

```
InvokeDynamic #0: makeConcat(String, int, long)
```

There is a need to break the circular reference. However, in the current JDK implementation, you cannot control what `java.invoke` calls from the complete JDK library. Also, removing the complete JDK library reference from `java.invoke` has severe side effects. We only need the `java.base` module for Indify String Concatenation, and if we can figure out a way to just call the `java.base` module, then it will significantly improve the performance and avoid unpleasant exceptions. I know what you are thinking. We just studied the coolest addition to Java 9, *Project Jigsaw*. It provides modular source code and now we can only accept the `java.base` module. This solves the biggest problem we were facing in terms of concatenating two strings, primitives, and so on.

After going through a couple of different strategies, the Java Performance Management team has settled on the following strategy:

1. Make a call to the `toString()` method on all reference args.
2. Make a call to the `tolength()` method or since all the underlying methods are exposed, just call `T.stringSize(T t)` on every args.
3. Figure out the coders and call `coder()` for all reference args.
4. Allocate `byte[]` storage and then copy all args. And then, convert primitives in-place.
5. Invoke a private constructor `String` by handing over the array for concatenation.

With this, we are able to get an optimized string concat in the same code and not in `C2 IR`. This strategy gives us 2.9x better performance and 6.4x less garbage.

Storing interned strings in CDS archives

The main goal of this feature is to reduce memory footprint caused by creating new instances of `String` in every JVM process. All the classes that are loaded in any JVM process can be shared with other JVM processes via **Class Data Sharing** (**CDS**) archives.

Oh, I did not tell you about CDS. I think it's important to spend some time to understand what CDS is, so you can understand the underlying performance improvement.

Many times, small applications in particular spend a comparatively long time on startup operations. To reduce this startup time, a concept called CDS was introduced. CDS enables sharing of a set of classes loaded from the system JAR file into a private internal representation during the JRE installation. This helps a lot as then any further JVM invocations can take advantage of these loaded classes' representation from the shared archive instead of loading these classes again. The metadata related to these classes is shared among multiple JVM processes.

CDS stores strings in the form of UTF-8 in the constant pool. When a class from these loaded classes begins the initialization process, these UTF-8 strings are converted into `String` objects on demand. In this structure, every character in every confined string takes 2 bytes in the `String` object and 1 byte to 3 bytes in the UTF-8, which essentially wastes memory. Since these strings are created dynamically, different JVM processes cannot share these strings.

Shared strings need a feature called *pinned regions* in order to make use of the garbage collector. Since the only HotSpot garbage collector that supports pinning is G1; it only works with the G1 garbage collector.

Concurrency performance

Multithreading is a very popular concept. It allows programs to run multiple tasks at the same time. These multithreaded programs may have more than one unit which can run concurrently. Every unit can handle a different task keeping the use of available resources optimal. This can be managed by multiple threads that can run in parallel.

Java 9 improved contended locking. You may be wondering what is contended locking. Let's explore. Each object has one monitor that can be owned by one thread at a time. Monitors are the basic building blocks of concurrency. In order for a thread to execute a block of code marked as synchronized on an object or a synchronized method declared by an object, it must own this object's monitor. Since there are multiple threads trying to get access to the mentioned monitor, JVM needs to orchestrate the process and only allow one thread at a time. It means the rest of threads go in a wait state. This monitor is then called contended. Because of this provision, the program wastes time in the waiting state.

Also, **Java Virtual Machine (JVM)** does some work orchestrating the lock contention. Additionally, it has to manage threads, so once the existing thread finishes its execution, it can allow a new thread to go in. This certainly adds overhead and affects performance adversely. Java 9 has taken a few steps to improve in this area. The provision refines the JVM's orchestration, which will ultimately result in performance improvement in highly contested code.

The following benchmarks and tests can be used to check the performance improvements of contented Java object monitors:

- `CallTimerGrid` (This is more of a stress test than a benchmark)
- `Dacapo-bach` (earlier dacapo2009)
- `_ avrora`
- `_ batik`
- `_ fop`
- `_ h2`
- `_ luindex`
- `_ lusearch`
- `_ pmd`
- `_ sunflow`
- `_ tomcat`
- `_ tradebeans`
- `_ tradesoap`
- `_ xalan`
- `DerbyContentionModelCounted`
- `HighContentionSimulator`
- `LockLoops-JSR166-Doug-Sept2009` (earlier LockLoops)
- `PointBase`
- `SPECjbb2013-critical` (earlier specjbb2005)
- `SPECjbb2013-max`
- `specjvm2008`
- `volano29` (earlier volano2509)

Compiler improvements

Several efforts have been made to improve the compiler's performance. In this section, we will focus on the improvements to the compiler side.

Tiered Attribution

The first and foremost change providing compiler improvement is related to **Tiered Attribution (TA)**. This change is more related to lambda expressions. At the moment, the type checking of poly expression is done by type checking the same tree multiple times against different targets. This process is called **Speculative Attribution (SA)**, which enables the use of different overload resolution targets to check a lambda expression.

This way of type checking, although a robust technique, adversely affects performance significantly. For example, with this approach, *n* number of overload candidates check against the same argument expression up to *n * 3* once per overload phase, strict, loose, and varargs. In addition to this, there is one final check phase. Where lambda returns a poly method call results in combinatorial explosion of attribution calls, this causes a huge performance problem. So we certainly need a different method of type checking for poly expressions.

The core idea is to make sure that a method call creates bottom-up structural types for each poly argument expression with every single details, which will be needed to execute the overload resolution applicability check before performing the overload resolution.

So in summary, the performance improvement was able to achieve an attribute of a given expression by decreasing the total number of tries.

Ahead-of-Time compilation

The second noticeable change for compiler improvement is Ahead-of-Time compilation. If you are not familiar with the term, let's see what AOT is. As you probably know, every program in any language needs a runtime environment to execute. Java also has its own runtime which is known as **Java Virtual Machine (JVM)**. The typical runtime that most of us use is a bytecode interpreter, which is JIT compiler as well. This runtime is known as *HotSpot JVM*.

This HotSpot JVM is famous for improving performance by JIT compilation as well as adaptive optimization. So far so good. However, this does not work well in practice for every single application. What if you have a very light program, say, a single method call? In this case, JIT compilation will not help you much. You need something that will load up faster. This is where AOT will help you. With AOT as opposed to JIT, instead of compiling to bytecode, you can compile into native machine code. The runtime then uses this native machine code to manage calls for new objects into mallocs as well as file access into system calls. This can improve performance.

Security manager improvements

Ok, let's talk about security. If you are not one of those who cares about application security over pushing more features in a release, then the expression on your face may be like *Uh! What's that?* If you are one those, then let's first understand the importance of security and find a way to consider this in your application development tasks. In today's SaaS-dominated world, everything is exposed to the outside world. A determined individual (a nice way of saying, a *malicious hacker*), can get access to your application and exploit the security holes you may have introduced through your negligence. I would love to talk about application security in depth as this is another area I am very much interested in. However, application security is out of the scope of this book. The reason we are talking about it here is that the JPM team has taken an initiative to improve the existing security manager. Hence, it is important to first understand the importance of security before talking about the security manager.

Hopefully, this one line of description may have generated secure programming interest in you. However, I do understand that sometimes you may not have enough time to implement a complete secure programming model due to tight schedules. So, let's find a way which can fit with your tight schedule. Let's think for a minute; is there any way to automate security? Can we have a way to create a blueprint and ask our program to stay within the boundaries? Well, you are in luck, Java does have a feature called *security manager*. It is nothing but a policy manager that defines a security policy for the application. It sounds exciting, doesn't it? But what does this policy look like? And what does it contain? Both are fair questions to ask. This security policy basically states actions that are dangerous or sensitive in nature. If your application does not comply with this policy, then the security manager throws `SecurityException`. On the other side, you can have your application call this security manager to learn about the permitted actions. Now, let's look at the security manager in detail.

In case of a web applet, a security manager is provided by the browser, or the Java Web Start plugin runs this policy. In many cases, applications other than web applets run without a security manager unless those applications implement one. It's a no brainer to say that if there is no security manager and no security policy attached, the application acts without restrictions.

Now we know a little about the security manager, let's look at the performance improvement in this area. As per the Java team, there may be a possibility that an application running with a security manager installed degrades performance by 10 percent to 15 percent. However, it is not possible to remove all the performance bottlenecks but narrowing this gap can assist in improving not only security but also performance.

The Java 9 team looked at some of the optimizations, including the enforcement of security policy and the evaluation of permissions, which will help improve the overall performance of using a security manager. During the performance testing phase, it was highlighted that even though the permission classes are thread safe, they show up as a HotSpot. Numerous improvements have been made to decrease thread contention and improve throughput.

Computing the `hashcode` method of `java.security.CodeSource` has been improved to use a string form of the code source URL to avoid potentially expensive DNS lookups. Also, the `checkPackageAccess` method of `java.lang.SecurityManager`, which contains the package checking algorithm, has been improved.

Some other noticeable changes in security manager improvements are as follows:

- The first noticeable change is that using `ConcurrentHashMap` in place of `Collections.synchronizedMap` helps improving throughput of the `Policy.implie` method. Look at the following graph, taken from the OpenJDK site, which highlights the significant increase in the throughput with `ConcurrentHashMap`:

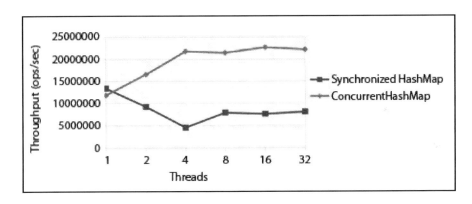

Source: `https://bugs.openjdk.java.net/browse/JDK-8055753`

- In addition to this, `HashMap`, which had been used for maintaining internal collection of `CodeSource` in `java.security.SecureClassLoader`, has been replaced by `ConcurrentHashMap`.
- There are a few other small improvements like an improvement in the throughput by removing the compatibility code from the `getPermissions` method (`CodeSource`), which synchronizes on identities.
- Another significant gain in performance is achieved using `ConcurrentHashMap` instead of `HashMap` surrounded by synchronized blocks in the permission checking code, which yielded in greater thread performance.

Graphics rasterizers

If you are into Java 2D and using OpenJDK, you will appreciate the efforts taken by the Java 9 team. Java 9 is mainly related to a graphics rasterizer, which is part of the current JDK. OpenJDK uses Pisces, whereas Oracle JDK uses Ductus. Oracle's closed-source Ductus rasterizer performs better than OpenJDK's Pisces.

These graphics rasterizers are useful for anti-aliased rendering except fonts. Hence, for a graphics-intensive application, the performance of this rasterizer is very important. However, Pisces is failing in many fronts and its performance problems are very visible. Hence, the team has decided to replace this with a different rasterizer called Marlin Graphics Renderer.

Marlin is developed in Java and, most importantly, it is the fork of the Pisces rasterizer. Various tests have been done on it and the results are very promising. It consistently performs better than Pisces. It demonstrates multithreaded scalability and even outperforms the closed-source Ductus rasterizer for a single-threaded application.

Summary

In this chapter, we have seen some of the exciting features that will improve your application's performance without making any effort from your end. In the next chapter, we will explore the various areas that will affect your application in an adverse way. We will look at causes and find solutions for the affected areas. Some of the topics covered are understanding the CPU infrastructure, memory utilization, optimization of heap and stack, escape analysis, common memory problems such as the `OutOfMemory` and `StackOverFlow` errors, and network-related performance bottlenecks.

2
Identifying Performance Bottlenecks

Before diving deep into understanding code-related performance problems, it is important to understand the platform on which the code is going to run. This not only includes the JVM, but also the underline operating system, hardware infrastructure, and network infrastructure. You may be wondering, why should I care about that? Isn't just focusing on the application code enough to make sure my application runs smoothly?

Unfortunately, the answer is no. No, it's not enough just to focus on improving your code. The reason is very simple--your code depends on the resources provided by JVM, operating system, and network infrastructure. When you write the REST client, you are relying on the underline network infrastructure to deliver the data. When you write the multithreaded code, you are relying on JVM and underlying operating system to serve your threads and provide them enough resources such as CPU time and memory allocation. When you create new objects, you are relying on JVM to provide your objects enough memory resources such as heap space. And hence, you cannot optimize your code if you do not understand the underline infrastructure properly. Therefore, you need to understand the inner working of these infrastructures to design your coding strategy.

In this section, we will learn about these infrastructures and try to understand the bottlenecks. Then, based on the findings, we will explore various strategies we can implement to optimize our code for these infrastructures. We are going to look into the following topics in detail:

- CPU infrastructure
- I/O operations
- Database operations

- Network utilization
- Memory utilization

CPU infrastructure

Central Processing Unit (CPU) is an integral part of the computer system. The core responsibility of a CPU is to handle all the instructions from hardware as well as software. It is beyond the scope of this book to explore the CPU in detail; however, we will study the basic architecture and underline functioning of a CPU in very high level. This will help us to understand the areas where we need to focus on utilizing a CPU optimally. Not every part of your code will be CPU-dependent, so it is important to find these areas and use a proper coding strategy to make sure we use CPU time more efficiently.

Let's first look at the high-level architecture of CPU. If you dissect the processing of a CPU, you will notice there are two main components, one is **Arithmetic Logic Unit (ALU)**, which is responsible for performing logical, mathematical, and comparison operations. And the second one is **Control Unit (CU)**, which is responsible for directing all of the processor's operations. Let's discuss these two main components:

- **The Control Unit**: The core function of this unit is to execute program instructions. As its name suggests, CU only directs and does not execute instructions by itself. It communicates with ALU and memory to perform its operation.
- **The Arithmetic/Logic Unit**: As you may have guessed already, ALU executes all arithmetic operations such as addition, subtraction, multiplication, and division and logical operations such as comparison. Without this unit, your application won't be able to perform calculations such as processing order payments and booking train or plane tickets. I hope now you can see the importance of this unit.

Now, let's look into how ALU and CU get their instructions. ALU and CU process one instruction at a time; so if there are multiple instructions coming at the same time, we need a way to manage this queue. I know what you are thinking. We need some kind of storage, right? Yes, you got it right. There are two types of storage available, primary and secondary.

Primary storage is more closer to CPU and hence faster to use by CPU to process data and instructions. This storage is a temporary storage whereas secondary storage, like a hard drive, is permanent. It is always more expensive to process instructions from secondary storage than primary. The primary storage includes CPU registers, cache, and **Random Access Memory (RAM)**. CPU registers are closer than cache and cache is closer than RAM. I know you can't wait to derive that CPU registers are faster than cache and cache is faster than RAM. You are absolutely correct. The farther away you go in the memory line, the more expensive it becomes to access data and instructions.

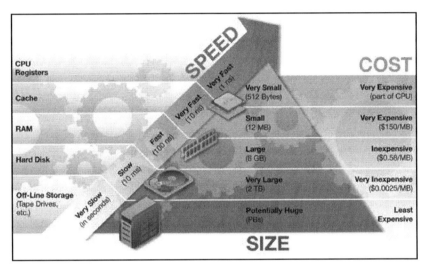

Image reference : http://neos-dev-web.neos-server.org/guide/?q=node/101

We will explore the memory optimizations in detail in the next section.

So far so good. Right? Now, let's see how your Java code runs on a CPU. When you execute your application, JVM looks for the main method and creates a thread, which is called the *main thread*. The main thread is then used to derive any new thread you create in the code. This main thread is a process for the underline operating system and the threads that you create are created as a lightweight process in the operating system. We will learn more about threads and various techniques to improve thread performance in Chapter 9, *Multithreading and Reactive Programming*. Hence, we will not get into detail about thread performance here. However, we will look into a few CPU-intensive code examples. This will help you to identify the areas that you will need to focus on optimizing. Note that the purpose of this exercise is not to teach you the best possible algorithm, but to highlight some of the small changes you can make to your code to gain significant performance improvement.

Let's look at an example of a prime number lookup algorithm. In this example, we will try to find all the possible prime numbers between 2 and 1 million. If you don't know what a prime number is, a prime number is a number greater than 1 which is divisible by itself or by 1. Prime number lookup is a very common example, but is very useful in software security and mathematical calculations. There are various algorithms available which improve the processing time. However, we will go from the worst case example and see what type of changes we can make to improve CPU utilization. So what would be your first go? Well, you may take a simple and naive approach as follows:

1. Take a number and loop through the series from 1 to 1 million and check if our number is divisible by the number in the sequence. If so, print it and move on:

```
public void lookupPrime(int start, int end) {
    for (int i = start; i <= end; i++)
    {
        int primeCheckCounter = 0;
        for(int j=i; j>=1; j--) {
            if(i%j == 0) {
                primeCheckCounter =  primeCheckCounter + 1;
            }
        }
        if(primeCheckCounter == 2){
            System.out.print(i + " ");
        }
    }
}
```

This code is very CPU intensive because it is totally dependent on ALU and CU units, which we studied earlier. This code is not optimized properly. See the following CPU usage for this code. We will also run JMH benchmarking. We will talk about JMH and micro benchmarking later in Chapter 6, *Optimizing Code with Microbenchmarking*.

2. Now, let's analyze this code and see how we can improve it. In the preceding example, we went through 1 to 1 million numbers. However, if 2 divides some integer n, it means n/2 divides n also. Hence, we don't need to iterate and check all numbers from 1 to 1 million. The modified code will look like the following:

```
public void lookupPrime(int start, int end) {
    for (int i = start; i <= end; i++)
    {
        int primeCheckCounter = 0;
        for(int j=i;2*j>=1;j--) {
            if(i%j == 0) {
                primeCheckCounter =  primeCheckCounter + 1;
            }
        }
```

```
        }
        if(primeCheckCounter == 2){
            System.out.print(i + " ");
        }
      }
    }
```

This code is significantly faster than the previous one and uses less CPU resources.

It looks good, doesn't it? With that small change, we saw a lot of improvement and now our code is utilizing less CPU resources. Are we done here? Can you think of anything else that will further reduce the processing time? Remember, our goal is to make sure we use optimum resources.

3. You may have got the answer by now. So, let's tally if our thinking processes match. For a given number, if you look closely on the factors, you will notice that the square root will always come in the middle. So it means, we only need to iterate up to the square root. Refer to the following example:

```
public static void lookupPrime(int start, int end) {

    for (int i = start; i <= end; i++)
    {
      int primeCheckCounter = 0;
      for(int j=i;(int)Math.sqrt(j)>=1;j --) {
          if(i%j == 0) {
              primeCheckCounter =  primeCheckCounter + 1;
          }
      }
      if(primeCheckCounter == 2){
          System.out.print(i + " ");
      }
    }
}
```

So, the purpose of this exercise is to guide your thought process when you write any algorithm. You do not want to make your algorithm eat the available CPU, or else your application will not respond to high load in the production environment. But you know that, right?

We can take advantage of multicore processor by running our algorithm on multiple core. We will cover multithreading in Chapter 9, *Multithreading and Reactive Programming*.

Memory utilization

In this section, we will explore another area which is susceptible to performance problems. More or less, each line of code is dependent on some data in the form of object, variable, and so on. Hence, JVM needs to have some type of provision to store this information so that it will be available to your code. This storage is mainly provided by the underline **Operating System (OS)**, which is based on physical memory such as **Random Access Memory (RAM)** and JVM is allocated to use a portion of it. This memory space is then available to your application running inside the JVM.

There are mainly two areas which you need to focus on:

- Heap
- Stack

Don't worry, we will take a closer look at these two areas, but before we jump into that, let's quickly review CPU memory that we briefly talked about in the previous section. Every time CPU executes the given instructions, it stores the results in registers. If you recall the diagram we saw in the earlier section, the registers are the closest memory to CPU and hence the fastest.

The next series in the CPU memory is RAM, which is accessible to CPU by the memory bus. Each CPU has a set size of physical address such as 16 bit, 32 bit, and 64 bit. Depending on this size, a CPU can access the physical memory. For example, a 16-bit address can access 2^{16} equivalent to 65.536 memory locations, a 32-bit address can access 2^{32} equivalent to 4.294.967.296 memory locations, and so on. The orchestration of memory is controlled by the underline operating system, which maps the physical memory to each process's memory. This can be achieved with the help of virtual memory. The OS does the underline wiring to assign each process a memory slot in a virtual memory space and maps this to the real physical memory like RAM.

Now, let's get back to heap and stack. It is important to understand these concepts properly as it will help you to design your coding strategy for the optimum memory management.

Java heap

As soon you start your application, JVM asks for some memory from the operating system. It then provides this space for your application. Part of this space is called as Java heap memory, which is located at the bottom of the address space. This place is used for storing all the objects created by using the operator `new`.

As long as you have an active reference to this newly created object, it uses memory space in heap. Once you remove this reference, this object becomes an orphan and available for removal so that JVM can claim this allocated memory and provide it to other objects. In order to clean this dead reference, Java has provided a tool called *garbage collector*. This garbage collector then collects all the orphan objects and frees up the memory that JVM can reuse.

If you are not familiar with garbage collector, don't sweat, we will cover this section in `Chapter 5`, *Understanding Garbage Collection and Making Use of it*.

And if you are curious, like George (you know Curious George ……... the monkey), you may jump ahead and read all about garbage collector and come back with your garbage collection wisdom. And you may respond like Edu (from the Curious George movie).

> Edu: Ted, The Man with the Yellow Hat: You know, the word Zagawa means enlightenment?
> Edu: Of course I know. I live here!

Ha ha ha…. but true. Knowing all about garbage collector will prepare you well for high performance coding. So be curious like George. It does pay in the long run.

Okay, enough fun time. Let's get back to the Java heap conversation. Managing heap space is the most important aspect of memory optimization. Hence, first and foremost, we need to make sure we allocate enough heap space to our JVM. Do not rely on the default heap space allocation as a part of memory optimization also involves making sure there is a proper estimation of the number of objects and their sizes. Depending on this, you can then allocate more memory using JVM options `-Xms` and `-Xmx`. You may be wondering, what are `-Xms` and `-Xmx` used for. If so, let's wear our Sherlocks hat--the clue is hidden in the last letter of these parameters. Did you get it? I knew… you would get it. `-Xms` is the minimum size of heap and `-Xmx` is the maximum size. Great job.

Also, note down one more parameter `-Xmn`, which sets the size of the new generation of heap space. If you are wondering what is new generation, you know what, you should first read `Chapter 5`, *Understanding Garbage Collection and Making Use of it*.

Java stack

Stack is another area you should focus on. It is the home of local variables and method invocations. Stack manages order as **Last-In-First-Out** (**LIFO**). Let's see how it works.

Your code calls a method, then its stack frame gets created and it gets put onto the top of the call stack. This stack frame maintains the state of the method. It also keeps track of the line of code currently getting executed and the values of all the local variables. For the method on stack, it also stores references to other objects in the heap. Once the method execution ends, the stack block gets claimed and becomes available for a new method. Compared to heap, stack has less memory allocated. As you may have figured out by now, the top of the stack contains the currently running method. Each thread has its own call stack.

Let's understand heap and stack with an example.

```
1.    public class HeapAndStack {
2.
3.    public static void main(String[] args) {
4.      String intro = "Call myAwesomeMethod";
5.      HeapAndStack has = new HeapAndStack();
6.      System.out.println(intro);
7.      LookupPrimeNumbers lpn = new LookupPrimeNumbers();
8.      has.myAwesomeMethod(lpn);
9.    }
10.
11.    private void myAwesomeMethod(LookupPrimeNumbers lpnParameter) {
12.      String message = "Let's generate some prime numbers";
13.      int start = 1;
14.      int end = 10000;
15.      System.out.println(message);
16.      lpnParameter.lookupPrime(start, end);
17.    }
18.      }
```

Let's analyze the preceding example with help of the following diagram:

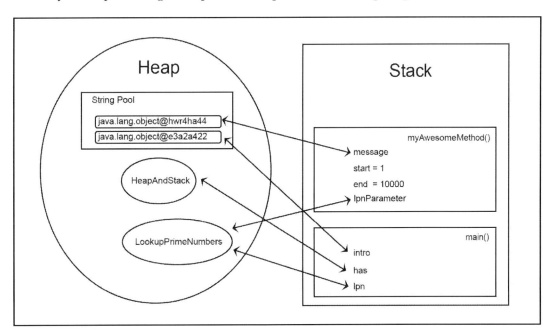

Can you make sense of this diagram? If not, let me take you through each step and show you what happens in the background.

1. When we run this program, JVM loads all the runtime classes into the heap space. As the JVM discovers our `main()` method in *line 3*, it immediately creates stack for the thread of the `main()` method.

2. On the *line 4*, we are creating a `String intro = "Call myAwesomeMethod"`; string variable. Hence, JVM creates a string object for `Call myAwesomeMethod` in the heap and puts it inside the `String` pool. Then, it creates a space in the stack space for the `intro` variable, which is referencing to this string object.

3. On the *line 5*, we are creating an object of the same `HeapAndStack has = new HeapAndStack()`; class. So, JVM allocates a memory location for this object in the heap. And it stores the `has` variable, which is referencing to this object in the stack memory.

4. After this, in *line 7*, we are creating a `LookupPrimeNumbers lpn = new LookupPrimeNumbers()`; object for the `LookupPrimeNumbers` class. Because of this, JVM allocates some space and puts this object in the heap. Also, it creates a space for the `lpn` reference variable in the stack space.

5. In *line 8*, we are calling the `myAwesomeMethod` method. At this stage, JVM creates a block in the top of the stack for the `myAwesomeMethod` method. As you already know, Java is pass by value, hence in *line 11*, a new reference to the object of `LookupPrimeNumbers` is created in the `myAwesomeMethod` stack block.

6. In *line 12*, we are creating a new string, which goes in the `String` pool in the heap. A new reference is created in the `myAwesomeMethod` stack and pointed back to this newly created string in the `String` pool.

7. On *line 13* and *line 14*, we are declaring new variables and assigning values to them. Since these are local variables, they go in the `myAwesomeMethod` stack.

8. In *line 16*, we are calling the `lookupPrime` method, so JVM creates a block in the top of the stack for the `lookupPrime` method. And, as we have seen in earlier stages, similar steps get followed for the method `lookupPrime`, like putting local variables in the `lookupPrime` stack, putting strings in the `String` pool and reference in `lookupPrime` stack, and so on.

9. In *line 17*, when JVM returns from the `lookupPrime` method, the `myAwesomeMethod` method is terminated and memory block for the `myAwesomeMethod` method gets freed up.

10. In *line 9*, when JVM returns from the `myAwesomeMethod` method, the `main` method terminates and the stack is destroyed. Also, the program ends and JVM clears all the memory and execution ends.

Java heap versus stack memory

I hope the preceding example and explanation gave you a good idea about how JVM uses heap and stack. So, let's just summarize these two points and note down a few key differences as follows:

- Stack is faster than heap memory.
- Stack provides a storage for local variables, including primitive and object variables referencing to objects in the heap memory.
- Stack is LIFO, whereas heap is not.
- Stack memory is smaller than heap memory.
- Stack is specific to one thread of execution, whereas Heap memory is available to all parts of the program.
- As mentioned earlier, stack is specific to one thread of execution so only the current executing thread can access stack memory whereas heap memory is accessible globally.

- Stack gets cleared up after the completion of currently executing method, whereas heap stays for a long time and depends on the garbage collector to free up some space.
- A very important point to note here is that it will help you to analyze the performance issue for your application. JVM throws `java.lang.StackOverFlowError` when the stack gets full and throws `java.lang.OutOfMemoryError` when the heap is full.

Escape analysis

As we have seen, objects live in the heap memory and heap memory is slower than stack. Every object on the heap has a lock, which ensures mutual exclusion upon invoke from a synchronized method or block. Heap and synchronization add performance overhead. Moreover, getting unused objects out of heap is very expensive from the performance point of view. On the other hand, stack memory is cheaper to clear as the JVM destroys the stack as soon as the method returns.

Also, JVM manages the stack memory properly and its deallocation is free, which speeds up the performance remarkably. I am sure you must be scratching your head and thinking, can we find a way to store an object in the stack memory than heap memory? If we could do so, wouldn't that improve the performance significantly? Well, as luck would have it, the Java team has provided a feature called escape analysis, which is enabled by default since Java 6.

Escape analysis can help determining if an object may escape the method, which is not local and may escape the thread that is its creator. If the object does not escape a method, it removes the need for creation of the object. In case of a thread, if the object does not escape a thread, then no other thread accesses the object, which means there is no need for synchronization for this object. Also, if the object is local to a thread, it means it can be allocated in the same memory location as the thread, which improves the data locality.

Although the result may vary from computer to computer, try running the following example on yours and analyze the performance gain.

For this example, we will modify the `HeapAndStack` class, which we used in the previous example. See the following modified version where we added a constructor and count the number of instances:

```
public class HeapAndStack {
    private static Long counter = 0l;
    public HeapAndStack() {
        ++counter;
    }
    public static void main(String[] args) {
        String intro = "Call myAwesomeMethod";
        HeapAndStack has = new HeapAndStack();
        System.out.println(intro);
        LookupPrimeNumbers lpn = new LookupPrimeNumbers();
        has.myAwesomeMethod(lpn);
    }
    private void myAwesomeMethod(LookupPrimeNumbers lpnParameter) {
        String message = "Let's generate some prime numbers";
        int start = 1;
        int end = 10000;
        System.out.println(message);
        lpnParameter.lookupPrime(start, end);
    }
    public static Long getCounter(){
        return counter;
    }
}
```

Now, let's see our escape analysis example, which uses the preceding class:

```
public class EscapeAnalysisTest {
    public static void main(String[] args) {
        System.out.println("Begin");
        for (long i = 0; i < 1000000001; i++) {
            HeapAndStack has = new HeapAndStack();
        }
        System.out.println("End of Test " + HeapAndStack.getCounter());
    }
}
```

In the preceding example, you will notice that we are creating one hundred million objects of the `HeapAndStack` class. It is a significant number, so it will give you a fair idea about the load. However, if your system cannot handle this, feel free to lower the number.

Try running the preceding example with the following parameters:

```
java -server -verbose:gc EscapeAnalysisTest|cat -n
```

```
mayur@mayur-VirtualBox:~$ java -server -verbose:gc EscapeAnalysisTest|cat -n
     1  [0.009s][info][gc] Using Serial
     2  Begin
     3  [0.172s][info][gc] GC(0) Pause Young (Allocation Failure) 4M->0M(15M) 1.646ms
     4  [0.177s][info][gc] GC(1) Pause Young (Allocation Failure) 5M->0M(15M) 1.146ms
     5  [0.178s][info][gc] GC(2) Pause Young (Allocation Failure) 5M->0M(15M) 0.178ms
     6  [0.179s][info][gc] GC(3) Pause Young (Allocation Failure) 5M->0M(15M) 0.149ms
     7  [0.180s][info][gc] GC(4) Pause Young (Allocation Failure) 5M->0M(15M) 0.129ms
     8  [0.190s][info][gc] GC(5) Pause Young (Allocation Failure) 5M->0M(15M) 0.237ms
     9  [0.194s][info][gc] GC(6) Pause Young (Allocation Failure) 5M->0M(15M) 0.219ms
    10  [0.194s][info][gc] GC(7) Pause Young (Allocation Failure) 5M->0M(15M) 0.171ms
    11  [0.195s][info][gc] GC(8) Pause Young (Allocation Failure) 5M->0M(15M) 0.137ms
    12  [0.196s][info][gc] GC(9) Pause Young (Allocation Failure) 5M->0M(15M) 0.129ms
    13  [0.197s][info][gc] GC(10) Pause Young (Allocation Failure) 5M->0M(15M) 0.165ms
    14  [0.198s][info][gc] GC(11) Pause Young (Allocation Failure) 5M->0M(15M) 0.130ms
    15  [0.203s][info][gc] GC(12) Pause Young (Allocation Failure) 5M->0M(15M) 0.145ms
    16  [0.204s][info][gc] GC(13) Pause Young (Allocation Failure) 5M->0M(15M) 0.157ms
    17  [0.204s][info][gc] GC(14) Pause Young (Allocation Failure) 5M->0M(15M) 0.189ms
    18  [0.205s][info][gc] GC(15) Pause Young (Allocation Failure) 5M->0M(15M) 0.227ms
    19  [0.207s][info][gc] GC(16) Pause Young (Allocation Failure) 5M->0M(15M) 0.248ms
    20  [0.211s][info][gc] GC(17) Pause Young (Allocation Failure) 5M->0M(15M) 0.165ms
    21  [0.212s][info][gc] GC(18) Pause Young (Allocation Failure) 5M->0M(15M) 0.161ms
    22  [0.213s][info][gc] GC(19) Pause Young (Allocation Failure) 5M->0M(15M) 0.131ms
    23  [0.214s][info][gc] GC(20) Pause Young (Allocation Failure) 5M->0M(15M) 0.161ms
    24  [0.215s][info][gc] GC(21) Pause Young (Allocation Failure) 5M->0M(15M) 0.173ms
    25  [0.217s][info][gc] GC(22) Pause Young (Allocation Failure) 5M->0M(15M) 0.142ms
    26  [0.218s][info][gc] GC(23) Pause Young (Allocation Failure) 5M->0M(15M) 0.138ms
    27  [0.219s][info][gc] GC(24) Pause Young (Allocation Failure) 5M->0M(15M) 0.128ms
    28  [0.220s][info][gc] GC(25) Pause Young (Allocation Failure) 5M->0M(15M) 0.123ms
    29  [0.220s][info][gc] GC(26) Pause Young (Allocation Failure) 5M->0M(15M) 0.125ms
    30  [0.221s][info][gc] GC(27) Pause Young (Allocation Failure) 5M->0M(15M) 0.150ms
    31  [0.233s][info][gc] GC(28) Pause Young (Allocation Failure) 5M->0M(15M) 0.315ms
    32  [0.248s][info][gc] GC(29) Pause Young (Allocation Failure) 5M->0M(15M) 0.274ms
    33  [0.249s][info][gc] GC(30) Pause Young (Allocation Failure) 5M->0M(15M) 0.325ms
    34  [0.250s][info][gc] GC(31) Pause Young (Allocation Failure) 5M->0M(15M) 0.286ms
    35  [0.251s][info][gc] GC(32) Pause Young (Allocation Failure) 5M->0M(15M) 0.160ms
    36  [0.256s][info][gc] GC(33) Pause Young (Allocation Failure) 5M->0M(15M) 0.258ms
    37  [0.257s][info][gc] GC(34) Pause Young (Allocation Failure) 5M->0M(15M) 0.194ms
    38  [0.258s][info][gc] GC(35) Pause Young (Allocation Failure) 5M->0M(15M) 0.215ms
    39  [0.263s][info][gc] GC(36) Pause Young (Allocation Failure) 5M->0M(15M) 0.182ms
    40  [0.265s][info][gc] GC(37) Pause Young (Allocation Failure) 5M->0M(15M) 0.183ms
    41  [0.268s][info][gc] GC(38) Pause Young (Allocation Failure) 5M->0M(15M) 0.193ms
    42  [0.269s][info][gc] GC(39) Pause Young (Allocation Failure) 5M->0M(15M) 0.176ms
    43  [0.270s][info][gc] GC(40) Pause Young (Allocation Failure) 5M->0M(15M) 0.165ms
    44  [0.275s][info][gc] GC(41) Pause Young (Allocation Failure) 5M->0M(15M) 0.213ms
    45  [0.276s][info][gc] GC(42) Pause Young (Allocation Failure) 5M->0M(15M) 0.203ms
    46  [0.277s][info][gc] GC(43) Pause Young (Allocation Failure) 5M->0M(15M) 0.159ms
    47  [0.278s][info][gc] GC(44) Pause Young (Allocation Failure) 5M->0M(15M) 0.159ms
    48  [0.279s][info][gc] GC(45) Pause Young (Allocation Failure) 5M->0M(15M) 0.159ms
    49  [0.282s][info][gc] GC(46) Pause Young (Allocation Failure) 5M->0M(15M) 0.166ms
    50  [0.284s][info][gc] GC(47) Pause Young (Allocation Failure) 5M->0M(15M) 0.173ms
    51  [0.285s][info][gc] GC(48) Pause Young (Allocation Failure) 5M->0M(15M) 0.155ms
    52  [0.286s][info][gc] GC(49) Pause Young (Allocation Failure) 5M->0M(15M) 0.149ms
    53  [0.290s][info][gc] GC(50) Pause Young (Allocation Failure) 5M->0M(15M) 0.209ms
    54  [0.304s][info][gc] GC(51) Pause Young (Allocation Failure) 5M->0M(15M) 0.250ms
    55  [0.305s][info][gc] GC(52) Pause Young (Allocation Failure) 5M->0M(15M) 0.190ms
    56  [0.306s][info][gc] GC(53) Pause Young (Allocation Failure) 5M->0M(15M) 0.149ms
    57  [0.308s][info][gc] GC(54) Pause Young (Allocation Failure) 5M->0M(15M) 1.507ms
```

And then, add the following:

```
java -server -verbose:gc -XX:+DoEscapeAnalysis EscapeAnalysisTest
```

```
mayur@mayur-VirtualBox:~$ java -server -verbose:gc -XX:+DoEscapeAnalysis EscapeAnalysisTest
[0.021s][info][gc] Using Serial
Begin
[0.239s][info][gc] GC(0) Pause Young (Allocation Failure) 4M->0M(15M) 5.339ms
[0.257s][info][gc] GC(1) Pause Young (Allocation Failure) 5M->0M(15M) 15.120ms
[0.259s][info][gc] GC(2) Pause Young (Allocation Failure) 5M->0M(15M) 0.272ms
[0.265s][info][gc] GC(3) Pause Young (Allocation Failure) 5M->0M(15M) 0.247ms
[0.275s][info][gc] GC(4) Pause Young (Allocation Failure) 5M->0M(15M) 0.266ms
[0.276s][info][gc] GC(5) Pause Young (Allocation Failure) 5M->0M(15M) 0.173ms
[0.277s][info][gc] GC(6) Pause Young (Allocation Failure) 5M->0M(15M) 0.218ms
[0.278s][info][gc] GC(7) Pause Young (Allocation Failure) 5M->0M(15M) 0.146ms
[0.280s][info][gc] GC(8) Pause Young (Allocation Failure) 5M->0M(15M) 1.717ms
[0.285s][info][gc] GC(9) Pause Young (Allocation Failure) 5M->0M(15M) 0.364ms
[0.286s][info][gc] GC(10) Pause Young (Allocation Failure) 5M->0M(15M) 0.301ms
[0.289s][info][gc] GC(11) Pause Young (Allocation Failure) 5M->0M(15M) 0.199ms
[0.300s][info][gc] GC(12) Pause Young (Allocation Failure) 5M->0M(15M) 0.232ms
[0.307s][info][gc] GC(13) Pause Young (Allocation Failure) 5M->0M(15M) 0.238ms
[0.308s][info][gc] GC(14) Pause Young (Allocation Failure) 5M->0M(15M) 0.175ms
[0.309s][info][gc] GC(15) Pause Young (Allocation Failure) 5M->0M(15M) 0.131ms
[0.309s][info][gc] GC(16) Pause Young (Allocation Failure) 5M->0M(15M) 0.127ms
[0.311s][info][gc] GC(17) Pause Young (Allocation Failure) 5M->0M(15M) 0.131ms
[0.312s][info][gc] GC(18) Pause Young (Allocation Failure) 5M->0M(15M) 0.150ms
[0.312s][info][gc] GC(19) Pause Young (Allocation Failure) 5M->0M(15M) 0.127ms
[0.317s][info][gc] GC(20) Pause Young (Allocation Failure) 5M->0M(15M) 0.227ms
[0.320s][info][gc] GC(21) Pause Young (Allocation Failure) 5M->0M(15M) 0.187ms
[0.324s][info][gc] GC(22) Pause Young (Allocation Failure) 5M->0M(15M) 0.195ms
[0.325s][info][gc] GC(23) Pause Young (Allocation Failure) 5M->0M(15M) 0.162ms
[0.326s][info][gc] GC(24) Pause Young (Allocation Failure) 5M->0M(15M) 0.136ms
[0.334s][info][gc] GC(25) Pause Young (Allocation Failure) 5M->0M(15M) 0.232ms
[0.335s][info][gc] GC(26) Pause Young (Allocation Failure) 5M->0M(15M) 0.152ms
[0.336s][info][gc] GC(27) Pause Young (Allocation Failure) 5M->0M(15M) 0.126ms
[0.337s][info][gc] GC(28) Pause Young (Allocation Failure) 5M->0M(15M) 0.237ms
[0.337s][info][gc] GC(29) Pause Young (Allocation Failure) 5M->0M(15M) 0.124ms
[0.338s][info][gc] GC(30) Pause Young (Allocation Failure) 5M->0M(15M) 0.128ms
[0.339s][info][gc] GC(31) Pause Young (Allocation Failure) 5M->0M(15M) 0.124ms
[0.339s][info][gc] GC(32) Pause Young (Allocation Failure) 5M->0M(15M) 0.120ms
[0.340s][info][gc] GC(33) Pause Young (Allocation Failure) 5M->0M(15M) 0.120ms
[0.341s][info][gc] GC(34) Pause Young (Allocation Failure) 5M->0M(15M) 0.119ms
[0.347s][info][gc] GC(35) Pause Young (Allocation Failure) 5M->0M(15M) 0.233ms
[0.355s][info][gc] GC(36) Pause Young (Allocation Failure) 5M->0M(15M) 0.208ms
[0.360s][info][gc] GC(37) Pause Young (Allocation Failure) 5M->0M(15M) 0.229ms
[0.361s][info][gc] GC(38) Pause Young (Allocation Failure) 5M->0M(15M) 0.172ms
[0.361s][info][gc] GC(39) Pause Young (Allocation Failure) 5M->0M(15M) 0.129ms
[0.362s][info][gc] GC(40) Pause Young (Allocation Failure) 5M->0M(15M) 0.122ms
[0.363s][info][gc] GC(41) Pause Young (Allocation Failure) 5M->0M(15M) 0.121ms
[0.364s][info][gc] GC(42) Pause Young (Allocation Failure) 5M->0M(15M) 0.199ms
[0.364s][info][gc] GC(43) Pause Young (Allocation Failure) 5M->0M(15M) 0.132ms
[0.365s][info][gc] GC(44) Pause Young (Allocation Failure) 5M->0M(15M) 0.131ms
[0.374s][info][gc] GC(45) Pause Young (Allocation Failure) 5M->0M(15M) 0.184ms
[0.375s][info][gc] GC(46) Pause Young (Allocation Failure) 5M->0M(15M) 0.156ms
[0.376s][info][gc] GC(47) Pause Young (Allocation Failure) 5M->0M(15M) 0.121ms
[0.377s][info][gc] GC(48) Pause Young (Allocation Failure) 5M->0M(15M) 0.190ms
[0.383s][info][gc] GC(49) Pause Young (Allocation Failure) 5M->0M(15M) 0.234ms
[0.383s][info][gc] GC(50) Pause Young (Allocation Failure) 5M->0M(15M) 0.171ms
[0.389s][info][gc] GC(51) Pause Young (Allocation Failure) 5M->0M(15M) 0.232ms
[0.390s][info][gc] GC(52) Pause Young (Allocation Failure) 5M->0M(15M) 0.205ms
[0.390s][info][gc] GC(53) Pause Young (Allocation Failure) 5M->0M(15M) 0.133ms
[0.391s][info][gc] GC(54) Pause Young (Allocation Failure) 5M->0M(15M) 0.126ms
```

Do you see the difference?

Without escape analysis, it is going to create one hundred million objects on the heap. With the help of escape analysis, the JVM can determine whether the object can go in the stack or heap. This will significantly help improve the performance.

If have several call levels in your code, with the help of escape analysis we can assign these objects on the stack as well, which can escape one method but not the calling method. For stream and optional, escape analysis proved to be very helpful in improving their performance.

Common memory problems

Now you know a little bit more about memory and how it's being used, let's see a few common memory errors.

OutOfMemory

If you are not new to development, you may have been bitten by the in famous `OutOfMemory` exception. This is the last thing you want to get on a production application as some companies may loose million dollars per minute in cases of server failure. You may have guessed the meaning of the `OutOfMemory` exception. Yes, you are right, your application has used up all the available memory allocated to JVM. You may be thinking, since the server resources are so cheap, you can just add more RAM and this problem will go away. Well, this approach may work for a couple of days. Increasing server resources is not the answer. If you have a memory leak in your code, then no matter how much memory you add, you are going to come to the same situation soon. Oh, you may be wondering, what is a memory leak? Ok, let's look into that. Every application needs to store data such as variables and objects temporarily. As you already know, applications running on JVM depend on it to provide sufficient memory. However, JVM's memory is also limited and largely depends on the underlying OS's memory. Hence, it is important for applications running on JVM to manage their memory properly. Applications are expected to release the memory resources after their use, but if an application does not release the memory then that application has memory leak, which eventually crashes with the `OutOfMemory` exception.

This is the most common performance-related error you can find. You see this error when JVM runs out of allocated memory and cannot allocate more objects. There are various ways by which you can get into this situation. Let's explore them one by one.

Mismanagement of object life cycle: java.lang.OutOfMemoryError: Java heap space

As we saw in the earlier chapter, when the application loads up, Java heap space is created. If for some reason your application is not making old unused objects available to the garbage collector, all these objects are going to consume this limited available space leaving no space for new objects. Hence, when a new object creation request comes in, JVM throws the OutOfMemoryError exception.

Also, in a typical web application scenario, if your application's traffic increases dramatically, it is going to consume all the available memory to serve these flooded requests. Hence, there will be a time when there won't be any memory available to support new requests and your application may crash for the OutOfMemoryError exception.

Refer to the following example, which generates the OutOfMemory: Java heap space error exception:

```java
public class OutOfMemoryError {
public static void main(String args[])
{
OutOfMemoryError ome = new OutOfMemoryError();
ome.generateMyIntArray(1,50);
}
public void generateMyIntArray(int start, int end){
int multiplier = 100;
for(int i = 1; i < end; i++)
{
System.out.println("Round " + i + " Memory: " +
Runtime.getRuntime().freeMemory());
int[] myIntList = new int[multiplier];
for(int j= i; j > 1; j--){
myIntList[j] = i;
}
multiplier = multiplier * 10;
}
}
}
```

Running the preceding example will provide the following output:

```
Round 1 Memory: 267253232
Round 2 Memory: 267253232
Round 3 Memory: 267249216
Round 4 Memory: 267209200
Round 5 Memory: 266809184
Round 6 Memory: 262809168
Round 7 Memory: 222809152
Round 8 Memory: 222840880
Exception in thread "main" java.lang.OutOfMemoryError: Java heap space
        at Java9PerformanceBook.OutOfMemoryError.generateMyIntArray(OutOfMemoryError.java:14)
        at Java9PerformanceBook.OutOfMemoryError.main(OutOfMemoryError.java:6)
```

This is just one example. However, there are many different scenarios which can cause the OutOfMemory exception. Pay close attention to object references. Make sure you clear the references once you are done using them.

java.lang.OutOfMemoryError: GC Overhead limit exceeded

This is a rather rare form of the exception OutOfMemoryError. As the name suggests, this error occurs when garbage collector has reached its overhead limit. This means, it is running all the time, but is very slow in collecting objects. See the following example;

```java
import java.util.Map;
import java.util.Random;

public class GCOverhead {
    public static void main(String args[]) throws Exception {
        Map map = System.getProperties();
        Random r = new Random();
        while (true) {
            map.put(r.nextInt(), "java 9");
        }
    }
}
```

Compile the previous program with javac and then use the following command:

```
java -Xmx100m -XX:+UseParallelGC GCOverhead
```

This will result in the `java.lang.OutOfMemoryError: GC overhead limit exceeded`. See the following output:

```
mayur@mayur-VirtualBox:~$ java -Xmx100m -XX:+UseParallelGC GCOverhead
Exception in thread "main" java.lang.OutOfMemoryError: GC overhead limit exceeded
        at java.base/java.lang.Integer.valueOf(Integer.java:1050)
        at GCOverhead.main(GCOverhead.java:9)
```

In order to improve the garbage collector's performance, the JVM is configured to detect whether during the garbage collection process, by default, the Java process recovers less than 2 percent of the heap by spending more than 98 percent of its processing time. When this happens, it throws the GC overhead limit exceeded error. This check is necessary because if GC is only going to recover 2 percent of the memory, there won't be much space for new objects. Hence, the JVM is going to run the GC process again and again only to claim this tiny space. This activity is going to utilize CPU resources fully and you will see that your application is not responding to user requests anymore. Hence, this check is necessary. However, you may be able to turn off this check by adding the `-XX:-UseGCOverheadLimit` flag to the `VM` parameter.

java.lang.OutOfMemoryError: Permgen space

This is applicable to JVM 7 and earlier. Java 8 has changed the memory model. This newer model does not have permanent generation region, which is replaced by Metaspace region. As we have learned, Java memory is divided into various regions. When JVM first initialized, it set the sizes of all these regions to platform-specific defaults. You can also specify the sizes in the `VM` parameter section, which will be used for the allocation over the platform-specific defaults. The preceding error is related to permanent generation area, which means the size of the permanent generation area in the memory is filled up. Permanent generation mostly stores the declarations, including name and fields of the class, methods with their bytecode, object arrays, constant pool information, and JIT compiler optimization of the loaded classes. This states that the permanent generation space is mainly affected by the number of classes and the size of each class. It means that a very big class or large number of classes are going to contribute to this type of error, `OutOfMemoryError`.

java.lang.OutOfMemoryError: Metaspace

One of the regions of the JVM memory is the Metaspace region. If it gets filled up, JVM throws this type of exception. Since this is the replacement of the permanent generation region, the Metaspace region now stores the information of permanent generation. It is used to store things like the declarations, including name and fields of the class, methods with their bytecode, object arrays, constant pool information and JIT compiler optimization of the loaded classes.

Hence, this type of error is thrown by JVM for having a large number of big classes. The following example uses `javassist` package from the link: `http://jboss-javassist.github.io/javassist/` which enables Java bytecode manipulation. This library is used for editing bytecodes. At runtime when JVM loads the classes, programs can define or modify new classes:

```
import javassist.*;

public class Metaspace {
    static ClassPool cp = ClassPool.getDefault();

    public static void main(String[] args) throws Exception{
        for (int i = 0; ; i++) {
            Class c = cp.makeClass("Java 9" + i).toClass();
        }
    }
}
```

In the previous program, the for loop runs without any limit and generates classes at the runtime. These classes definitions then consume `Metaspace` and eventually throw the `OutOfMemoryError: Metaspace` exception. See the following output:

```
Error occurred during initialization of VM
OutOfMemoryError: Metaspace
```

java.lang.OutOfMemoryError: Unable to create new native thread

As you know every Java program runs in a new thread. Java supports multithreading so you can create as many threads as you like till you consume all the available memory for the JVM. Once the memory limit is reached, JVM native code can no longer create a new native thread from the underlying operating system. In order to identify the problem, you can take a thread dump and analyze it. If you are new to Java, you may be wondering what a thread dump is. You can refer to `Chapter 3`, *Learning How to Troubleshoot Code* where we have covered this section in more detail.

Please see the following example which will end up in throwing
`java.lang.OutOfMemoryError: unable to create new native thread`:

```
public class NativeThread {
    public static void main(String[] args){
        NativeThread nt = new NativeThread();
        nt.runThreads();
    }
    public void runThreads(){

        while(true){
            new Thread(new Runnable(){
                public void run() {
                    try {
                        Thread.sleep(10000000);
                    } catch(InterruptedException e) { }
                }
            }).start();
        }
    }
}
```

As mentioned earlier, the precceding program is going to throw
`java.lang.OutOfMemoryError: unable to create new native thread`. Please
note that the native thread limit is platform-dependent so it will take a different number of
threads in order to reach to the limit:

```
Exception in thread "main" java.lang.OutOfMemoryError: unable to create new native thread
        at java.lang.Thread.start0(Native Method)
        at java.lang.Thread.start(Thread.java:714)
        at Java9PerformanceBook.NativeThread.runThreads(NativeThread.java:18)
        at Java9PerformanceBook.NativeThread.main(NativeThread.java:7)
```

java.lang.OutOfMemoryError: request size bytes for reason

If you are not new to computers, you may already know what swap space is. It is a space
used by the underlying operating system to store the contents in lieu of RAM in case it fills
up. Every time you start your application, JVM allocates the appropriate amount of
memory to all the regions depending on your VM parameter. This means, your application
has an upper limit for the memory it can use. Hence, if your application happens to request
more memory than the allocated limit, the operating system uses the swap space from the
hard drive as a virtual memory. If the swap memory space is also fully consumed, JVM
throws the error `java.lang.OutOfMemoryError: request size bytes for reason`.
Are you out of swap space?

java.lang.OutOfMemoryError: Requested array size exceeds VM limit

As everything with the JVM memory regions, there is a limit on the number of array size that the program can allocate. This limit is platform specific. If your application uses an array size more than the allowed size for the underlying platform, you will see this error. The following code will help you understand this error:

```
public class ArraySizeExceedsLimit {
    public static void main(String[] args){
        ArraySizeExceedsLimit arr = new ArraySizeExceedsLimit();
        arr.arraySizeChecker();
    }

    public void arraySizeChecker(){
        int[] myIntArray = new int[Integer.MAX_VALUE-1];
    }
}
```

If you run the preceding program, it is going to throw the desired error as the `int` primitives that we are trying to generate requires more memory than the defaults allocated by the JVM:

```
Exception in thread "main" java.lang.OutOfMemoryError: Requested array size exceeds VM limit
        at Java9PerformanceBook.ArraySizeExceedsLimit.arraySizeChecker(ArraySizeExceedsLimit.java:10)
        at Java9PerformanceBook.ArraySizeExceedsLimit.main(ArraySizeExceedsLimit.java:6)
```

Out of memory: kill process or sacrifice child

This error is thrown by the operating system. The operating system has processes which are governed by various kernel jobs. One of these jobs is out of memory killer. This job monitors the low memory situation and kills the rogue process which is consuming more memory resources. See the following example, which runs a loop and adds `int` array to a list. Eventually, you will get this error. Please note that you may need to tweak the swap file and heap sizes on your system:

```
import java.util.ArrayList;
import java.util.List;

public class KillProcess {
    public static void main(String[] args){
        List<int[]> myArrayList = new ArrayList();
        KillProcess kp = new KillProcess();
        kp.processKillLoop(myArrayList);
    }
    public void processKillLoop(List<int[]> l){
```

```
        for (int i = 1; ; i++) {
            try{
                l.add(new int[Integer.MAX_VALUE-3]);
            }catch(Throwable t){
                t.printStackTrace();
            }
        }
    }
}
```

StackOverFlow

As we learned in the previous section, stack is the home of the parameters and local variables of an object which have references to that object on the heap. Heap and stack are important parts of memory allocated to JVM. Each thread created by your program gets its own stack and this memory is limited by its creator thread. As you learned earlier, when we call a method, JVM reserves a block on top of the stack where it stores local variables. And if our method fills up this allocated block, JVM throws an StackOverFlow error.

There are many possibilities for getting an StackOverflow error; however, having a recursive call without any proper termination condition is a very common reason. As you may have figured out, a recursive call can consume the allocated memory and leaves no room for new threads. Refer to the following example to understand the bad recursion problem:

```
1.      public class StackOverflowExample {
2.
3.      public static void main(String args[]){
4.        StackOverflowExample sfe = new StackOverflowExample();
5.        int num = 10;
6.        System.out.println("Factorial of " + num + " is " +
sfe.computeFactorial(10));
7.      }
8.
9.      private int computeFactorial(int num) {
10.             if ( num == 1)
11.             {
12.                 return 1;
13.             }
14.
15.             return computeFactorial (num + 1) * num;
16.        }
17.
18.      }
```

The preceding example computes the factorial of a given number. It is a very common and simple example. In this example, we are passing a number and calculating the factorial of that number. In the `computeFactorial(int num)` method, we are saying if the number is 1, then just return 1. So this is a good terminating condition. However, if we pass in anything other than 1, then the program is going to skip this condition. *Line 15*, makes the recursive call by adding 1 to the given number and passing it as a parameter and multiplying it by the same number. This is where we have a problem. To compute a factorial, we need to subtract 1 and not add 1. By adding 1, we are creating a non-terminating recursion. This program will never end and hence will end up using the allocated stack memory and eventually throws an `StackOverflow` error.

```
Exception in thread "main" java.lang.StackOverflowError
    at StackOverflowExample.computeFactorial(StackOverflowExample.java:15)
    at StackOverflowExample.computeFactorial(StackOverflowExample.java:15)
    at StackOverflowExample.computeFactorial(StackOverflowExample.java:15)
    at StackOverflowExample.computeFactorial(StackOverflowExample.java:15)
    at StackOverflowExample.computeFactorial(StackOverflowExample.java:15)
```

We can fix this problem by replacing + with – and that way we are adding a terminating condition.

Another common example that can cause the `StackOverflow` error is circular dependency. Refer to the following example:

```
1.    public class StackOverflowCircularDependencyExample {
2.
3.     public MyAwesomeClass mwc;
4.
5.     public static void main(String args[])
6.     {
7.       StackOverflowCircularDependencyExample scde = new
StackOverflowCircularDependencyExample();
8.       scde.printHello();
9.     }
10.
11.    public StackOverflowCircularDependencyExample()
12.    {
13.      mwc = new MyAwesomeClass();
14.    }
15.
16.    public void printHello()
17.    {
18.      System.out.println("Hello Friend !!!");
19.    }
20.   }
21.
```

```
22.    class MyAwesomeClass
23.    {
24.     public StackOverflowCircularDependencyExample scde;
25.
26.     public MyAwesomeClass()
27.     {
28.      scde = new StackOverflowCircularDependencyExample();
29.     }
30.
31.    }
```

In the preceding example, we are creating a cyclic dependency. The constructor of the StackOverflowCircularDependencyExample class is calling the constructor of the MyAwesomeClass class. And the constructor of MyAwesomeClass is calling the constructor of the StackOverflowCircularDependencyExample class. So by running the StackOverflowCircularDependencyExample class throws an StackOverflow error.

```
Exception in thread "main" java.lang.StackOverflowError
     at
MyAwesomeClass.<init>(StackOverflowCircularDependencyExample.java:28)
     at
StackOverflowCircularDependencyExample.<init>(StackOverflowCircularDependen
cyExample.java:13)
     at
MyAwesomeClass.<init>(StackOverflowCircularDependencyExample.java:28)
     at
StackOverflowCircularDependencyExample.<init>(StackOverflowCircularDependen
cyExample.java:13)
     at
MyAwesomeClass.<init>(StackOverflowCircularDependencyExample.java:28)
     at
StackOverflowCircularDependencyExample.<init>(StackOverflowCircularDependen
cyExample.java:13)
     at
MyAwesomeClass.<init>(StackOverflowCircularDependencyExample.java:28)
     at
StackOverflowCircularDependencyExample.<init>(StackOverflowCircularDependen
cyExample.java:13)
     at
MyAwesomeClass.<init>(StackOverflowCircularDependencyExample.java:28)
```

These are very basic examples and we can easily spot the problem by just inspecting them. However, in real production applications, many times it is not possible to spot these problems easily as they may not be visible during your normal development or QA test. Often some type of scenario triggers this condition and throws an `StackOverflow` error. Hence, it is important to train your eyes to look for terminating the condition and the possibility to meet that condition using your program. For example, in our first example, we put in a terminating condition but in reality that condition may not trigger at all.

Also, even if your application is not using any recursion or creating a cyclic dependency, there is a possibility that your application is calling another library and that library is making a call to your application. This can also trigger the `StackOverflow` error. Hence, look for these clues as well.

Database operations

So far we have seen various code-level optimizations related to CPU and memory that we can perform to improve an application's performance. However, the overall performance of the application is dependent on various factors such as database, IO, and network.

In the SaaS world, almost every application out there is database dependent. This means, we need to focus on various aspects related to database optimization. Several performance issues are the result of poor architectural decisions, the wrong use of design patterns, improper database configurations, and sometimes incorrect database type selection. In this section, we will focus on identifying various database-related bottlenecks and briefly discuss the areas of improvements. Database optimization itself is a vast topic and out of the scope of this section. In order to optimize the database you need to look at various different aspects such as cache management, JDBC batching, connection pool management, indexing, query optimization, including `N+1` query problem, prepared statements, ORM configuration and optimization, failover and redundancy management, and cluster configuration and optimization.

I am sure you must be bouncing off the walls to learn more about the database optimization. However, before you go crazy on dissecting your database, it is important for us to first understand the bottlenecks, identify the problem areas and design strategies around it.

Most often you will hear your customer service and marketing team complain about slow application performance, server crash during busy times, the system does not store users' responses, and so on. All these problems are generally related to the database and can be fixed by taking appropriate measures. Let's explore more to see the underlying causes of the earlier mentioned problems.

All the end user visible performance problems have several underlying reasons. Let's look at them one by one:

- **Slow application performance**: This issue may be related to slow query performance, which may be caused by incorrect design of the query; for example, using improper join statements and retrieving values from various tables which are not normalized. Also, there are other factors that could contribute to the slow application performance such as inadequate indexing, poor application and database logic, faulty database framework configurations, and so on. Application performance can be improved by moving some of the logic to the database layer by creating store procedures. This way we can balance the load. Indexing is the most essential part of the database design. Indexing helps to reduce the full table scan, which contributes significantly to the slower performance of large records.

- **Server crash during busy times**: The most common reason for this failure is the excessive use of memory and CPU resources. If not managed properly, the application eventually consumes all the resources and makes database servers go down. This could happen due to the insufficient availability of connections from the connection pool, poor memory allocation, or not enough disk space allocation. Excessive logging, poor indexing, improper normalization, and non-optimized complex join statements can also contribute to server crash.

- **System does not store the user's response**: These types of problems occurred mainly due to the failure to manage the SQL transactions properly. In rare cases, the developer's inability to use proper exception handling can lead to this type of problem. For example, swallowing of a database exception in a catch block, in other words, a catch block does not have code to handle this exception and silently fails to report this problem. Because of this, the system runs as usual but the database transaction fails. These are common signs of database performance issues. If you are experiencing performance issues with your application, it may be a good idea to look for the following signs to identify database-related issues.

- **Missing table indexes**: This is the area you should focus on first. It should not take much time to optimize your table indexes. If you are not familiar with database indexing, let's spend some time to understand the concept. Indexing is nothing but sorting a particular column. This is helpful when you try to retrieve values from the table as the database can easily find the sorted values. In order to create proper indexes, you need to analyze the table and figure out the most commonly used columns in your queries. These columns are the right candidate for adding indexes. Without indexes, the database has to do a full table scan of every row and every value of each and every column. As you can see, this is very expensive. On the other hand, if you add an index to a column, then that column gets sorted in natural sort order. Because of this, the database is able to do a binary search on the column, which is *O(log n)* versus going through every row and every value, which is *O(n)* search.

- **Many complex join statements**: These are the queries you should be focusing on to identify query-related issues. Oftentimes, an improper join type can lead to excessive data pull. This slows down the application as now your code has to go through a lot more data than required.

- **Execution of multiple SQL statements**: Look for transactions using multiple SQL statements. In many situations, using multiple statements in one transaction may not be necessary. You should be able to optimize it by combining it with joins, or if data is not getting updated frequently, then creating materialized views and using that instead of making multiple calls for each transaction.

- **Creating N+1 query problem**: These types of problems occur when the same SQL statement is getting executed multiple times. Look for patterns in your code which are making multiple calls. The best candidates would be the loops. For example, consider a case where you are sending a newsletter to all your customers. For that you need to fetch their email addresses and use that to email them your awesome newsletter. Since you can have multiple email addresses, you are storing the email addresses in a different table with associated customer ID. For this, you come up with the following code:

```
1.    public static void main(String args[]){
2.      List<Customer> customers = getAllCustomers();
3.      for(Customer customer : customers){
4.          String email = customer.getEmailAddress();
5.          AwesomeNewsLetter.send(email);
6.      }
7.    }
```

Line 2 gives you all the customers from the database. For this, say for example, you are directly calling the database like this `SELECT * FROM customer`. In *line 3*, you are looping through the `Customer` array. In *line 4*, you are fetching the first email address for that customer by triggering `SELECT email FROM customer WHERE customerid = ?` and passing `customer id` from the `customer` object.

In this example, you are firing `N+1` queries where `N` is the number of customers:

```
SELECT email FROM customer WHERE customerid = 1
SELECT email FROM customer WHERE customerid = 2
SELECT email FROM customer WHERE customerid = 3
SELECT email FROM customer WHERE customerid = 4
SELECT email FROM customer WHERE customerid = 5
SELECT email FROM customer WHERE customerid = 6
SELECT email FROM customer WHERE customerid = 7
SELECT email FROM customer WHERE customerid = 8
    .
    .
    .
    .
SELECT email FROM customer WHERE customerid = N
```

Can you see the problem with the preceding code? In order to get the email addresses for all customers, we are generating `N` number of queries where as we can easily retrieve all the emails in one single query. And this single query will be much faster than firing all the queries.

- **Too many open connections**: This problem is very common as many application developers don't pay attention to the connection pool. You need to make sure you are explicitly closing the connections after use. Not doing that will result in consuming all the available connections and denying access to your application.

These are some of the areas one should focus to improve the database performance.

I/O operations

This is another area that is important from the performance optimization point of view. If you need to read or write files to your server, you need to rely on Java's I/O APIs. The I/O operations are resource intensive and may consume a large amount of processing time. This can turn into a big performance bottleneck, and hence, it is important to tune this area to improve the overall application performance.

Most Java developers still rely on the basic I/O APIs, which are more than adequate to perform any file related operations. However, they do have some performance issues, for example, `InputStream.read()` performs character-by-character reading or the method `Reader.read()` reads one character at a time. Then there are stream-related APIs. Most of them read or write one byte at a time, which contributes to performance problems as it takes a long time to go byte by byte on a large dataset. This led to the birth of buffered streams which buffer the data (as if you did not get that from the name). Naturally, this gives better results compared to the normal stream APIs. For example, `FileInputStream` helps reading from a file and `FileOutputStream` helps writing to a file. These are basic stream APIs one would use. However, Java has provided a buffered version of these APIs `BufferedInputStream` and `BufferedOutputStream`. Let's take the following example and see the difference:

```
public class JavaIOPerformanceTest {
public static void main(String args[]) {
JavaIOPerformanceTest iotest = new JavaIOPerformanceTest();
 try{
 FileOutputStream foStream = new
FileOutputStream("/Users/MayurRamgir/fileoutputstream.txt");
 iotest.write(foStream);
 BufferedOutputStream boStream = new BufferedOutputStream(new
FileOutputStream("/Users/MayurRamgir/bufferedoutputstream.txt"));
 iotest.write(boStream);
 } catch (IOException e) {
 e.printStackTrace();
 }
 }
 private void write(OutputStream os) {
 long startTime = Instant.now().toEpochMilli();
 try {
 for (int i = 0; i < 99999999; i++) {
 os.write(1);
 }
 os.close();
 } catch (IOException e) {
 e.printStackTrace();
 }
 long endTime = Instant.now().toEpochMilli();
 long totalTimeSpent = endTime - startTime;
 System.out.format("Program took %02d min, %02d sec, %02d
millisec",
 TimeUnit.MILLISECONDS.toMinutes(totalTimeSpent),
 TimeUnit.MILLISECONDS.toSeconds(totalTimeSpent) -
TimeUnit.MINUTES.toSeconds(TimeUnit.MILLISECONDS.toMinutes(totalTimeSpe
nt)),
 TimeUnit.MILLISECONDS.toMillis(totalTimeSpent)
```

```
);
System.out.println(" for " + os.toString());
    }
}
```

If I run the preceding program on my machine (MacBook Pro macOS Sierra v10.12.6, 2.7 GHz Intel Core i7, 16 GB 2133 MHz LPDDR3), I see the following output:

```
Program took 02 min, 06 sec, 126886 millisec for java.io.FileOutputStream@7852e922
Program took 00 min, 00 sec, 309 millisec for java.io.BufferedOutputStream@4e25154f
```

So, from the preceding example, you can see that the use of a buffered version of I/O API gives us much better results. However, Java has progressed further than this and added NIO and NIO.2 packages which in some cases give a significant performance boost for I/O-related operations. These packages provide low-level access to underlying operating system. Although it gives us more control over I/O, it requires us to pay more attention to using these APIs than basic I/O. The NIO package is platform dependent not only to hardware but to the underlying operating system and JVM. The NIO package introduces a few new concepts such as channels and selectors, buffers, and charset. On the other hand, the NIO2 package was introduced in Java 7, which offers support for using symbolic links and file attributes access. The NIO2 package offers file management-related functionalities such as channel based and buffer-oriented techniques to handle input or output. However, in many cases, stream based I/O is more efficient than NIO and NIO2 packages. Refer to the preceding example with the addition of the NIO package as follows:

```
public class JavaIOPerformanceTest {
public static void main(String args[]) {
JavaIOPerformanceTest iotest = new JavaIOPerformanceTest();
try{
FileOutputStream foStream = new
FileOutputStream("/Users/MayurRamgir/fileoutputstream.txt");
iotest.write(foStream);
BufferedOutputStream boStream = new BufferedOutputStream(new
FileOutputStream("/Users/MayurRamgir/bufferedoutputstream.txt"));
iotest.write(boStream);
Path nioFilePath = Paths.get("/Users/MayurRamgir/niotest.txt");
OutputStream nioStream = Files.newOutputStream(nioFilePath);
iotest.write(nioStream);
} catch (IOException e) { e.printStackTrace();
}
}
private void write(OutputStream os) {
long startTime = Instant.now().toEpochMilli();
```

```
        try {
        for (int i = 0; i < 99999999; i++) {
        os.write(1);
        }
        os.close();
        } catch (IOException e) {
        e.printStackTrace(); }
        long endTime = Instant.now().toEpochMilli();
        long totalTimeSpent = endTime - startTime;
        System.out.format("Program took %02d min, %02d sec, %02d millisec",
        TimeUnit.MILLISECONDS.toMinutes(totalTimeSpent),
        TimeUnit.MILLISECONDS.toSeconds(totalTimeSpent) -
  TimeUnit.MINUTES.toSeconds(TimeUnit.MILLISECONDS.toMinutes(totalTimeSpent))
,
        TimeUnit.MILLISECONDS.toMillis(totalTimeSpent)
        );
        System.out.println(" for " + os.toString());
        }
        }
```

Refer to the following output from the same machine:

```
Program took 02 min, 16 sec, 136081 millisec for java.io.FileOutputStream@7852e922
Program took 00 min, 00 sec, 326 millisec for java.io.BufferedOutputStream@4e25154f
Program took 02 min, 17 sec, 137597 millisec for java.nio.channels.Channels$1@55f96302
```

From the preceding output, you can see that for our example, BufferedOutputStream gave us a good performance boost even over the new package NIO. However, for many concurrent connections, NIO and NIO2 packages can perform better. The NIO2 package specifically adds value in the following ways:

- It delegates I/O buffering activities to the underlying operating system
- It streams data in blocks versus sequential streaming used by old I/O streams, which is good for chained filtering but bad for manipulating cached data
- It processes data in blocks, which are generated through buffers
- It uses channel streaming in which a single thread can manage multiple threads

Hence, you cannot just rely on the updated package to give you the performance boost you were expecting. You need to perform a thorough evaluation of your targeted production system and also perform performance benchmarking in order to understand which type of I/O package you should use for your specific needs.

Network operations

As the world is progressing toward the SaaS application's paradigm, it is imperative to pay close attention to network utilization of your program. In this typical client-server architecture, in many cases, every event is processed on the server side and the data constantly flows over the wire, across the oceans, miles away from its origin. On top of this, the world is becoming impatient regarding speed and performance. With the advent of social media and the love of video and photo sharing, data usage has sky rocketed and is using up almost all the bandwidth a user can get. Hence, it is extremely important to use network resources as efficiently as possible.

In order to squeeze every possible performance gain from the available network resources, we need to implement various strategies and design patterns. This section will highlight some of the new additions to latest Java releases, which we could use to optimize the network dependencies and speed up the data sharing between a client and a server. Note that the aim of this section is not to look into optimizing your network but to focus on the application areas which can be improved to get most from even the slowest network.

This heavy use of data requires us to rethink about the existing HTTP API, which has several drawbacks. The `HttpURLConnection` is provided since JDK1.1 to create a single request per thread. This API provides an abstract class `URLConnection`, which was designed for various protocols such as ftp and gopher, which are now obsolete. This API is not suitable for modern day usage where the user is creating multiple data requests. If your application is relying on connecting to various other web resources, you need to pay close attention to optimizing these connections. The `HttpURLConnection` API works on HTTP/1.1 protocol and offers various methods to connect and fetch data from remote resources. Also you need to make sure you properly close the unused connections in order to save on server resources. Various open connections will certainly affect the application's performance and create performance bottlenecks.

In order to overcome these drawbacks, Java 9 has introduced a new HTTP client API, which includes HTTP/2 and WebSocket. HTTP/2 is designed by considering the network latency, utilization of server resources, and overall performance and offers single connection between the user's web browser and web server. WebSocket, on the other hand, provides a single full-duplex connection to communicate interactively over a TCP connection. In contrast to the traditional HTTP, it streamlines the client and server communication by enabling the client to receive responses without any need to poll the server. This will significantly reduce the connection and request or response time between a client and a server. With this reduced network latency, web applications can now offer a desktop application feel in terms of request or response delays.

This API is not part of the standard JDK package. It is included in the `java.httpclient` incubator module. Hence, it will not be resolved automatically at compile and runtime. We need to explicitly add this in our application's `info.java` module file.

The following is a quick rundown on how to use this client. First, we create an URI object, which is then passed to the `HttpRequest` class's static create method to create a request object. This request object has GET, POST, and PUT methods. In case of POST, we can send a JSON string for which we need to set the content type as `application/json` for our request header.

The following shows an example with the GET method:

```
URI getAllURI = new URI("http://www.zonopact.com/getAllBooks");
HttpRequest request = HttpRequest.create(getAllURI) ;
request.GET();
```

The following shows an example with the POST method:

```
URI getAllURI = new URI("http://www.zonopact.com/getAllBooks");
String myJSONString = "
{"Books": {
        "author": "Mayur Ramgir",
        "book": {
            "title": "Java 9 High Performance",
            "version": "1.0",
            "published": true,
            "pages": 400
        },
    "book": {
            "title": "Unbarred Innovation: A Pathway to Greatest
Discoveries",
            "version": "1.0",
            "published": true,
            "pages": 232
        }
}";
HttpRequest request = HttpRequest.create(getAllURI);
 request.header("Accept", "application/json");
request.header("Content-Type", "application/json");
request.body(HttpRequest.fromString(myJSONString)) ;
request.POST();
```

It also offers the `responseAsync` method, which is useful for composing and combining multiple `HttpResponses`. It returns an instance of `CompletableFuture<HttpResponse>`, as shown in the following:

```
URI getAllURI = new URI("http://www.zonopact.com/getAllBooks");
    URI processAllURI = new URI("http://www.zonopact.com/processAllBooks");
    List bookRequestList = List.of(getAllURI, processAllURI);
    CompletableFuture<?>[] bookRequests = bookRequestList.stream().map(uri
-> HttpRequest.create(uri).GET().responseAsync()).map(f -> f.thenCompose(r
-> r.bodyAsync(HttpResponse.asString()))).map(f ->
f.thenAccept(System.out::println)).toArray(CompletableFuture<?>[]::new);
    CompletableFuture.allOf(bookRequests).join();
```

In the preceding example, we are passing two `URI` and combining the responses at the end.

WebSocket Client API

WebSocket API is another addition to the `java.httpclient` package. As explained earlier, it enables having full duplex communication between the client and the server. This package provides various methods to help build messages, listen for events and messages, and handle partial messages. This is one of the important additions to the Java network API as it can process client's requests seamlessly. Let's take the following example:

```
public class MyFirstWebSocketListener implements WebSocket.Listner{
    @Override public CompletionStage<?> onText(WebSocket webSocket,
CharSequence message, WebSocket.MessagePart part){
        //Process the message here
    }
  }
```

The client can then use the following code to call this:

```
        URI processAllURI = new
URI("http://www.zonopact.com/processAllBooks");
    WebSocket.newBuilder(processAllURI, new
MyFirstWebSocketListener()).buildAsync().join();
```

Summary

In this chapter, we learned about various bottlenecks which can cause performance issues. In particular, you need to focus on various areas such as CPU infrastructure, I/O operations, database operations, network utilization, and memory utilization. It is important to understand the type of operation your algorithm is performing. Based on that you need to optimize your code, so it wont take much of the resources.

In the next chapter, we will learn about the various troubleshooting and error handling techniques, logging, and then about thread dump and how to analyze it.

3

Learning How to Troubleshoot Code

"Ah-ah-ah. First rule of leadership: everything is your fault."- A Bug's Life (1998)

This is what your manager thinks but in a slightly different way. You might have heard me saying in my speeches or read in my leadership book and articles that a manager may not be a good leader. So, they may interpret this as *everything is your fault*. And after every client and management meeting, they come to you and shout like *P.T.* from the movie, *A Bug's Life, We're losin' the audience! You clowns get out there now!*

Sadly this is the reality, hence you and only you are responsible for controlling bugs in your code.

"It's a bug-eat-bug world out there, Princess. One of those 'circle of life' kind of things. Now let me tell you how things are supposed to work out: the sun grows the food, the ants pick the food, the grasshoppers eat the food..." - A Bug's Life (1998)

Very well said Mr. Grasshopper, the world is very buggy; so we can at least make sure we don't add more to it with our awesome application. As a developer, you have to take charge and learn how to find them and get rid of them.

A developer's life always crosses paths with a bug's life. Well, not a real-life bug, but a bug in your application. No matter how hard you try, they are inevitable, and so, learning how to keep them under control is one of the best moves you can make in your software development career. But don't feel bad--you have contributed significantly towards creating jobs beause of these bugs. (You know who I am referring to.....testers.)

These guys are the lousiest circus bugs you've ever seen! AND THEY'RE GONNA MAKE ME RICH!" - P.T

A tester may be thinking like this while testing your application code.

OK, enough of our silly jokes. Let's get back to business. From my sarcastic examples, you have learned that we have and will have bugs in our code. So, how will you find bugs? Troubleshooting is the answer. It is one of the most important parts of the development cycle. The more code you write, the more problems come to the surface. It is often difficult to identify the root cause of the bug, so you need to implement proper troubleshooting techniques.

In this chapter, you will learn various techniques to troubleshoot your code to identify root causes of bugs. Troubleshooting is a systematic process through which functionality problems in machines, electronic devices, software systems, and computers are identified and resolved. This involves, firstly, identifying the troubleshooting problem and gathering as much information as possible to accurately decide what action will help resolve the issue. This may also comprise of an understanding of the related circumstances and symptoms that have given rise to the problem.

Measuring performance

Performance measurement in software development can be defined as a method of gathering information about objects, classes, threads, and various other resources to examine the problematic areas that cause the underlying performance issue and find the root cause in order to solve the issue. Troubleshooting can be used as an instrument to measure performance. In a later section, you will learn about troubleshooting and how it can be used as a channel to fix performance issues.

Performance checklist

Before we begin with this chapter, let's first understand if we really have a performance issue with our application. How would you define a performance issue? To answer this question, you need to have a blueprint, which will be used as a base to measure performance. So, let's learn how to create this blueprint (or in other words, *checklist*) so we can understand if we really have a performance issue or not.

The first step in creating a performance checklist is to draft our objectives clearly. Let's explore this further:

1. Specify the acceptable response time based on the intended use of our application, such as the target user, target platform, and so on. For example, for an e-commerce application 3 seconds to 5 seconds processing time may be acceptable, but the same may be disastrous for an investment portal.

2. Consider scaling expectations. For example, what type of load our application should take and how much leverage we should have in order to expand the resources in real-time. By specifying the correct scaling expectation, we can measure the performance properly.

3. The third step is to incorporate user feedback. Involve your target users in the early release phase. This will give you an idea about user's expectations and their response to your application performance. You can use this feedback to set up your performance target.

4. Set performance targets per module. Always set performance targets for each module. For example, if your application contains an account opening module and a payment processing module then it is important to measure the performance of the account opening module and payment processing module separately as it will help us to pin point the problem effectively.

Basic principles of troubleshooting

To troubleshoot issues in your application, not only do you need to know the right means of fixing each individual problem, but you also need to have the correct mindset in understanding and resolving them. There are a number of principles you need to fulfill so that you can solve problems and differentiate simple troubleshooting errors from more serious ones:

1. You need to remember to always resort to a logical method when troubleshooting a problem. This means that you should employ a structured method in understanding the context and cause of the problem and use it to determine the right solution to fix it. Without using this logical approach, you will most likely become overwhelmed with the issues.

2. Using the philosophical principle of Occam's razor is also helpful. This implies that the explanation with the least variables and assumptions is most likely the correct one. In the context of Java troubleshooting, this may mean that the most obvious explanation of a problem is generally the truth. Employing this principle can help you understand and solve issues faster.

3. Make sure that you always verify the information before you resort to the right course of action. A reason why operators often cannot troubleshoot a problem is because they rely on incomplete or inaccurate information of the symptoms of problems. To resolve a specific issue or problem, make sure that every instruction you input adheres to specific objects and classes.

Why some developers find troubleshooting difficult?

The difficulties associated with Java troubleshooting mainly relate to the complexity of the Java programming language itself. Although the programming language is thought to be less complex than other languages, such as C++, Java utilizes object-oriented mechanics, which means that every programming input has to abide by formal rules in terms of objects and classes. Think of it as a bureaucratic approach to fixing computer problems.

This highly formalized process of using the right methods and objects can render troubleshooting painstaking work. The added emphasis on typing specific instructions with regards to objects and pointers can be daunting and overwhelming. Each command or instruction has to be laid out in highly clear terms so as to minimize or eliminate ambiguity.

The Java programming language tends to conceal memory management and pointers from coders. Programmers who don't possess sufficient knowledge of these aspects can find troubleshooting particularly challenging. This is because Java's object-oriented programming is immersed in logic. Without understanding logic, any attempt to diagnose and troubleshooting issues becomes almost impossible.

Understanding the intricacies of objects, references, and memory allocation requires a lot of time and effort to make troubleshooting seem second nature. We need to input all instructions in carefully coded frameworks that have as few implementation dependencies as possible and are consistent across all applications.

This methodical and structured manner of troubleshooting errors and inconsistencies requires you to take certain rules for granted. There are various components and aspects of the language that need to be understood to make clear troubleshooting instructions. For example, error handling, logging, thread dumps, and heap dumps, which will be covered in the next sections.

Setting up the environment for troubleshooting

Many IDEs have an in-built debugging engine that allows developers to debug their application with ease. However, before you begin, it is important to make sure that your application is set up properly and has the right classpath. Depending on the complexity of your application, you may need to use different techniques. For example, if your application is running on a different server, you may need to use a remote debugging technique. In this case, you attach the debugger to the remote server by specifying the server's IP address and the listening port number. In this case, you need to make sure that you have the right source code. The source code version must match in order to get the correct debugging feedback from the debugger or else the line numbers won't match and the debugger will highlight the wrong area.

Importance of error handling

Error handling refers to the systematic approach of monitoring, identifying, and fixing errors in application and programming. Despite the ease of the Java programming language, application and programming errors are unavoidable. This is because each application or program is developed, modified, and updated by hundreds of users, and inconsistencies of logic and the use of that application or program gives rise to multiple errors and problems.

This can cause the program or application to crash and increases the risk of losing all customers. Through the use of error handling, programmers can prevent or fix errors in an application. If this is not possible, then the application is terminated as a last resort. Error handling helps programmers meet the following objectives:

- Helps in the identification and anticipation of an application or programming error. This enables programmers to employ specialized error handlers to eliminate the problem as quickly as possible, allowing the program or application to be resolved to meet excellent customer service.
- Enables the functionality and maintenance of the program or application to be enhanced through a detailed understanding of the problem or error.

More importantly, error handling allows programmers to utilize a comprehensive resolution method by identifying and fixing all kinds of errors. These consist of development errors, syntax errors, logic errors, and runtime errors. By taking all such errors into account, error handling provides a more thorough and effective means of troubleshooting Java inconsistencies and problems.

There are a few best practices when resolving such kinds of errors. To resolve syntax or development errors, programmers need to proofread each detail of the error in great detail. For logic errors, debugging the program or application is best for ensuring proper execution of code.

As for runtime errors, these can be fixed through the use of error handler code. This is known as exception handling and requires the use of `try-catch-finally` blocks.

A basic try-catch-finally block and its usages

As useful error handling is in troubleshooting Java problems and inconsistencies, there is a need for creating exceptions to a general instruction or rule. This is because whenever an instruction is input in Java programming, the rules are applied instantly across the entire spectrum. In many instances, programmers require exceptions to a general rule for added flexibility and convenience. This is where exception handling is essential.

An exception in a Java program or application bypasses the standardized and formalized rules of the program instruction. Having an exception executed prior to troubleshooting means that the effect of the new instruction is implemented through particular conditions. The `try-catch-finally` blocks are a form of exceptional handling that is beneficial for differentiating between a set of codes and various types of errors.

What are try-catch-finally blocks?

A `try` block consists of a series of program statements that include exceptions. Try blocks are followed by `catch` blocks, which are used to process the exception contained in the `try` blocks. In many instances, the `catch` block is then followed by a `finally` block that has the function of executing essential Java code, such as a stream or a closing connection. It is important to note that the individual blocks may not always follow a sequence. In many cases, a `try-catch` block will be sufficient. In other cases, it will require using all `try-catch-finally` blocks.

Usage of try-catch-finally blocks

The following are examples of the syntax used for each `try`, `catch`, and `finally` blocks:

```
Try-Block
 try{
     //Code goes here
   }
```

```
Catch-Block
 catch(Exception e){
     //Handle the exception here
 }
Finally-Block
 finally{
     // Do the clean up here
 }
```

Mistakes programmers make when using error handling

Regardless of what their skill level may be in using Java programming, there are a number of common mistakes that all programmers make when it comes to error handling. If you are new to error handling in Java programming and wish to avoid taking the long route to mastering your error handling skills, learning about these common mistakes can provide a good foundation to begin with.

- **Problems accessing member variable from main static methods**:
  Programmers often experience issues in accessing variables that are non-static from their main static methods. The term `main` is used to infer that there is no requirement for creating a separate class instance to accessing the main method. However, because some applications do not consist of an instance, it prevents programmers from accessing any member variables.

- **Overriding codes by mistyping method names**:
  When using error handling, overriding may be required for replacing an existing method's codes. However, a common mistake that many programmers fall into is using the incorrect spelling for a given method instruction. When this is done, the method fails to override the required code. The problem is that programmers will often fail to account for this possibility and experience a lot of frustration. It is thus important to be aware of any spelling mistakes when overriding codes.

- **Making capitalization errors**:
  Capitalization errors are among the most frequent mistakes that programmers make. Just as important as it is to have the right spelling of the method name when overriding codes, ensuring a method or variable is capitalized can be equally essential. Capitalization errors, unfortunately, are the most difficult to spot since it can be easy to keep track of capitalized letter or words in a large code or instruction, especially when each method or variable has to conform to other crucial patterns and formats.

- **Equating exceptions as conditions**:
  We have mentioned how using a `try-catch` block can be useful for creating exceptions to general rules or codes. However, programmers need to be aware not to use it in every case. In the case of managing null values, using `try-catch` blocks should not be used to specify conditions. Instead, a simple `if-else` statement will be enough. Of course, there are situations in which a `try-catch` block will be relevant to use for specifying conditions, but these will only be in cases that cannot be handled through simple `if-else` statements.

- **Generalizing exceptions**:
  There is also a risk that programmers generalize exceptions to a code by resorting to catching blocks or clauses. This presents a host of problems that can be difficult to identify and rectify. Firstly, the generalized exception can result in the code being executed across formats that the programmer had no intention of. Another problem that it can lead to is that the code can fail to account for the very exceptions that the developer had in mind.

Why swallowing exception is bad?

Considering the complexity of using exception handling, programmers often take the shortcut to error handling problems by swallowing exceptions. In this, they continue to process and run programs and applications by pretending there are no issues or inconsistencies to begin with. Seeing that monitoring, identifying, and solving errors at every step of the way is time-consuming and frustrating, programmers assume that swallowing exceptions helps eliminate further risks.

However, this is considered a bad practice for a number of reasons. Swallowing exceptions is firstly viewed as expensive, since it can lead to greater problems in the future that can take a lot more time and effort to fix. Programmers need to ensure that they resolve exception problems as soon as they come to know it. If ignored, the exception will not make the application or program run any better.

In fact, it can lead to unexpected failure or result in a problem that has no relation to the source. This can severely compromise customer service and your reputation. Instead of swallowing exceptions, be sure to log it along with the entire trace of the stack. This will make tracking and solving the issue a lot easier.

Use of logging

Logging in Java programming refers to recording activities for the purpose of tracking and resolving problems and errors in applications and programs. It involves the recording of data structures and events pertaining to the program for the purpose of easier auditing. Programmers can come across multiple errors and inconsistencies in the form of logic errors, syntax errors, and runtime errors, and logging these issues can help minimize the time required for troubleshooting.

Logging is useful for serving a variety of purposes such as keeping maintenance application logs to tuning and system failure identification. Programmers who underestimate the value of logging fail to troubleshoot Java problems and inconsistencies effectively and face the risk of losing customer satisfaction.

It consists of either inputting text messages on files or transmitting the data to various monitoring applications. Logging is particularly useful in Java programming to keep track of various problems. Programmers have recourse to a range of logging methods, some of which include the use of threading behavior, call stack logging support, application data monitoring support, and more.

Logging vs Debugging

As a developer, you may be in love with debugging and may not imagine a development day without a debugger at your disposal. Trust me, I can understand. Debugging is the most important part of the development activity. When in development, it is an easier and, most importantly, a faster way of finding bugs than any other method. However, what if your application leaves the development environment? What about QA or the production environment? You certainly do not have access or complete control to debug the application to find bugs. Moreover, it is not at all feasible to debug on a live customer data or a production cloned environment like QA. So, what would you do in that case? How will you find bugs that are causing various issues in your application? Well, you guessed it right, you have to rely on logging. There are several advantages of using logging over debugging. Some of them are as follows:

- **Manual Involvement**: Logging will not take as much time as debugging will take. Logging is more of an automated process. Once configured properly, logging will capture the desired data and store it in a log file for later review.
- **Record Storage**: Debugging cannot store data in any medium. Logging will store data in various mediums like as files, in database, and so on.
- **Auditing**: Debugging cannot be used for auditing purpose. However, logging can be used for auditing if configured properly.

In addition to this, logging data can be used for pattern finding, anomaly detection for web applications, and profiling particular components.

What are the main components?

The recording of activity through logging has three components:

- **The Logger**: This stores the message that needs to be logged into the logging framework by capturing specific metadata.
- **The Formatter**: Upon the storage of the error message, the formatter is then approached to process it for output, usually by converting the binary object of the message into string representation.
- **The Handler**: Its function is to post the message effectively according to a specific structure or format. This can involve representing the data in the form of a database table, email, socket, or bitbucket.

How to do logging?

In addition to realizing the importance of logging, programmers also need to ensure that they log messages and errors in the right manner. There are various Java logging tools that programmers must choose from to be able to record events and data structures efficiently and accurately. The steps involved in logging include:

1. **Create a logger**:
   The first step you need to follow is to create a logger in your own code. To do this, you can use the following instruction:

```
import java.util.logging.Logger;
//our logger class name is MyLogger
private final static Logger logger =
Logger.getLogger(MyLogger.class.getName());
```

2. **Choose the appropriate message level**:
   When logging messages, it is important to determine the severity level of it. These are as follows in descending order:

- FATAL
- ERROR
- WARNING
- INFO

- DEBUG
- TRACE

Choosing the rank of the level, it will then determine the right course of action that needs to be taken. For instance, if the severity level of an error is considered FATAL, it can be set as visible as quickly as possible. On the other hand, if the severity level is TRACE, then these can be stored as log files only and require more information for proper handling.

3. **Know what you are logging**:
Every effort should be made to ensure the process of logging is not done so in a careless manner. Programmers need to ensure what message details or specific metadata are being accessed and stored into logs for future use. It is thus important to stop and double check that all details of the message are being recorded accurately to avoid the possibility of mistyping or incorrect sentences. Care should also be taken to avoid logging collections. This happens when a programmer gathers and stores a set of domain objects into a logging database without accurate log details, increasing the possibility of memory errors, thread starvation issues, and other problems.

4. **Be wary of side-effects:**
You should also be careful not to drag in other side effects when logging by ensuring that the message you wish to log does not lead to an unfavorable impact on the application or program. It is perfectly possible for a logging message to cause lazy initialization data to creep into an application session.
In this particular circumstance, the logging threat level would increase and cause great difficulty for the programmer to locate a bug or other inconsistency.
There is also the case of a performance side-effect that you should be careful of. This can slow down the speed of the system or cause the server to restart every few minutes as a result of a thread starvation problem. Here, excessive logging can be a culprit, so you should be careful about how much information should be stored into the logging database.
Another side-effect of logging is the termination of the business process itself, which should be avoided at all costs through the use of descriptive and detailed logging information.

5. Incorporate return values and method arguments into logs:
   Programmers would often resort to a debugger upon discovering a bug in an application in order to find the source of the problem. However, in certain cases, a debugger may not be available for use due to the bug infecting a customer application. Relying solely on debuggers in this case will leave you without any details to track the problem source.

   As a contingency, you should also make sure to include both return values and method arguments and not rely on a debugger every other time. Doing so will allow you to track and identify the source of the bug in every circumstance and not leave you vulnerable for system failure.

The process of troubleshooting and error handling will become a lot smoother as you will simply have to read blogs using relevant names. This does not render the use of debuggers completely unnecessary. Rather, you should know to use them in special cases and not become over-reliant on them.

What logging frameworks are available?

There is a wide range of logging frameworks that programmers can use to log messages for audit purposes. Prior to logging, the appropriate framework for logging should be selected to record events or data structures. Now the biggest question is which framework to choose. As a developer, you should evaluate the frameworks based on performance, support, and ease of use. There are three popular logging frameworks--Java Util Logging, Log4j 2, and Logback. They rank high on these three criteria. However, they do have some pros and cons of their own. Let's take a deep dive into each one to understand the best possible option for your project.

Java Util Logging

This is the core logging offering of Java and is maintained by the Java team, so you can rely on the support. However, this framework has some limitations, which are discussed in the *Performance* section.

The following is an example of using JUL in your code:

```
import java.util.logging.*;

public class JULExample1 {
    private static final Logger logger =
Logger.getLogger(JULExample1.class.getName());

    public static void main(String[] args) {
```

```
        logger.info("Info logging level example");
        try {
           Object o = null;
           if(o == null){
               logger.log(Level.WARNING, "Object is null");
           }
           o.toString();   //this line is going to throw a null pointer
exception
        } catch (Exception ex){
           logger.log(Level.SEVERE, ex.getMessage(), ex);
        }
     }
  }
```

The previous algorithm produces the following result.

```
Oct 09, 2017 12:05:58 PM Java9PerformanceBook.JULExample1 main
INFO: Info logging level example
Oct 09, 2017 12:05:58 PM Java9PerformanceBook.JULExample1 main
WARNING: Object is null
Oct 09, 2017 12:05:58 PM Java9PerformanceBook.JULExample1 main
SEVERE: null
java.lang.NullPointerException
        at Java9PerformanceBook.JULExample1.main(JULExample1.java:17)
```

We will now have a look at a handler example. The following algorithm shows the use of handler to store the logs in a user defined file:

```
import java.io.IOException;
import java.util.logging.*;

public class JULHandlerExample {
   private static final Logger logger =
Logger.getLogger(JULHandlerExample.class.getName());

   public static void main(String[] args) throws IOException {
       Handler fileHandler = new
FileHandler("/Users/ramgirm/handlerexample.log", true);  //create a handler
       logger.addHandler(fileHandler);     //add the handler to the logger
       logger.setLevel(Level.INFO);

       logger.info("Before try block");
       try {
          Object o = null;
          if(o == null){
               logger.log(Level.WARNING, "Object is null");
          }
```

```
            o.toString();    //this line is going to throw a null pointer
exception
        } catch (Exception ex){
            logger.log(Level.SEVERE, ex.getMessage(), ex);
        }
        fileHandler.flush();
        fileHandler.close();
    }
}
```

The previous algorithm produces the following result;

```
Oct 09, 2017 12:18:36 PM Java9PerformanceBook.JULHandlerExample main
INFO: Before try block
Oct 09, 2017 12:18:36 PM Java9PerformanceBook.JULHandlerExample main
WARNING: Object is null
Oct 09, 2017 12:18:36 PM Java9PerformanceBook.JULHandlerExample main
SEVERE: null
java.lang.NullPointerException
        at Java9PerformanceBook.JULHandlerExample.main(JULHandlerExample.java:20)
```

Log4j 2

This project is the Apache software foundation project and is supported by an active development team. It is a widely used and well documented framework. The updated version Log4j 2 brought more functionality and can be used as an audit logging framework. There is an interesting upgrade in Log4j 2 that is missing from Log4j 1.x and Logback. In Log4j 1.x and Logback, while re-configuring the framework, they are losing events; however, Log4j 2.x has overcome this problem.

Generally, Logback ignores the exceptions that occurred in Appenders whereas Log4j 2 allows configuring the exceptions to be bubbled to the application. Appenders is a mechanism in the logging framework that helps to deliver log events to their destination. They are only responsible for the delivery of the log events and not responsible for formatting the log events. For this, they delegate the responsibility to a layout. Asynchronous loggers are a new addition to Log4j 2, which are based on *LMAX Disruptor library*. This is where Log4j 2 is leading the field. Its asynchronous loggers give 10 times higher throughput and orders of magnitude lower latency compared to Log4j 1.x and Logback.

 You can find all the information about this at: `https://logging.apache.org/log4j/2.x/index.html`

Logback

Logback is based on `log4j`. Logback is designed to be a fast and generic framework which can work in different environments. There are three main modules of Logback. They are as follows:

- `logback-core` : This is the core module needed for Logback
- `logback-classic`: This module requires `logback-core` to provide logging services
- `logback-access`: This module assists servlet containers such as tomcat to capture HTTP access log

Logback implements the **Simple Logging Facade for Java** (**SL4J**) API natively, which is a facade for various logging frameworks.

Before we can compare these three frameworks, let's first understand the common factors. All these frameworks are hierarchical, which offers configuration files to make runtime modifications; for example, the ability to change the logging level at runtime. They offer similar features but use different terminology; for example, Handler or Appender records the log messages to the log file while Formatter or Layout formats log messages.

Although many features are quite similar or can be coded around easily, there is one feature that we should compare, which is **Mapped Diagnostic Contexts** (**MDCs**). MDCs empower the log messages with the information that is not available to the code block where logging takes place. To understand this better, let's look into a scenario: as part of an audit process, you are required to capture a user's location and device information while making an online payment. However, the application code that is accepting payment may not be allowed to forward this information to the code that processes the payment and logs the activity. In this case, MDC is helpful, as the application then inserts the user's location and device information into the MDC, which will then be available to the logging code on the same request handling thread.

Let's see the program for the earlier mentioned scenario. In this example, we will use the Log4J 2.x framework.

Following is the `Payment` class, which will be passed to the service:

```java
public class Payment {
    private String sender;
    private Long amount;
    public Payment(String sender, long amount) {
        this.sender = sender;
        this.amount = amount;
    }
    public String getSender() {
        return sender;
    }

    public Long getAmount() {
        return amount;
    }
}
```

This is the `UserIdentity` class to collect `location` and `device` info:

```java
public class UserIdentity {
    private String location;
    private String device;
    public UserIdentity(String location, String device){
        this.location = location;
        this.device = device;
    }
    public String getLocation() {
        return location;
    }
    public void setLocation(String location) {
        this.location = location;
    }
    public String getDevice() {
        return device;
    }
    public void setDevice(String device) {
        this.device = device;
    }
}
```

This is `PaymentProcessorController`, which will call the service to process the `Payment`:

```
import org.apache.log4j.Logger;
import org.apache.log4j.MDC;

public class PaymentProcessorController {
    private static Logger logger =
Logger.getLogger(PaymentProcessorController.class);
    public static void main(String[] args){
        Payment payment = mockPaymentObject();
        UserIdentity ui = mockUserIdentity();
        PaymentProcessorService pps = new PaymentProcessorService();
        MDC.put("location", ui.getLocation());
        MDC.put("device", ui.getDevice());
        pps.process(payment);
        MDC.clear();
    }

    private static UserIdentity mockUserIdentity() {
        UserIdentity ui = new UserIdentity("New York", "iPhone 8");
        return ui;
    }

    private static Payment mockPaymentObject() {
        Payment pay= new Payment("Mayur Ramgir", 100);
        return pay;
    }
}
```

This is the `Payment` service:

```
import org.apache.log4j.Logger;

public class PaymentProcessorService {
    private Logger logger =
Logger.getLogger(PaymentProcessorService.class);

    public boolean process(Payment payment) {
        logger.info("Processing payment for " + payment.getSender() + "
amount " + payment.getAmount());
        // process payment here
        return true;
    }

}
```

However, there may be a few scenarios where you don't need MDC support. For example, in standalone applications where a state is not transferred, all the information is available to all the code blocks. Hence, there is no need to inject the information into MDC.

Performance

This would be the most important criterion. To understand the performance impact of each logging framework, it is required that you do benchmarking on each one. For this, the **Java Microbenchmark Harness (JMH)** toolkit will be useful. This toolkit is designed by the JVM team, so you can rely on this to give you accurate benchmarking. If you are an experienced developer, you know that measuring performance of a small part of a larger application via writing benchmarks is not only difficult but also seems impractical. This is because you need to take a lot of care while writing benchmarks for your program. You need to make sure the JVM and underline hardware do not apply optimization during the microbenchmark execution. We will learn more about JMH in `Chapter 6`, *Optimizing code with Microbenchmarking*.

As per the *Java Logging Benchmarks* project on GitHub by *Stephen Connolly* (`https://github.com/stephenc/java-logging-benchmarks/`), **Java Util Logging (JUL)** does not meet the performance threshold. JUL lacks in buffered handler implementation, which impacts the logging performance. Buffer file I/O is the most important factor for logging and may impact adversely if not implemented properly. However, there is a downside for buffering log files--in the case of a crash, the last statements may not get pushed to the log file, and because of which the cause of the crash will be lost completely.

As per the study, when compared the synchronous logger, Apache Log4J leads the area with a 25 percent lead over Logback. As per Log4J 2.x documentation, Asynchronous logging has been added, which will boost the application's performance by executing I/O operations in a different thread. Logback and Log4J 2.x asynchronous logging comparison is not available so it is hard to claim a winner. However, overall, Log4J 2.x looks promising.

Support

It is important to make sure the logging framework project is operational in development and is supported by an active development team. A framework should have frequent updates and respond quickly to the bug requests. Failing to achieve this may result in abandoning the support for that framework, which ultimately affects your project. All three projects are quite active in development and are well supported by the experienced community. So, there is no loser for this criterion.

Ease of Use

This part can be evaluated on two factors--how easy it is to configure and how easy it is to code. All the frameworks provide good configuration options but they all lack on the documentation part. A developer has to go through JavaDocs to find the required options.

In terms of easy to coding, all three frameworks rank quite highly on this point, so there is no loser for this criterion either.

Although each logging framework differs in its features, configuration options, and ease of use, if you are just starting out, Log4J 2.x is the one you should opt for. It consists of a range of interesting features and is constantly updated and can provide a richer and more convenient user experience.

Best use case for logging

When logging, it is not enough simply to store the message. Rather, programmers need to apply context to be able to increase value and make it easier to perform troubleshooting. For example, if an application leads to a failed transaction, it will look like the following:

```
Transaction Failed
```

Logging the problem as shown previously will not be sufficient or clear enough for troubleshooting.

```
Transaction failed 2342624 : cc number checksum
```

Messages that are logged like the previous log will be more useful in clarifying the details of the problem or error and will make it easier to troubleshoot.
Furthermore, when logging a message, it is advised that you perform automated processing. This is because the log message needs to adhere to a machine parseable format. Otherwise, the log entry will become difficult to parse and become more error prone.

More importantly, logging should not be limited for auditing or troubleshooting purposes only. It can also be used to profile logs to make it easier to identify certain sections of the application or program. Through logging, you can mark a starting and end point of an activity and also monitor performance metrics to ensure the application conforms to a user or customer's requirements.

Analyzing thread dump

Thread dump analysis is one of the more important techniques of troubleshooting. The Java language is designed as a multi-threaded language. Many business-critical Java applications are designed as to run in multiple threads. This way, your program can perform many different tasks simultaneously. For example, connecting to database, fetching data, processing algorithms, and so on. All these tasks can be performed without waiting on finishing the previous task as each task can run in its own thread. Hence, thread dump can give us a snapshot of each thread's current execution step in the JVM. It can provide some information about each thread like, such as its `id`, `name`, `current state`, and `call stack`. The `call stack` can give us information about the monitor it has locked on as well as if that thread is waiting on other monitor to be released. This can expose the problematic areas that are causing various problems like deadlock. If you don't know what deadlock is, let's take a quick look. Deadlock is a state where two threads are waiting on each other to release their locks on resources that the other thread is waiting to enter. Take the example of a doghouse. There are two doghouses in front of each other and each dog from each doghouse is waiting for the other dog to come out of that house so he can enter the other doghouse. Since both the dogs are standing on the door and waiting on each other to come out, no dog is able to take any step so they are stuck in their respecting houses. Now, let's take a more in-depth look at thread dump.

What is a thread dump?

All commands in Java programming are the by-product of threads and processes. Threads are similar to processes except they are lighter in weight and require fewer resources to create a new one. Every process that is used to execute a command consists of at least one thread that contains valuable resources, such as open files and memory.

Since each thread has the capacity to provide additional threads, programmers need to know the intricacies of a process and the various threads to avoid the possibility of communication errors. This is where thread dumps are important.

A thread dump, as the name suggests, is a collection of all threads in a Java programming system that are part of a specific process. Analyzing thread dumps allows the programmer to view the stack trace details and understand the thread stack's contents.

Benefits of thread dump analysis

Analyzing thread dumps gives programmers essential the information of Java threads at a particular point in time. Thread dump analysis provides the following pieces of information:

- **Thread name**: You will be presented with a number of a thread if you are using `java.lang.Thread` for thread generation. However, if you use the class `java.util.concurrent.ThreadFactory`, you will get a pool name along with a thread number.
- **Thread priority**: This will show the priority of a thread.
- **Thread ID**: This displays a thread's unique ID that can provide essential information in terms of thread memory or CPU usage.
- **Stack trace**: This is a report that shows a snapshot of an active stack frame at a particular point in time.

Upon discovering the details of the aforementioned pieces of information, programmers can quickly identify and deeply understand various usage patterns of a thread, in addition to the state of thread groups, hotspots, and of patterns that are executed in an advisory list.

The identification of thread groups allow you to organize multiple threads of the same type together. This can allow programmers to understand how Engine and BPEL Invoke threads are being utilized in terms of the quantity of JMS producers and consumers, as well as the condition of Muxer threads and other thread groups.

Thread dump analysis is also useful for exposing threads problems. These could relate to code portions that are used excessively and consist of hung applications, along with thread synchronization and locking application issues. Upon evaluation of a merged report, a programmer can get insight and updates on whether threads that are critical to a function are functioning smoothly or not. This can be particularly useful for diagnosing spikes in CPU performance, memory problems, deadlocks, poor response times, unresponsive applications, and problems in the Java system itself.

How to collect a thread dump

Thread dumps can be collected either through the system or by the programmer himself. To generate a thread dump, the programmer needs to send a request to JVM by specifying an exception. It is important to bear in mind that the thread can be collected only if the process is linked to a command line console in the foreground.

However, the very act of collecting or generating a thread dump will depend on the command line tool or operating system you use. There are many options that you can choose from, such as jstack, JVisualVM, Windows, ThreadMXBean, and more.

If you wish to collect a thread dump in the Windows operating system, you will first need to choose the command line application window and use the *Ctrl + Break* instruction. Once you give this command, you will produce a thread dump that will be displayed on the console window.

 Bear in mind that since it is displayed in the console window, you will have the disadvantage of not being able to access it as a separate file. To prevent this, you will have to issue the command in the following manner:
```
java -classpath . MyThreadProgram >
/home/me/myThreadDump.txt 2>&1
```

If you wish to generate a thread dump using `jstack`, simply use the PID of the current process in the Java application, extract it, and use it as a parameters to generate a thread dump. Look at the following example:

```
jstack -f 1111
```

How to analyze a thread dump

The process of analyzing a thread dump can be a complex one for beginners. However, with a little practice and the right tools, you will be able to understand the different constituents of a thread dump. An easy way is to resort to Java analysis tools that can list the different threads in a thread dump according to name and priority.

Tools, such as Thread Dump Analyzer and Samurai, for instance, can help analyze your thread dumps. These are easy to install and use and can help save time. Be mindful that these tools work as business intelligence or analytics tools. Rather, they provide a simple means of navigating through various stack traces that makes thread dump analysis a lot easier and more convenient.

One crucial aspect of analyzing thread dumps are stack traces. These need to be read from the bottom up as it can help you understand the code execution path and the exception contained in it. Reading from the bottom first will also be crucial in the identification of the Java EE container or custom thread originator, after which determining the request of the thread and the particular application modules should be followed.

You should then locate the protocol by looking at around 10 to 20 lines before the first line. After reading the first line, you will then have a clearer picture of what the thread dump entails.

Best practices

To ensure programmers are able to analyze thread dumps as effectively as possible, it is important to highlight a few best practices that should be implemented. Firstly, programmers should make sure not to keep default thread names. When a thread is generated, it is named according to a named pool and thread number. However, in the event of analyzing hundreds of threads, keeping track of specific ones is most likely to become challenging. Therefore, you should name the threads using a custom name as soon it is generated.

Secondly, you can also use specific tools for obtaining detailed thread dump information. Tools such as MBean and ThreadInfo can be particularly beneficial in acquiring pieces of information that cannot be obtained as quickly or efficiently otherwise. If you use ThreadInfo, for instance, you can access information on the number of inactive threads.

Analyzing heap dump

Heap dump analysis is another important step in troubleshooting your Java application. As we have seen earlier, thread dump gives us a snapshot of the threads running in the JVM. This greatly helps us to identify the problematic areas of threads execution. A heap dump snapshot is little bit different to the thread dump snapshot. It gives us a snapshot of the heap memory. As you may recall, heap memory stores information about objects. This snapshot gives us very low-level information about objects like class, fields, primitive values, static fields, and references. It helps to identify various performance leaks such as class loader leaks, memory leaks due to not clearing an object reference after use, and so on. Now, let's understand the heap dump in detail.

What is a heap dump

A heap dump is a collection of memory processes in the Java heap system. It is a snapshot of all Java classes and objects up to the point the snapshot is made. A heap dump does not determine the allocation of memory; rather, it provides information on a range of useful information such as the following:

- Java objects in terms of fields, classes, references, and primitive values

- Garbage collection objects or roots that can be accessed outside the heap system, such as threads, JNI, and Java locals
- Thread related stacks and data

Benefits of analyzing heap dumps

There are a range of benefits that programmers can achieve upon analyzing heap dumps. It allows programmers to minimize the risks of performance problems in applications and programs and enhances the value of work and improves customer service and satisfaction through efficient IT management procedures.

It also helps them identify the root cause of problems, such as footprint issues and memory leaks, which compromise the client IT environment. Furthermore, it provides a considerable boost to programming and IT skills through the identification and analysis of performance analysis concepts and techniques.

By having a greater understanding of garbage collection tools, JVM, and Java object and class cycles, you can help foster JVM skills, resulting in a higher quality of the overall IT service and customer satisfaction.

When do you analyze a heap dump

Despite the many benefits that heap dump analysis can provide, it is not recommended for programmers to analyze heap dumps in every Java heap issue or problem. This is because performing heap dump analysis is a lengthy and time-consuming task and can lead to unnecessary disruptions in Java applications or programs.

Programmers should conduct heap dump analysis only in the following scenarios:

- Troubleshooting Java leaks in heap memory and classloader memory
- Understanding and tuning the application or program along with the surrounding memory footprint of the Java EE container or API

Using heap dump analysis for any reason other than the aforementioned ones can lead to various limitations and drawbacks, such as causing your Java system to hang or become unresponsive, and making it difficult for you to retrieve the entire process memory footprint.

How to collect heap dump

A heap dump can be generated either manually or through automated processes. To do so manually, you can execute the following command:

```
sudo -u <username> jmap -dump:file=headdump.hdprof,format=b <pid>
```

Taking the preceding command as an example, you need to make sure that the relevant process ID is used in place of the `pid`, as shown previously. Also, the process owner should be replaced with the user to ensure the correct instructions. Otherwise, you will not be able to generate a valid heap dump.

To generate heap dumps using automated processes, you will need to use either the JRockiet R28+ or the HotSpot Java VM 1.5+ and include the parameter shown as follows:

```
-XX:+HeapDumpOnOutOfMemoryError
```

This will cause the Java system to automatically produce a heap dump after an error `OutOfMemory`. It is advisable that you generate a heat dump through automated processes. Doing so can prove to be a lot more convenient and more effective in analyzing performance problems in the heap memory.

How to analyze heap dump

In the same way tools are required for analyzing thread dumps, the same is important when analyzing heap dumps. By far the most useful and efficient analysis tool is the Eclipse Memory Analyzer. After downloading and installing it on your desktop, access the tool by choosing **Open Heap Dump** under the **File Menu** option. Once opened, the analyzing tool will then access a number of default reports open parsing the heap dump.

It will then highlight the memory distribution retained based on objects and show memory leaks in the form of a pie chart in the leak suspect report. This will only be in the case if the memory leak is induced by one or more objects. If this doesn't occur, then the leak could be the result of a class of objects and may not be visible in the reports.

In this case, you will need to use a dominator tree and choose *Group result by* and then *Group by class*. This will then change the retained memory distribution to be shown according to class instead of object.

The Eclipse Memory Analyzer also provides a histogram that highlights the number of class instances, in addition to a top components list.

Best practices

There are a number of best practices when it comes to the effective use of heap dump analysis. Firstly, you need to always make use of **Object Query Language (OQL)** for processing custom queries. This is because it is often that custom queries become loaded with workflow steps. This tends to happen if scripts are uploaded excessively or if workflow steps are used too much.

You should also check for performance issues by obtaining a list of threads running during the time of the problem. To do this, choose **Java Basics** and then select **Thread Overview**. **Java Collection** can also be utilized to obtain deeper insights into each data collection. Among these pieces of information include collision map ratio, fill ratio per collection, and size per collection.

Summary

In this chapter, we have learned about the importance of troubleshooting, why developers are struggling with troubleshooting, and how to set up the right environment to troubleshoot your application. Furthermore, we looked into the importance of error handling and how it can help to identify the problematic areas and why developers should incorporate error handling in their day-to-day development. Then we learned the other helpful part of error handling, which is logging. We have seen how to create a logger and use the appropriate message level. We have also explored various other logging libraries that we can use in our application development. After that, we learned two important techniques in troubleshooting--thread dump and heap dump.

In the next chapter, we will explore the role of profiling and how it is useful to you as a developer to improve the performance of your code.

4
Learning How to Use Profiling Tools

In the previous chapter, you learned about troubleshooting and how it can help us identify problems in our code. However, the biggest question is--*How would you define a problem?* If you don't have a performance measurement checklist that shows you what to expect from the program and doesn't collect supporting data that can be used to validate the checklist, then you will not be able to define the performance problem properly. And if you don't define the problem properly, then what will you fix? It will be like the following experience published in *Reader's Digest*:

> *My mother was rushed to the hospital following a serious tumble. There the staff placed a band around her wrist with large letters warning: Fall Risk.*
>
> *Unimpressed, Mom said to me, "I'll have them know I'm a winter, spring, and summer risk too."*

> *-Betty Heim-Campbell, Fairhope, Alabama*

Hence, understanding the problem properly would be the first step. In order to complete this first step successfully, you need to collect a lot of data about your application. You need to understand the amount of memory as well as the amount of CPU your code is consuming while running in an ideal environment. Now, you may be wondering what the ideal environment is. The simplest answer would be *it depends*. It depends on your application. This is where your performance checklist will come handy. It will help you define the ideal environment for your application based on the performance requirements. The process of collecting and analyzing (comparing it with your performance checklist) all the required data in a given environment in order to check the performance of your application is called profiling.

Profiling can help you identify performance bottlenecks. It can highlight the areas that are causing throughput and latency issues in your application. Throughput is a method of measuring the number of messages that a server can process in a given time interval. And latency can be defined as a method of measuring the complete processing time of a given operation. Hence, profiling can help you find the cheapest possible way to fix your performance problem, like the following joke published in a *Reader's Digest* issue:

> *Lenny tells the psychiatrist, "Every time I get into bed, I think there's somebody under it."*
>
> *"Come to me three times a week for two years, and I'll cure your fears," says the shrink. "And I'll charge you only $200 a visit."*
>
> *Lenny says he'll think about it. Six months later, he runs into the doctor, who asks why he never came back. "For $200 a visit?" says Lenny. "A bartender cured me for $10."*
>
> *"Is that so! How?"*
>
> *"He told me to cut the legs off the bed."*

In this chapter, we will focus on understanding the importance of using various profiling tools and how to use these to improve our code quality. In this chapter, you will come across the following topics:

- The first section talks about what profiling is, followed by a discussion on why a developer should use profiling tools.
- You will learn about various advantages and disadvantages of using a profiling tool.
- Then, you will learn about the various profiling tools, including jmap, VisualVM, JProfiler, XRebel, YourKit, JRockit, BTrace, and AQtime.

By the end of this chapter, you will be able to select the right profiling tool for your needs and be able to identify performance issues.

Introducing profiling

Now, let's understand profiling in a little more detail. In the context of software engineering and development, profiling is a form of dynamic program analysis that may be used as a means of measurement regarding certain parameters such as memory, CPU time, and so on.

Here, profiling may also be defined as the use of a specific set of instructions in a program, along with the length or the regularity of function calls. However, profiling is most often undertaken as an aid to the optimization of any computer software.

Profiling is typically conducted by a specific tool that is referred to as a *profiler*. This tool may utilize multiple methods based on either statistical simulation or even many event-based techniques to create such profiles.

Furthermore, profiling helps address the cumbersome task of having to perform memory management on its own. In most computer languages, the programmers manually apportion hardware memory to build any object that is stored in the system. Subsequently, they have to deallocate the memory to delete the object associated with it.

If the programmer forgets the crucial task of deallocating memory or creates threads that are not designed to do so themselves once their tasks are done, there is high potential for memory leakage. In other words, the program may go on consuming memory in even greater amounts.

Moreover, if a particular chunk of memory is repeatedly deallocated, it increases the system's instability to a very high degree, and as a direct result, the program can become unstable, and may even crash and take the whole system with it. Furthermore, in non-garbage collection languages, the code is considerably more complicated, and the user has to track and finalize memory allocations on their own.

However, Java has a built-in automatic garbage collection, thereby effectively bypassing all such issues. The programmer is responsible for deciding when precisely objects are created, while Java runtime determines, as well as manages, the object's time frame and its duration.

A program created in the Java language can locate an object by holding a reference to it in its database. Once the reference to that specific object is gone, Java's garbage collector methodically removes the unreachable object automatically. The resultant freed memory helps avoid a memory leak. Theoretically, it is possible to compare Java and C++, since it is possible in the latter to implement such functions, albeit with added complexity and development time. While in Java, on the other hand, garbage collection is not only built-in but discreet enough to be almost invisible to the programmer.

Since developers do not have to perform garbage collection on their own, they can utilize their time for higher development activities and thus curb overall costs.

Why a developer should use a profiling tool

It does not matter how proficient a developer is; the fact remains that in spite of the most meticulous attention to detail, the odds are that actual code will not run at peak performance levels around which it has been designed, at least not the first time in its generation. The actual speed of the code versus its theoretical speed tends to differ to a great degree.

This is because there are a lot of elements that combine to create a visible gap between the two. In order to substantially decrease that gap (with the core aim of ultimately closing it altogether), all code must be debugged, analyzed, and reviewed again and again until it has been determined that all of its bugs have been removed and it is running as fast and as efficiently as it had been initially designed to do so.

But the question is how to go about achieving this? That is, how can a Java developer figure out that their code is not just efficient but both swift and bug free? This is where a profiling tool comes into the picture. This tool can closely analyze and examine an application's code both quickly and methodically and figure out where the bottlenecks are so that they can be safely removed, so as to lead to an overall increase in the application's performance. The diagnostic abilities of most well-known profilers enables them to narrow down and pinpoint the exact locations where faults lie so that the software being developed may be streamlined and may even exceed (the previously mentioned theoretical) design parameters.

There are a myriad number of reasons to convince the developer to opt for a profiling tool. Some of them include the following:

- **Short development cycles**: Today's customer wants his app and he wants it yesterday! This means that there is little room for back and forth communication that used to lead to the fine-tuning of the program. Now, time constraints mean that there is very little space for errors that may require refactoring or performance tweaks. This is why the developer has to make sure that the software program runs flawlessly, right from the onset.
- **Lack of patience among end users**: Today's users are simply not interested in looking at the World Wide Web, as it has turned into the *World Wide Wait*. In the late 90s, research indicated that most web surfers would patiently wait up to 8 seconds or so for a site to load. However, within only a few short years, that time period had substantially shrunk to a mere 4 seconds or so, or effectively half of the total in the previous century, and it is shrinking steadily even today. Bad and inefficient code means slower loading times that, in turn, mean less hits and, even worse, overall conversions. What to talk about referrals! A vast majority of surfers simply don't bother clicking on a website that has given them a bad experience. And why should they? After all, there are other faster sites available that may well be carrying the same kind of information. If a site were not to pay attention to its loading time, it may as well not be on the internet altogether.

- **Too much of a good thing**: Sometimes, a news site may have many hits in too short a time span, which makes it slower to respond, and ultimately, it may crash altogether (for example, the Canadian immigration site crashed when Donald Trump was elected president of the United States). This is because a function is sometimes dependent on user execution, ergo when too many users try to execute it simultaneously, the code simply cannot cope and this leads to a progressive slowdown of the entire site. This is why it is absolutely necessary to optimize code right from the onset.

The disadvantages of not using a profiling tool are as follows:

- **The challenge of not optimizing code**: All tasks require the relevant tools to ensure on-time completion, and Java software is no different. Without the availability of a profiler tool, a software programmer may have to fall back to more traditional (read old-fashioned) techniques so as to ensure the optimization of their applications. They may try to guess the issues, such as attempting to figure out where the key problem may occur, or alternately they may look at their own part of the code while effectively ignoring the rest, thus creating potential integration issues. Without using a high-end profiling tool, it will only lead to near endless delays.

- **The main drawback of a profiler tool**: Many senior programmers eschew profiling tools because they believe that a typical profiler is not only highly invasive but also uses too many system resources, effectively slowing down the program itslef.

- **The birth of integrated profiling**: Recently, however, an all new generation of profiling tools has begun to make its presence felt in this arena. This latest generation of profiling tools for a JVM are not subject to the many problems and inherent limitations of their predecessors and, moreover, actually have the ability to speed up the software during development (by fixing the issues in the development phase during its operational life cycle, as well). As a matter of fact, the ideal profiling tool ensures smooth integration throughout the process of development of the program and, in this way, allows very precise and pinpoint measurements of the program code's overall performance.

- **Minimally invasive profiling:** When shopping for that ideal profiling tool, it is crucial to select a profiler that is as minimally invasive as possible. As a matter of fact, there exists many highly invasive profilers with regards to the source code of the application. Furthermore, many such profiling tools in effect may actually require that the program code itself be modified in order to ensure that the profiling tool can do the needful or even take any measurements with a certain degree of accuracy. Since it is essentially impossible to do this manually, the code has to be modified at the source by the relevant tool, effectively ensuring that a code is writing another code (so to speak) and the developer himself is shut out of the loop. This leads to questions regarding not just the efficacy of the profiler, but also the fact that it might inadvertently insert bugs in the source code. This is why it is considered crucial that any profiling tool chosen should first and foremost not require any changes in source code, nor should it take up so many system resources that it slows down the whole process altogether.

- **User-friendly software:** This is why software developers working in the Java real-time environment (along with any other applications) should select a profile tool that enables them to seamlessly figure out performance-related issues in their code. This is because any developer tasked with creating the code is already doing a very difficult job indeed, which is why he would want something that would make his life easier rather than adding unnecessary complications. Moreover, he would be more interested in working with the tools he already has rather than attempting to master a whole new set of complicated tools with their own instructions regarding their usage and utilities. As a matter of fact, before selecting a profiling tool, it is imperative to understand that it is supposed to not just speed up the software development process, but also optimize its performance as well. If, on the other hand, it creates more lag than if the same were not used, then that is definitely not the right profiler for the job. Furthermore, a profiler should not only have a minimal learning curve, but the developer should be able to use it as soon as it has been ingenerated into the system so as to minimize the valuable work hours lost when learning to use it.

- **Ability to conduct multiple measurements:** Ideally, a good Java profiling tool would allow a developer to profile his (source) code in several different ways. The key word here is versatility, since having a versatile profiler means that a developer can not only be sure of the performance of the code he is generating, but also that he can observe in real time many issues that tend to crop up, such as the allocation of system memory, CPU resource utilization, overall OS use, as well as the performance of the application program itself. Moreover, it is also necessary to ensure that all the performance parameters (in which the profiler operates), as well as the different measurements, are easy to understand while being both fast and intuitive, so as to save the programmers the time and hours required to run it.

- **The right reporting formats:** All the information generated by just about any Java profiling tool is completely worthless unless it is able to display the data it has gathered in a lucid and clearly understandable format. It may be an MS Word file or even a hypertext page; unless the data is actionable, that is, it can be used to allow the programmer to take the relevant action and thereby rectify the anomaly, it is functionally useless. Actionable data means that it should be robust and flexible, and furthermore, the profiler should only showcase the most relevant data rather than inundating the system (and the developer) with reams of useless information. Moreover, it has to be graded according to its relevance, with the most important and pressing information filtered first.

The art of profiling

By going through the earlier section, hopefully you have convinced yourself that you are going to need to use a profiling tool to improve the performance of your application. Now, let's look into the art behind profiling. In other words, let's see how our applications are profiled. As you have learned, the main purpose of a profiler is to measure resource usage in your application like CPU utilization, memory consumption, I/O utilization, and so on.

In simpler terms, the profiler needs to record methods that are getting invoked and the time they took to complete the processing. To do this, the profiler needs to collect data; this process is called *sampling*. The data collection, like call stack, occurs at specified intervals. This is a more passive technique where we are not meddling with the application code. Hence, this approach has less impact on application execution.

The other technique is more of an active technique where code can be injected into the application code to count calls and calculate execution time into prologs and epilogs of methods. It is also known as *instrumentation* and is treated as the more accurate approach. However, you need to be cautious when using this in your code. Let's take an example to understand this well. Say you have method that uses five CPU cycles. Now, in that method, you are going to add profiling code, which is going to add five more CPU cycles. So, this means you have doubled the load. On top of this, capturing execution time is done by a system call so that is an additional burden. Hence, you should think of using a mix of these two strategies, like instrumentation on a few selected methods and sampling for others.

Profiling areas

In order to improve your application performance or investigate performance issues, you need to focus on various different areas like CPU, memory, threads, exceptions, databases, I/O, and so on. Each area has various elements that can affect the performance of your application. Lets take a deep dive into each area.

CPU profiling

Any application is going to need to use the CPU time of your application server. So there is a high probability of your application getting affected by poor use of the CPU's resources. Moreover, the underlying operating system of your application server controls the CPU scheduling, so you as a developer don't have any control over which process will get priority, and the amount of CPU time and waiting time. In `Chapter 9`, *Multithreading and Reactive Programming,* you will learn about specifying thread priorities, but that is more of a request and not a guarantee. Hence, the best strategy would be to look into using less CPU time by optimizing your application code. Before you perform any CPU profiling, lets first understand a few concepts related to the CPU:

- **CPU utilization**: It is the amount of load the CPU is going to take. It is a good practice to make sure the application is less dependent on the CPU.
- **Throughput**: It is defined as the number of processes completed in a given amount of time.
- **Turnaround time**: The amount of time required by the CPU to complete a particular process.
- **Waiting time**: It is the time spent by a process waiting in the ready queue to get some CPU time.
- **Load average**: It is the average of the number of processes waiting in the ready queue to get some CPU time.
- **Response time**: It is the amount of time between the request submission and the first response by the CPU.

In order to optimize the CPU, you need to focus on increasing utilization and throughput and look into ways of reducing turnaround time, waiting time, load averages, and response time. Now lets look into a few points you need pay close attention to in order to perform effective CPU profiling.

Any profiler is going to add some processing overhead. Hence, you need to make sure you eliminate the profiler's methods. Make sure you focus on a few methods at a time to see the amount of impact they have on your application. You can filter the other methods to get the result for your selected methods.

Memory profiling

Another important area to look into is memory profiling. Every application is going to use memory and hence it is important to find an optimum way of using this resource. Memory leaks can make your application crawl and eventually crash on you. As we discussed earlier, Java is blessed with a **Garbage Collector** (**GC**), which clears up unused memory. However, if your application is allocating memory faster than GC can collect, then you may see some visible slowness.

Using memory profiling, you can uncover the areas of your code which are causing memory leaks. Memory profiling will let you do the following:

- Track memory allocation to see the patterns which are affecting your application
- Capture heap dumps to see which object is using up memory
- GC activity to see how objects are getting collected and at what speed GC is running
- Monitor object creation speed to see how fast your application is creating new objects and consuming memory

Use periodic memory dumps to identity a pattern to find the actual cause of the memory leak. Perform a couple of tests using different number of loads. For example, simulate system load by making 50, 100, 200, and so on. calls and check the object creation speed and memory consumption speed.

In order to analyze heap dump you are going to need to use **Object Query Language** (**OQL**) language, which has built in functions to query the heap dump. It looks lot more like SQL queries. Classes are like tables which you query, fields as columns, and objects are rows.

The sample query looks like the following:

```
SELECT * FROM [ INSTANCEOF ] <class_name> [ WHERE <filter-expression>]
```

See the following example:

```
SELECT x FROM java.io.File x
```

Which gives the following result in VisualVM (which we will explore in the later section):

```
java.io.File#1 – /Library/Java/JavaVirtualMachines/jdk1.8.0_05.jdk/Contents/Home/jre/lib/ext/localedata.jar
java.io.File#2 – /Library/Java/JavaVirtualMachines/jdk1.8.0_05.jdk/Contents/Home/jre/lib/ext/nashorn.jar
java.io.File#3 – /Library/Java/JavaVirtualMachines/jdk1.8.0_05.jdk/Contents/Home/jre/lib/ext/dnsns.jar
java.io.File#4 – /Library/Java/JavaVirtualMachines/jdk1.8.0_05.jdk/Contents/Home/jre/lib/ext/sunpkcs11.jar
java.io.File#5 – /Library/Java/JavaVirtualMachines/jdk1.8.0_05.jdk/Contents/Home/jre/lib/ext/zipfs.jar
java.io.File#6 – /Library/Java/JavaVirtualMachines/jdk1.8.0_05.jdk/Contents/Home/jre/lib/ext/sunjce_provider.jar
java.io.File#7 – /Library/Java/JavaVirtualMachines/jdk1.8.0_05.jdk/Contents/Home/jre/lib/ext/cldrdata.jar
java.io.File#8 – /Library/Java/JavaVirtualMachines/jdk1.8.0_05.jdk/Contents/Home/jre/lib/ext/jfxrt.jar
java.io.File#9 – /Library/Java/JavaVirtualMachines/jdk1.8.0_05.jdk/Contents/Home/jre/lib/ext/sunec.jar
java.io.File#10 – /Users/ramgirm/Documents/ClintraWebServices/TestSorting/bin
java.io.File#11 – /Library/Java/JavaVirtualMachines/jdk1.8.0_05.jdk/Contents/Home/jre/lib/jfr.jar
java.io.File#12 – /Library/Java/JavaVirtualMachines/jdk1.8.0_05.jdk/Contents/Home/jre/lib/jsse.jar
java.io.File#13 – /Library/Java/JavaVirtualMachines/jdk1.8.0_05.jdk/Contents/Home/jre/lib/rt.jar
java.io.File#14 – /Library/Java/JavaVirtualMachines/jdk1.8.0_05.jdk/Contents/Home/jre/lib/resources.jar
java.io.File#15 – /Library/Java/JavaVirtualMachines/jdk1.8.0_05.jdk/Contents/Home/jre/lib/jce.jar
java.io.File#16 – /Library/Java/JavaVirtualMachines/jdk1.8.0_05.jdk/Contents/Home/jre/lib/charsets.jar
java.io.File#17 – /dev/urandom
java.io.File#18 – /dev/random
java.io.File#19 – /dev/random
java.io.File#20 – /var/folders/01/ytcqsv756gv2nkyr_7y2s64c0000gq/T
java.io.File#21 – /var/folders/01/ytcqsv756gv2nkyr_7y2s64c0000gq/T/jfluidbuf8568835627257287074.tmp
```

There are various built-in functions supported in OQL that can operate on Java objects and arrays.

The following functions are for Java objects:

- `sizeof(o)`: This function gives object's size in bytes
- `objectid(o)`: This function gives unique id of the specified object
- `classof(o)`: This returns class object for a given object
- `identical(o1, o2)`: This return Boolean value to check if two given objects are identical or not
- `referrers(o)`: This gives an array of objects referring to the given object
- `referees(o)`: This gives an array of objects referred by the given object
- `reachables(o)`: This gives an array of objects directly or indirectly referred from the given object

The following functions are for Java arrays:

- `contains(array, expr)`: This gives an array contains an element that satisfies the given expression.
- `count(array, [expr])`: This gives number of elements satisfying the given expression.
- `filter(array, expr)`: This gives a new array containing elements satisfying the given expression.
- `map(array, expr)`: This function applies the given expression on each element of input array and gives a new array back.
- `sort(array, [expr])`: This function sorts the given array. You may also supply a comparison expression, otherwise it will use numerical comparison
- `sum(array)`: This gives sums of all elements of array.

Thread profiling

In a multi-threaded application, it is important to monitor a thread's life cycle to avoid possible race condition or monitor contention. You can periodically capture the stack traces of all currently alive threads. Further, we can also collect information such as CPU consumption from these threads. Again, as we have discussed in the earlier sections, this type of task is going to add processing overhead. So, make sure you consider this when evaluating the results. However, in order to get accurate results you need to repeat this process frequently.

Collect periodic samples in order to correctly identify thread behaviors. For the sampling, make sure you use the exact same system environment.

For monitor contention, you can perform monitor profiling which will help you analyze synchronization issues like calling of the `wait()` method by threads and the time they took to come out of it. This will also uncover the threads that are blocked trying to acquire a monitor held by another thread, and the time they took to come out of it. For example, synchronized blocks and methods.

The different types of Java profiling tool

If a program is plagued with slow service, the system unexpectedly crashes and is prone to hanging and pausing on its own, or takes up excessive CPU power and memory; the odds are that there are certain bugs in it that need to be removed as soon as possible. However, for debugging, it is necessary that you have the requisite data before you commence any rectification procedures.

Fortunately, there exists a vast number of tools that may potentially help provide all the necessary information that you need to be able to fix the program. Some of these tools may be part of the JVM itself, while some tools have been developed by third-party specialists.

We will look at some of the most simple ones that may prove to be helpful once the program or application (as the case may be) starts performing unexpectedly.

Jmap

Let's start with *jmap*. Oracle states (in its constructor summary) that it creates a convenient script object to deal with the instance `java.util.Map`. They further describe it as an application that prints shared object memory maps or heap memory details of a given process, core file, or remote debug server.

In order to run the jmap utility successfully, it is necessary to know the required **Product ID (PID)** of the application that you want to run this tool against. This may be speedily accomplished by using a tool called **Java Virtual Machine Process Status Tool (JPS)**, which is already available in the JVM. Basically, JPS may be used to create a list of each and every JVM process currently running on the system along with every process's very own PID. You may also use the `ps -ef | grep java` command on Linux platforms, which will give you the PIDs of Java processes as shown here:

```
$ ps -ef | grep java
501 1079 1044   0 10:35AM ttys000   0:00.00 grep java
```

The PID can be retrieved with the `jps` command as well. See the following:

```
$ jps
1077 Jps
```

You may also use various other options with `jps` as follows:

- Option `–l` gives us the PID and fully-qualified Java `main` class name as shown in the following code:

```
$ jps -l
1103 sun.tools.jps.Jps
```

- Option `–lm` gives us the PID, fully-qualified Java `main` class name, and application arguments as shown in the following code:

```
$ jps -lm
1107 sun.tools.jps.Jps -lm
```

- Option `–v` gives us the PID and JVM options as shown in the following code:

```
$ jps -v
1112 Jps -
Dapplication.home=/Library/Java/JavaVirtualMachines/jdk1.8.0_45.jdk/Content
s/Home -Xms8m
```

The `jmap` command-line utility will print the memory-related statistics. The jmap tool can also be used to collect information from a remote machine using the `jsadebugd` demon. However, it takes a long time to print the output. JDK 8 brought new utilities such as `jcmd`, which takes less overhead than `jmap` and provides enhanced diagnostics. Hence, it is advisable to use jcmd over jmap.

However, if you are really interested in using the jmap tool, then let's dive deep into it. There are various options you can use with `jmap` such as `–heap`, `–histo`, `–permstat`, and so on. If no option is provided, then it will print the list of shared objects loaded. You can also store the output in a file for which you will need JDK 7 or higher. Use the `–dump:format=b, file=<filename>` option with `jmap`, which will dump the Java heap in the binary HPROF format. You may use that tool to analyze this file later.

- The `–heap` option:

  ```
  $ jmap -heap 54510
  ```

  This option gives us the information on the garbage collection algorithm and its details, such as the number of threads. Further, it gives us information on heap usage such as the total heap capacity, free memory, and in-use memory.

- The -histo option:

  ```
  $ jmap -histo 54510
  ```

  This option gives us a class-specific histogram of the heap by printing memory size, a number of objects, and a fully qualified name for every class.

- The -permstat option:

  ```
  $ jmap -permstat 29620
  ```

  This option gives us the information on the objects in the permanent generation area. For big and complex applications, it is possible to load a large number of classes in the permanent generation area, which may fill up the available space and throw an OutofMemroyError exception. Hence, it is important to monitor the permanent generation space.

VisualVM

Another tool that is indigenous to the **Java Virtual Machine (JVM)** is VisualVM. Its developers tout it as a visual tool integrating several command-line JDK tools and lightweight profiling capabilities. This makes it a very handy tool indeed to conduct a postmortem after an application crash, or in a less serious case, once a critical error or performance issue has been clearly understood. As a general rule, customers are the first people to point out any faults in an application, and moreover, they want them resolved as soon as possible. VisualVM can be of great help in this regard.

However, the biggest issue by far with VisualVM is that it is essentially what many professional developers colloquially refer to as a brute force profiler and actually results in a slowdown of any application that the system may be running at that particular point in time. This is why it is very important to realize that VisualVM is not considered a full feature profiler in any sense of the term.

On the other hand, it also has a whole unique set of features that are highly underappreciated by a vast majority of the users for the perfectly simple reason that most of them don't even know they exist. For example, it can actually monitor MXBeans (in real time) while simultaneously showing the user different management components such as memory pools statistics, thread pools usage, along with extensive details regarding irrelevant threads as well as the overall frequency of garbage collection and so forth.

It also takes a closer look at many memory-consuming issues such as heap dump, and it also has the ability to analyze the same, so as to inform the user of the existence of many objects that created such a dump in the same place, and thus, slow down the process memory of the JVM.

There are many other, more advanced profilers out there that may offer more to the developer (especially in terms of application profiling). However, when it comes to (level one) first tier profiling tools, VisualVM has few equals and even fewer superiors, especially when it comes to checking the overall performance of the code itself. Moreover, it is one of the most convenient applications around in the profiling world, since it's already bundled with the **Java SE Development Kit (JDK)** distribution. It is exceptionally user-friendly and can be easily accessed with a single click of the relevant tab, a feature that effectively makes it one of the most popular profilers in the world today, especially when used in collision with other, more advanced profilers. However, that does not mean that it cannot be used as a standalone on its own either, at least until there is an absolute need to use something a lot heavier for some really deep digging.

However, a point to be noted is that while VisualVM may be a highly popular profiler in its own right (on the basis of usage statistics), its performance cannot be compared to other, more heavier applications since it does not fare all that well when it comes to discovering those irksome performance bugs. In fact, it is known to find far fewer bugs than many contemporary profilers. However, when used along with other, more advanced profilers, this issue is automatically rectified, and in the discovering performance bugs department, it works reasonably well when paired with other profiling tools.

Let's use VisualVM with our *Prime Number Generator* example we have seen in `Chapter 2, Identifying Performance Bottlenecks`.

You can use the following command to start the VisualVM on Mac, Windows and Linux. Go to command prompt or terminal window and navigate to the latest JDK's bin directory and type the following command:

```
$ jvisualvm
```

- The overview view:

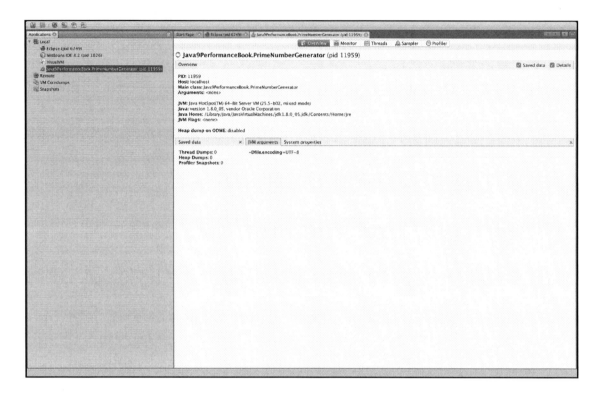

- The monitor view:

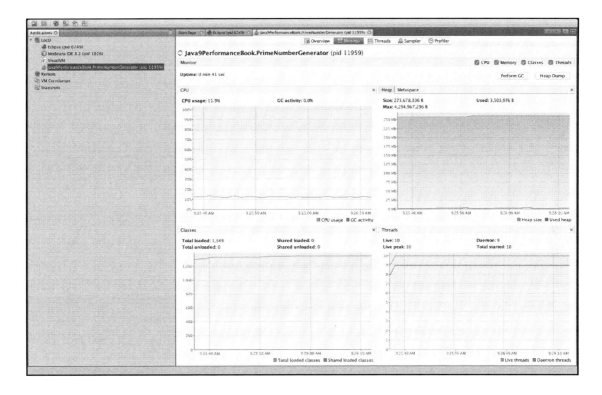

- The threads view:

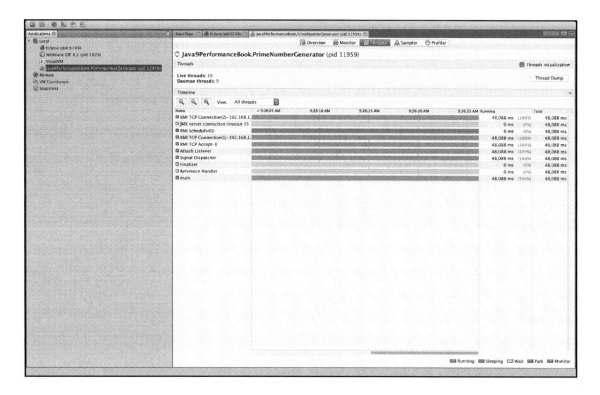

- The sampler view:

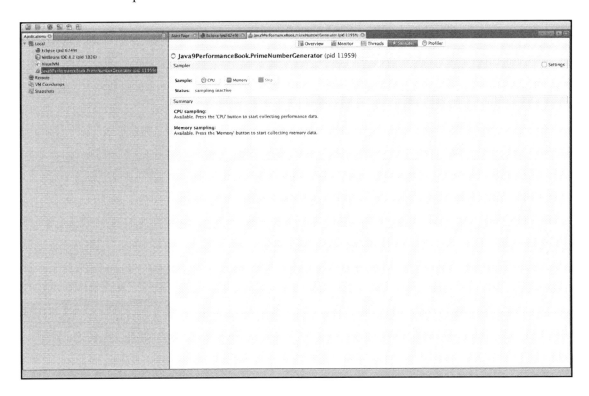

- The profiler view:

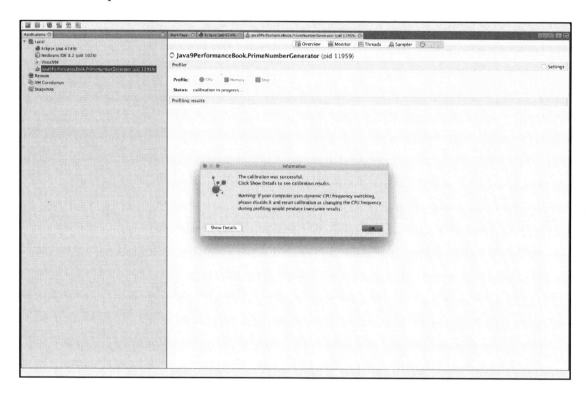

- The monitor view after executing Perform GC:

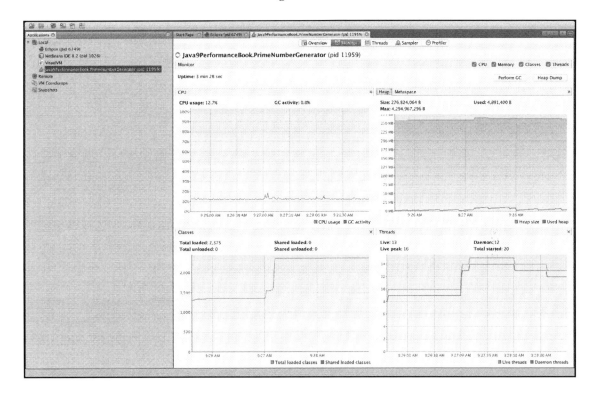

- The monitor metaspace view after executing Perform GC:

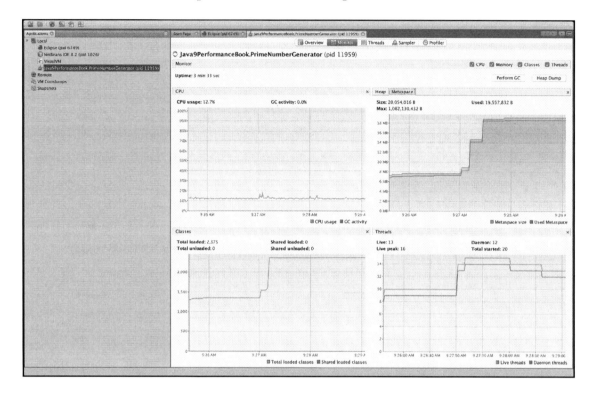

- The thread dump view:

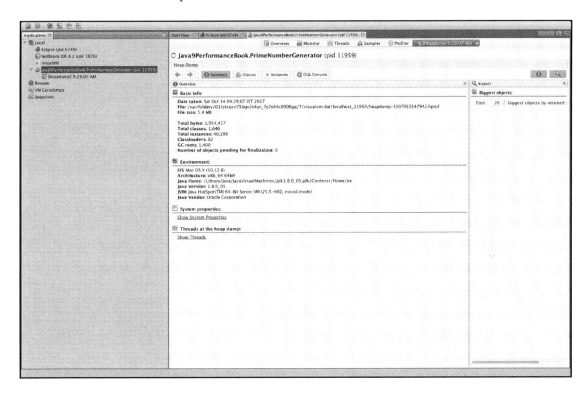

- The thread dump classes view:

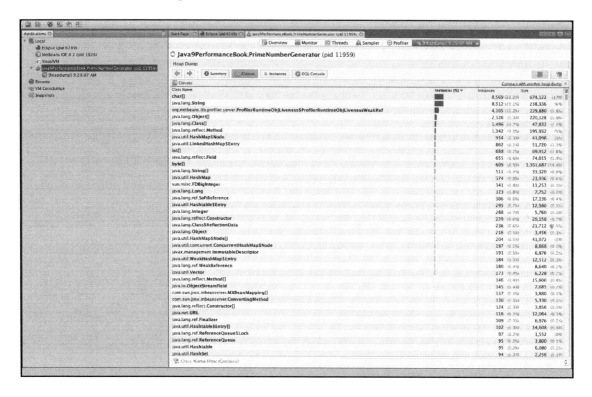

- The OQL console view:

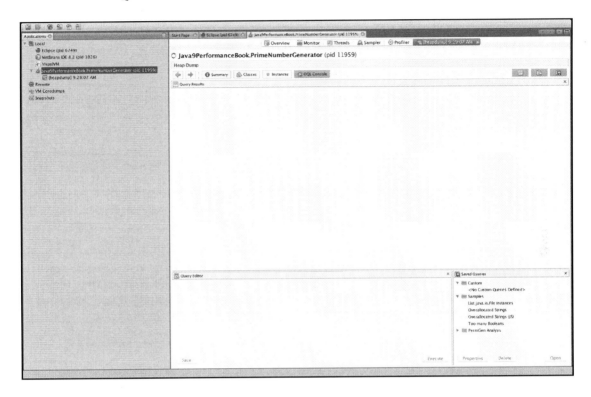

- The OQL console view with saved queries:

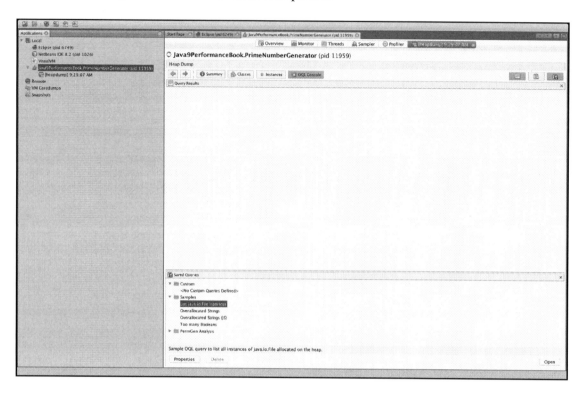

- The OQL console view with command:

- The OQL command result view:

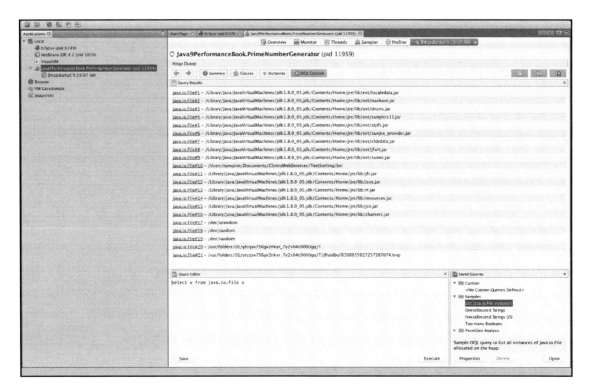

JProfiler

JProfiler is one of the most comprehensive profilers that has been built specifically for Java SE and Java EE applications. This is why it is fully equipped with built-in plugins for all major IDEs that help provide improved scrutiny for all the profile data collected by the app.

In keeping with just about every profiler created for the Java environment, CPU profiling is arguably one of the most important and practical uses of just about any profiling tool. Moreover, JProfiler is capable of showing a comprehensive call graph view, where all the different techniques are vividly represented by numerous rectangles in different colors, so as to be able to give near instantaneous and graphic visual feedback about the location of all slow codes in their method call chains, effectively making the whole task of finding and subsequently removing any bottlenecks from the code a whole lot easier.

Another nifty feature of the JProfiler is its memory profiling feature that is capable of different customization options and can be easily tuned to display lesser or greater details as per the preferences of the user. It may be fine-tuned to convey more data, or alternately, it may also be able to reduce the overall performance overhead as well. Another handy ability of this tool is that it can create snapshots of the dump heap (though HPROF) and can also collect and analyze these in real time. In fact, the JProfiler is ranked only second when it comes to popularity among the myriad of profilers used today.

Finding bugs is part of the job description of most profilers, and JProfiler is not lacked when it comes to ferreting out bugs. And as a matter of fact, apart from custom in-house tools, few third-party profilers come close to its bug-finding abilities.

Let's see the JProfile interface. We will run their demo project so we can see all the functionalities that JProfile is offering:

- The telemetries overview:

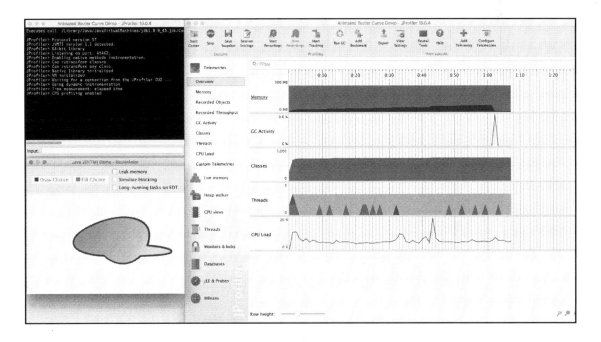

- The telemetries memory view:

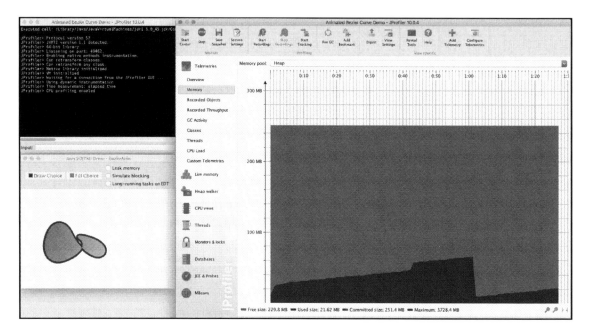

- The telemetries recorded objects view:

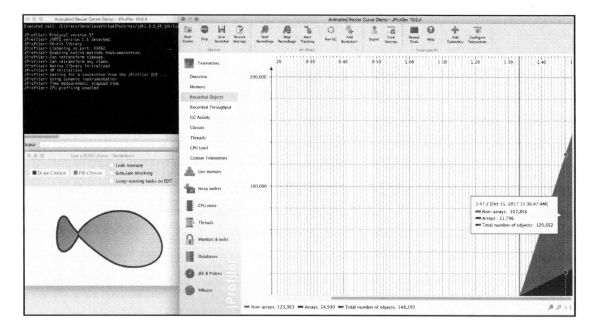

- The telemetries recorded throughput view:

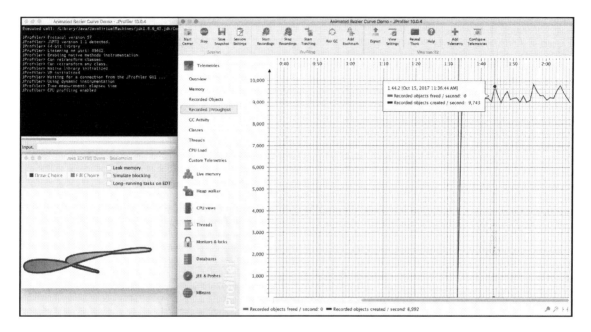

- The telemetries GC activity:

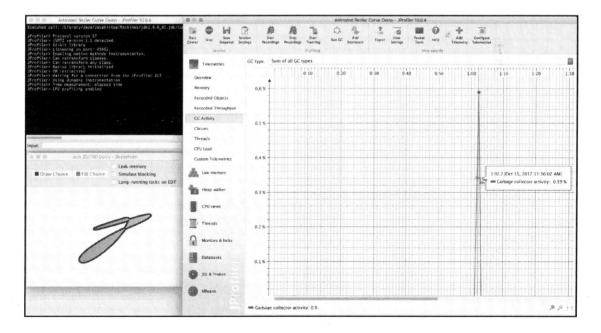

- The telemetries classes view:

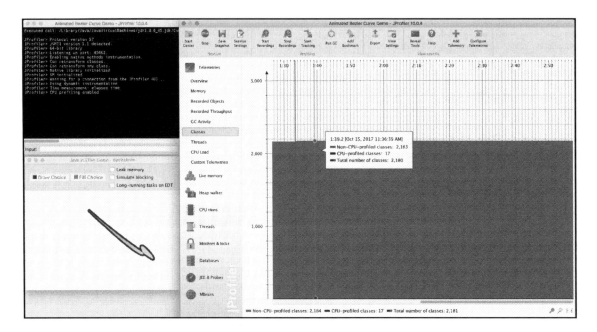

- The telemetries threads:

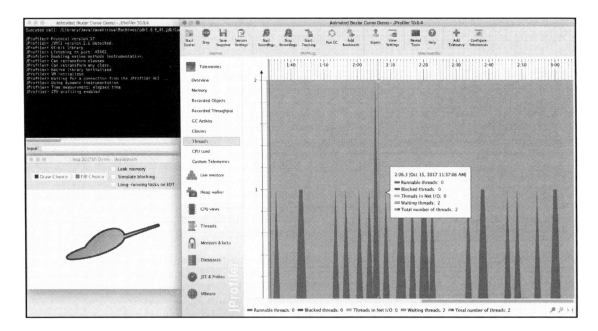

- The telemetries CPU load view:

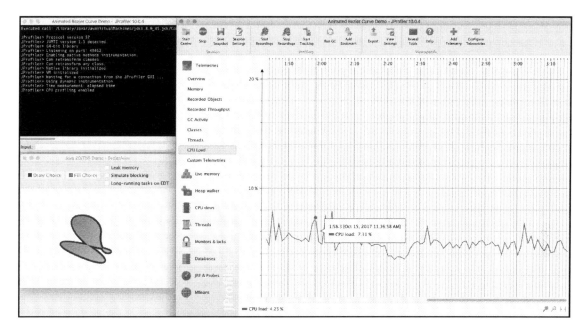

- The live memory all objects view:

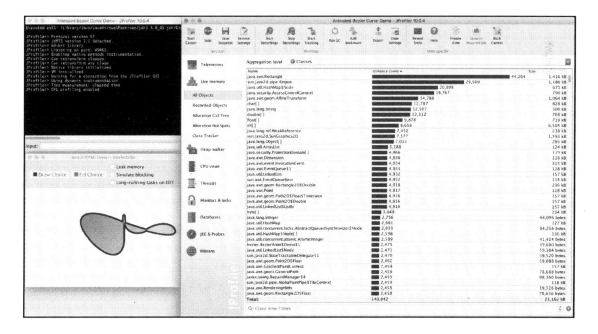

- The heap walker classes view:

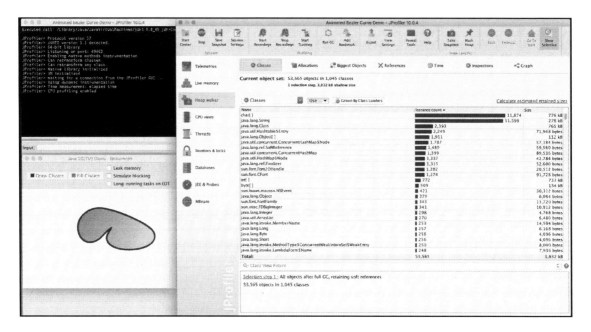

- The heap walker allocations view:

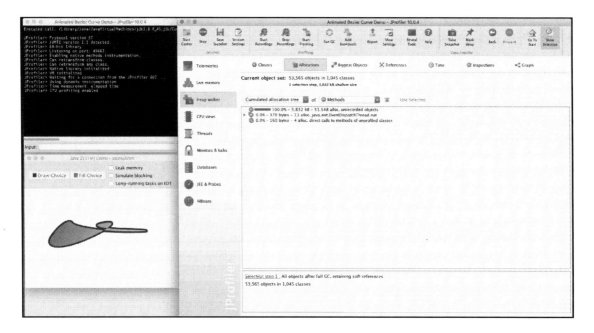

- The heap walker biggest objects view:

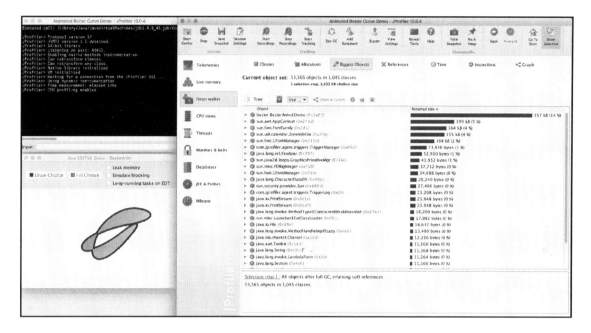

- The heap walker references view:

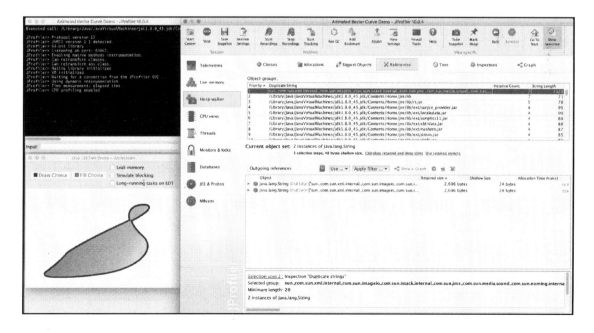

- The CPU views--Call Tree:

- The CPU views--Hot Spots:

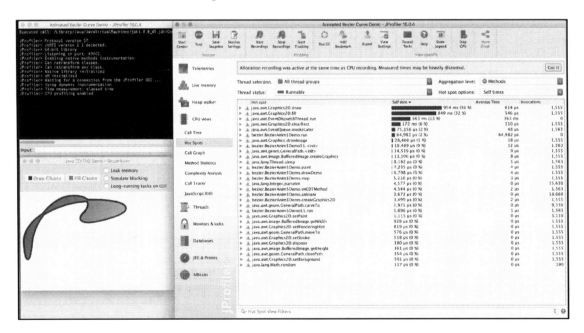

- The CPU views--Call Graph:

- The CPU views--Method Statistics:

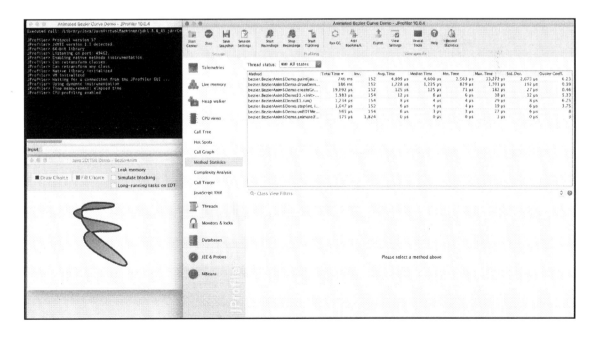

- The CPU views--Call Tracer:

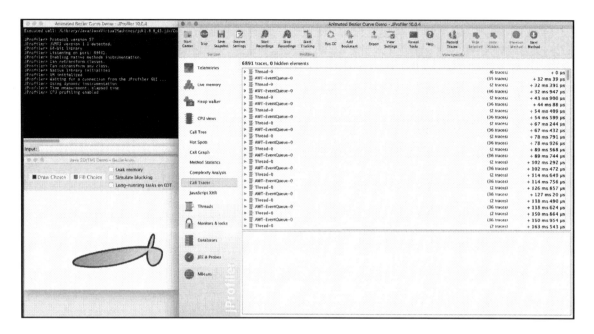

- The threads view--Thread Monitor:

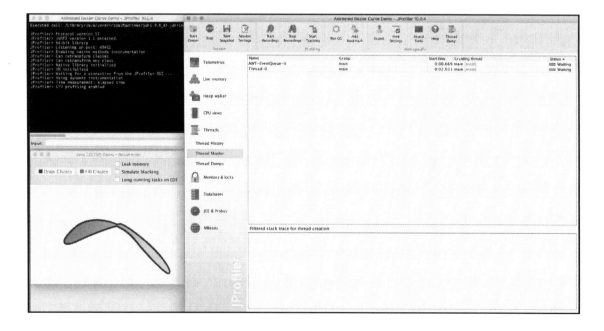

- The threads view--Thread Dumps:

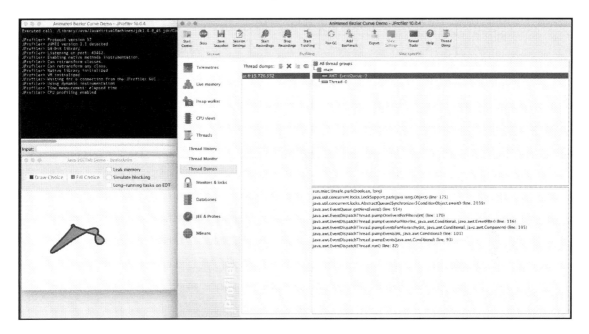

- The monitors and locks view--Current Locking Graph:

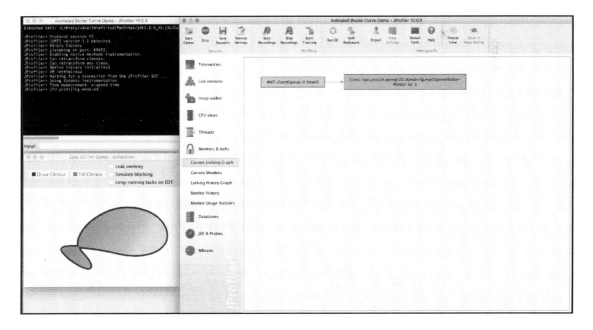

- The monitors and locks view--Current Monitors:

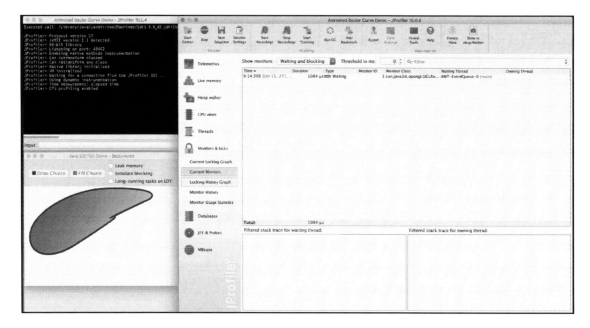

- The monitors and locks view--Locking History Graph:

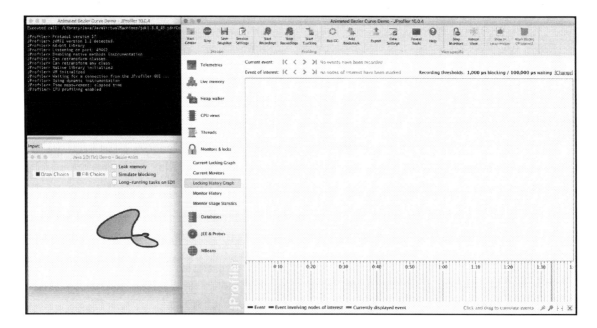

- **Long Running Tasks**: This view shows the activities when long running tasks on EDT is ticked on the demo application window. It shows the difference in CPU load:

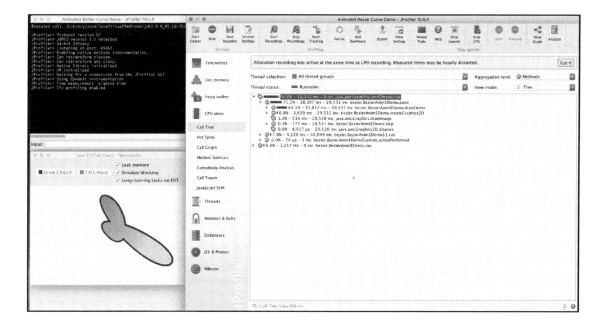

- **Simulated blocking**: This option, when ticked on the demo application show the blocking behavior for threads. See the following screenshot:

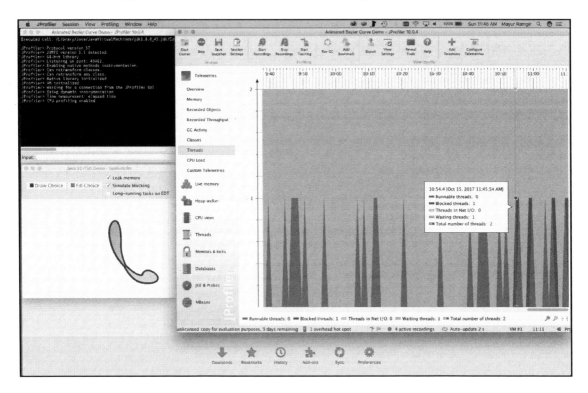

XRebel

XRebel (built by Zero Turnaround) is a high-end performance tool for Java applications that has been created for extensive usage in a Java development environment. In fact, this particular Java agent is ideal for many Java web-based applications and automatically inserts a *reporting console* in the form of a virtual widget. This widget is embedded in the application view and simultaneously showcases all the relevant data regarding the performance of the application being run on the Java platform. XRebel's core advantage stems from the fact that just about any Java developing professional can easily rectify the worst of the performance-related problems without incorporating the poor code (that may well have led to these issues to begin with) in the overall runtime environment.

Its most unique ability is the fact that it is capable of both gathering and presenting the hours used, critically serving every request. These requests are then further broken down into the appropriate method calls. XRebel's trace contains all the necessary information regarding both total time as well as the self-time along with the process itself.

Moreover, it presents all the relevant information both intelligently and concisely so as to be able to determine which processes or methods are degrading the performance of the whole app. At the same time, XRebel also shows method information and the time spans they consume, and in this way, it is able to scale the apps in which it is run.

Apart from that, this tool is fully integrated with the system's database drivers and common HTTP querying solutions, which means it can both collect and subsequently display all relevant the database actions that were either initiated or created in the application along with any requests to third-party based web services.

As a matter of fact, it is a known fact that primarily database access (or lack of it thereof), as well as associated **Hypertext Transfer Protocol** (**HTTP**) calls, are the most widespread as well as the most well-known causes for bad performance. This is an area in which the XRebel tool really shines, since it presents the developer with highly accessible data about these two common problems in real time, thus effectively making it very easy indeed to avoid many such performance-related problems both quickly and easily. In fact, XRebel ferrets out excessive database access (even for third-party applications), even as it exposes many N+1 query related issues right in their development stage. This is because it has the unique ability to understand which objects create a memory bottleneck in the HTTP session even as they occur (both during and after development testing). Finally, it single-handedly allows Java developers to see all exceptions naturally occurring in the application in real time, and yes, that includes hidden apps as well.

YourKit

The YourKit profiler is arguably one of the most well-known tools in the pantheon of relatively well-known Java profilers. It is known for its high degree of versatility, such as its ability to conduct on the spot CPU and memory profiling as well. Moreover, it is a highly versatile profiler with near seamless integration across the spectrum of well-known Java applications, such as **Java Database Connectivity** (**JDBC**), an API application programming interface for Java, as well as many other frameworks for top-end performance analysis such as (difficult to find and curb) synchronization issues and even excessive database access.

YourKit has two different modes of operation:

- Sampling
- Tracing

This effectively means that it is pretty good at extracting the best of both worlds, that is, it can quite comfortably run both tracing and sampling profiling modes. In fact, this dual ability means it can precisely trace the execution of commands controlling actual code while simultaneously managing overhead profiling, too.

The memory profiling feature in this profiling tool can also detect memory leaks in the system and subsequently trace them back to the **Garbage Collection (GC)** roots to give the user a bird's-eye view as to why the tool is not collecting the objects.

Furthermore, its automatic memory snapshot generation, as well as memory snapshot comparison, features can help guide the user when the system is low on memory, thereby helping them determine the status of the application's heap. Thanks to that, the tool is highly individual when demand profiling, as the profiled application can be run with effectively zero overheads. This is because actual profiling may be triggered only as and when required instead of running continuously in the background and draining system resources. The tool may be switched on and off only when needed so that overhead control is always maintained in the system. However, one of its biggest cons is that there have been a lot of performance issues and bugs in virtually every release.

JRockit

JRockit is a proprietary JVM originally developed by Appeal Virtual Machines and is currently part of the Oracle group. Oracle's JRockit is widely considered to be a comprehensive, across the board solution for the **Java Standard Edition (SE)**. Bundled under the hood is a full JVM, along with monitoring, profiling, and diagnostics tools as well. It is also capable of predicting latency in most Java applications. The current iteration of the JRockit toolkit has been fully decked out with a set of tools that are collectively referred to as JRockit Mission Control. This mission control suite includes the following:

- An independent console used for overall management of the toolkit and its many auxiliary applications management
- The capability of visualizing garbage collection and many other important performance statistics
- Runtime analyzer for the analysis of overall runtime performance
- Memory analyzer to easily analyze memory issues

BTrace

BTrace is another powerful profiling tool that has the ability to communicate with the JVM and thereby extract all relevant information from it. This way, the user is able to guess what needs to be ignored and shunted aside and what information is crucial and therefore needs to be gathered and evaluated.

As a rule, BTrace can help find out the following:

- The memory usage for the application (both heap and non heap)
- The real-world number of thread activities being run in an application--the many different types of threads with each thread are counted individually
- The total CPU load of the Java runtime machine
- The system's load average, that is, the total load on the CPU at any particular point in time
- The average self-execution time
- Average wall clock time
- The invocation counts and the execution times for all SQL calls

The execution timelines for both internal or external disk-based as well as network-based operations BTrace is fully capable of gathering and analyzing all of the earlier mentioned data, and since it is equipped with BTrace scripts, it lets the user specify relevant queries to ensure that only the required data has been gathered. A typical BTrace script consists of multiple parts that, when taken together, are essentially designed to give you an accurate analysis of your JVM. However, it should be kept in mind that since BTrace is only an agent, its task is considered complete once it has shown you its results. This is why it is not capable of any dynamic real-time functional ability, but rather relies solely on text-based output. As a matter of fact, the default mode for BTrace is that the text file is found next to the BTrace class file.

While it is certainly possible to press in an extra parameter to this profiling tool so as to make it log rotate all of its log files, it will only log rotate across 100 files after reaching `*.class.btrace.99`. The tool will automatically overwrite the `*.class.btrace.00` file.

Apart from that, one of the biggest drawbacks of this tool is that it is considered to be relatively primitive when compared to other Java profilers. Moreover, its static, text-oriented output format is not conducive to dynamic output. The GUI concept has been around since the 1970s, and yet BTrace seems to have refrained from climbing the graphical user interface bandwagon. Moreover, its inability to send alerts when key thresholds are breached is also a negative aspect of this profiler.

AQtime

The AQtime profiler never modifies the source code of the program. As a matter of fact, this profiler tends to use the most minimally intrusive type of operation to gather and analyze the required data. This effectively makes it one of the least intrusive methods to achieve the requested results.

Java developers and programmers have no need to learn complex shell commands or proprietary programming languages when it comes to profiling any sort of source code with this profiling tool. This is because it has a very user-friendly interface that was designed specifically keeping the needs of most software developers in mind. By clicking just a few tabs, the programmer can easily pinpoint both resource allocation problems as well as performance-related problems far faster than many other profilers.

Reporting issues

The Achilles heel of many profiling tools is reporting issues, and in fact, there exists a lot of tools that do not have the ability to report all errors and problems in a manner that would allow the developer to take immediate action. This is where AQtime comes into its own. Once a profiling session is complete, this profiler shows a summary report of all its findings. Furthermore, the summary generated is designed in a manner that helps programmers pin-point the various problems in the code and therefore rectify them on an as-needed basis by showing the most relevant data in order of importance. Moreover, all such summaries may be easily stored in many different formats such as XML, HTML, or text.

Summary

Without the extensive utilization of a Java profiling tool, many programs would be prone to bugs as well as degradation of code, which would in turn lead to the program hanging or even crashing. Initially, when profiling tools were created, many developers were quite weary of using them due to the fact that they made the whole process considerably slower. Furthermore, there was the added fear that the profiler would insert issues in the code itself.

However, with the passage of time, a whole new generation of profiling tools has changed this equation, and now it has become imperative for software developers to use them when developing new programs or even when fine-tuning old ones.

In the next chapter, we will learn about garbage collector, benefits of using garbage collector and carious garbage collection methods like escape analysis and reference counting. We will also look into disadvantages of reference counting like space reduction, cycles, and atomic tasks. Further, we will learn about parallelism and the importance of it followed by exploring the new **Garbage-First** (**G1**) collector along with a few **Garbage Collector** (**GC**) tuning techniques. You will also learn about ParallelGC and understand how it is different from G1.

5
Understanding Garbage Collection and Making Use of It

Everything we do, we leave behind a mess that we never want to clean. And that is where we rely on someone to do the job for us. Imagine your house without someone cleaning it every day. Yes, you got it. It may soon look like a garbage truck and will not leave any room for humans to survive.

The same is also true for software development. Imagine the world without a cleaner called a garbage collector. You have developed an awesome software, which is running with all its grace on the most advanced server with a lot of RAM and a large number of CPU cores. In all its glory, it is helping a lot of users get the most out of their software investment. At its peak, inside the application server, your code is loading a lot of classes and creating a lot of objects to support the complex operations your algorithm is supposed to perform. However, soon, your server goes down with the exception `OutOfMemoryError` without any warning. Now, you may be wondering why? It's because your server becomes like a garbage truck, a lot of unused objects lying around consuming valuable resources, leaving no room for new objects. It's not a pretty picture, right? And that's why a cleaner is important.

In this chapter, we will cover the following topics:

- What is a garbage collector?
- What are the features of a garbage collector?
- Principals of a garbage collector
- Benefits and demerits of garbage collection
- Various garbage collection methods, such as escape analysis and reference counting

- Disadvantages of reference counting, such as space reduction, cycles, and atomic tasks
- Understanding the current `ParallelGC`
- What is parallelism and why it is useful?
- New G1 collector and its impact
- Comparison of G1 collector and Parallel GC

Understanding the Java 9 garbage collector for top optimization

Garbage collection is an important technique used for automatic reallocation of memory. The new JDK 9 is a project that requires implementation of the Java SE 9 platform. It is defined in the Java community as the JSR 379 process and serves as the key to implementing the JEP 2.0 proposal.

One of the important ideas is to find the ideal and the most optimized method for memory allocation. We will discuss different garbage collector algorithms in this article. The important and proven technique of Parallel GC will be explained here as well while discussing concepts such as parallelism, heap sizing, and G1 collector facilities.

Different failures will also be discussed here, and then, further details of the new garbage collection mechanism will be explained.

Garbage Collection

Garbage Collection (GC) is important in computer programming and development. A garbage collector tries to reclaim the garbage memory, which contains objects that will no longer be used during a computer program. Its concept was presented by John McCarthy in 1959 to improve manual memory management processes.

Although garbage collection aims to automatically manage memory, most real solutions use a combination of different approaches. GC processes take up a lot of computing power, so it is essential to use highly optimized solutions in this regard. Garbage collection is only faster if it is properly designed, according to the available program and optimized for a universal standard.

Sometimes, there are different resources such as network sockets and user interaction tools that also require management. A method used to take care of these resources may often have the capacity of managing memory as well, therefore eliminating the need for separate GC methods.

On the other hand, there are GC systems where the recollection of a particular memory region may automatically help in the reclamation of other resources. This process is termed finalization. It can be difficult to control this process since there can be a latency between the reclamation and the actual availability of resources. Now we will describe the main principle behind garbage collection.

The principle of GC

The main principle of GC is to automatically identify data objects in a program which will not be accessed in the future. This is followed up by the reclamation of resources under these objects.

Java is a programming language that requires the availability of GC methods. These methods, in fact, are described in the specification. Garbage collection is essential in Java since it is a scripting language. The GC is developed with the runtime system of Java, which ensures that it is associated directly with the memory allocation method of the programming language.

Benefits and demerits of garbage collection

GC methods are required by the Java community since they ensure that the programmer does not have to deal with memory allocation issues within the programming language.

Here are the different benefits on offer:

- Different bugs and programming discrepancies reduce due to the presence of automatic memory management.
- Pointer bug issues are resolved, which occur when free memory still has pointers towards it. The memory may have been reassigned, but the presence of multiple pointers causes bugs in normal allocation.
- Double free bugs are also reduced. This occurs when the program tries to attempt to use memory that was already free and used again by the program earlier.
- It stops memory leaks. These leaks occur when a program does not free up memory that contains unreachable objects.
- It allows for the better implementation of large data structures.

- Program security and efficiency are significantly improved.

There are a few demerits as well when using GC. Here are some of the top disadvantages:

- GC methods employ additional resources. This means that programs require more computational power as a result. They are not compatible with manual resource management.
- GC processes also impact the performance of Java programs since greater resources are consumed. The program may take a longer time to carry out subsequent processing tasks but require less overall memory.
- GC can also require additional memory, as some experts believe that it may require greater memory to speed up the process of automatic memory management. The lack of memory may produce program stalls.
- It may produce unforeseen errors that are hard to predict during the traditional testing phase.

Unpredictability

The exact moment of GC remains undefined, which is the main reason for causing stalls through a program operation. Some environments cannot tolerate even minor stalls, such as interactive programs, which make it difficult to efficiently employ GC in Java.

GC is significantly improved in the new collector, which is explained later in this detailed article. It works the most on background elements by selecting different threads that are marked for collection during application processing. Programs with large quantities of objects may still produce a slow resolve during a GC event.

GC methods

There are different methods that are employed to improve and carry out GC. Here, we will take a look at some of these methods.

Escape analysis

This is a method that allows the conversion of memory heap allocations to stack allocations. This reduces the object size of the garbage collection by performing a single-time analysis. This analysis finds whether a particular object is not accessible in other functions.

The object identified in this method may then be allocated to a thread stack for release, and this decreases the activities that group up together for GC.

Reference counting

This is an excellent GC method where all objects are identified according to the number of references. A garbage object is the one that does not have any associated references and has a zero count. Each time an object is referenced, the count is increased. The count decreases whenever a particular reference is eliminated.

The memory is only reclaimed when a particular object's reference count approaches zero. This method does not require the tracing of objects for GC as reference counting destroys objects the moment their references are eliminated completely. This reduces the need for virtual memory as well as CPU cache required for better computational power.

This method has some disadvantages that are avoided with the use of sophisticated GC algorithms, and some of the algorithms are explained in the following sections.

Space reduction

Since this method requires the counting of references, this count also needs to be efficiently stored. One way of reducing this count is to not use a separate memory for this purpose, but to rather employ the free system memory through the use of memory pointers that point towards empty spaces.

A tagged pointer is excellent since it is usually available in different programming languages. The reference count may only require 32 bits of storage, but the pointer can mean the use of even smaller space already available to the program.

Any reliable pointer available to objects can be used to store the reference count. In fact, additional pointer space can also be employed for storing the count and eliminate the need for extra memory altogether.

Cycles

Sometimes, a never-ending cycle can be created due to two objects that only refer to each other. Their count will never reach zero for both of them, resulting in an active status throughout the program and inefficient memory allocation.

Cycles are removed through specific algorithms that are able to detect such instances. One strategy is to use back pointers and create weak references when a cycle position is achievable in two objects. A weak reference does not increment the count; therefore, it can reach a null reference count value.

Atomic tasks

Using the reference counting method required atomic operations, especially when using large programs with multiple threads. Objects that are cross-referenced but shared in different threads can really increase the load on a processor. They can especially slow down software emulations.

The issue is resolved by adding reference counts in each thread and only using the global count when the local count reaches zero. This decreases the instances that require greater processing power but can increase the need for a larger memory head.

GC in Java

Java focuses greatly on using automatic memory allocation systems, which means that it employs an automatic garbage collector. The GC in Java recovers the memory after the runtime evaluates that certain objects are no longer in computational use. It uses a method of reference, such as the one that may be employed in a manual scheme.

Once all the references to an object are eliminated, the memory location is marked for automatic freeing by the garbage collector. A memory leak occurs when inefficient code by a programmer references an object that is actually not required. A null pointer exception method is usually employed in Java for identifying non-existent objects.

The main idea behind the use of different GC methods in Java is to take away the burden of memory management from the programmers. In some languages, objects are allocated from heaps and deallocated from them as well. This means that the programmer must manually perform the memory allocation of the relevant object heaps.

The issue with manual management is that if the program addresses de-allocated memory during execution, then unpredictable results appear, and it can hang up or crash altogether. The use of smart pointers can resolve this issue, but it produces its own space overhead and increases the complexity of the programming solution.

GC in Java needs to be carefully used since it does not stop the programmer from performing logical memory leaks. This occurs when objects in the memory are referenced but never employed in the program. Since GC methods depend on the absence of references to reclaim the memory, it remains and increases the overall space required for running the program.

GC can occur at any time in a running Java program, but should ideally happen when the program is in the idle position. GC is triggered when there is insufficient free memory to allocate a new object on the heap. However, triggering at the time of need may stall the program for a memory.

However, there is no way around this problem, since Java does not support or exhibit explicit memory management. Java is different from its parent C language since it does not support the use of pointers in addressing objects in terms of a class of unsigned integers. This lack of support is essential for the working of the GC in a safe and secure manner.

Understanding the current Parallel GC

The Parallel GC collector can be defined as a generational connector and uses multiple threads for improving the GC, which is inherently a difficult problem. The connection is activated using the command-line. Minor and major collections occur in parallel in this method, which reduces the overall overhead present in GC in Java.

This collector method uses a fixed fraction of the total number of hardware threads that are available in a program. It usually selects around 5/8 threads for garbage collection out of the total data threads. This fraction may be reduced in special applications to 5/16, which decreases the load that the data collector has to handle, especially in large programs with many threads.

The parallel collector is designed to efficiently work with multi-processor systems since it is possible to execute the collection simultaneously on different processors when working on large heap sizes. A serial collector, on the other hand, is ideal when there is a single processor that has the ability to work fast, but in a continuous manner.

The command-line options can be used to control the `ParallelGC` threads in Java. This means that this method can be easily tuned to meet the particular needs of a Java program for improved performance. Collection pauses are efficient and shorter since they occur in a parallel fashion and spread over different computational capacity.

The `ParallelGC` method also allows coders to select the number of threads. This can be done with a simple command-line selection. The heap can be explicitly tuned up with these options, and it may work in the same manner as a serial collector.

The `ParallelGC` method makes the collection pauses shorter, which was the reason behind its initial application. Multiple collectors work at the same time when this method works, which may cause some fragmentation to develop. This happens when there is a transfer of generations in each collection attempt.

The minor collection always reserves a part for future promotions and divides the available free space. This essentially may cause fragmentation but is necessary for a parallel method. A coder can easily reduce the number of these collector threads while also increasing the size of the tenure generation to get more control over fragmentation.

Generations

The `ParallelGC` method significantly depends on the ideal use of collection generations. The parallel collector works by using several server machines. It is also available with an automatic tuning method that allows the use of specific behaviors rather than explicit control over generation size.

This lets you set up details such as the maximum GC pause time and the heap size of the memory reallocation.

The `ParallelGC` method allows the setting up of a maximum garbage collection pause time in milliseconds. The selection of a particular size means that other important parameters, such as heap size, will be automatically adjusted to ensure shorter pauses than the specified time.

These adjustments may reduce the original throughput of an application. The desired pause time objective may not be achievable in such a case due to the lack of available physical resources.

The throughput goal determines the time spent in performing garbage collection when it is compared with the time of application that occurs outside of the garbage collection. The default value for garbage collection is 99, which describes an objective of 1 percent time spent in GC mode.

The footprint of the `ParallelGC` method can also be specified using the command-line. The collector automatically attempts to minimize the size of the heap, which we will explain later within this section.

There is a priority method followed in `ParallelGC` since it may not always be possible to achieve all the mentioned objectives when setting up manual tuning of the method. There are three settings available and discussed here, in order of their priority.

The maximum pause time is the most important goal, and the GC always attempts to achieve this goal above others. The second priority is to achieve the throughput goal explained on the command-line. The last priority is to maintain a minimum footprint.

The adjustment of generation size is an important characteristic of the `ParallelGC` method. This method uses the available statistics that are updated after each collection cycle. Tests are carried out after each cycle to ensure that GC goals have been achieved or if there is a need to adjust the generation size in the next attempt.

However, there are also exceptions when the program calls out for explicit garbage collection, which ignores the current statistics and the need for adjustments. Generation size always changes in an incremental value that is always a fixed percentage of the desired size that needs to go up or down.

The default change in generation size is to grow 20 percent in each cycle, while the shrinking has a default value of 5 percent of the generation size. These values can also be fixed for the new and the tenured generation.

If there is a need to grow the initial generation, then a supplementation increment is set up. This supplemental value drops down with each collection and therefore does not have a long-term implication. This technique is not available for shrinking.

The size of one generation is reduced if the GC cannot meet the goal of the maximum pause time. There are multiple generations crossing the goal pause time; the generation with the higher pause time is first shrunk to meet the objective.

The size of both generations is increased if the throughput goal is not achieved. Each increase happens according to the contribution towards the total garbage collection time.

Heap sizing

The heap size refers to the memory allocated to different parts of your program. The heap sizes can be specified in your program using the command-line. The maximum heap size is that half of the available physical memory that may go up to 192 MB (megabytes). The capacity remains at one-fourth the value if the physical memory goes up to 1 GB (gigabyte).

In fact, the maximum heap size is seldom used by the JVM. It is only used when there are enough objects in the program to actually require additional memory. The JVM does not obtain the maximum amount at the start, as it may obtain resources that may not be required at all.

The lowest initial size is 8 MB, while it may have the value of 1/64 of the physical memory available up to the limit of 1 GB. The space allocated to the young generation is maximized at one-third of the total heap size.

The initial and maximum heap size allocations work similarly on server and client JVMs. Exceptions only occur when these values increase to higher values. The default maximum heap size can go up to 1 GB on 32-bit JVMs only if there is at least 4 GB of available physical memory. On the other hand, 64-bit JVMs can go a lot higher, with the maximum heap size going up to 32 GB if there is at least 128 GB of physical memory. These values can be set up in JVM in order to best employ the available memory resources.

There are flags that can be used to alter the initial and maximum heap sizes. Coders who are aware of how much memory is required for their application are able to set up custom memory sizes. The two values can be the same as well. In a normal function, the JVM starts with the initial heap size value and starts to grow until a balance is achieved between the use of heap and the JVM performance.

There are also other parameters that may change these values. It is always possible to check the heap in Java and ensure that it is set to default values.

The `ParallelGC` method is able to produce an error if it takes more time to perform the garbage collection. The `OutOfMemoryError` is shown if over 98 percent of the time is spent collecting garbage. It also appears if less than 2 percent heap is recovered.

This feature allows applications to stop running for longer periods when the heap has a limited capacity. It can also be disabled in the JVM by adding a command-line option. These options allow the Parallel GC to perform the same as a serial collector. The next section describes the whole concept of parallelism in greater detail.

Parallelism

Parallel computing is an important concept that describes the use of creating a set of smaller problems in order to quickly process a larger program. This option is essential in speeding up the overall process by allowing its different elements to get processed at the same time. Parallel computing has especially found more power, as all JVMs now have access to multiple processors.

The Java framework essentially takes the advantage of parallelism and implements it into all of its functionalities, including garbage collection. However, this means that you have to partition your programs, functions, and memory objects in order to run them in a parallel operation. The Java runtime usually performs the actual partitioning and the recombining of these divisions to create the final output.

Parallelism is difficult to implement in JVM where collections are employed. Collections are groups of related functions whose safety is not guaranteed when threaded multiple times since it produces interference and consistency errors.

There is the collections framework to resolve this issue, which adds automatic synchronization to a collection. However, this process produces thread contention, which makes it impossible to run them in a parallel computing method. The availability of parallel streams and aggregate operations allows programmers to use parallelism while using collections that are not safe for thread generation.

An important point to remember is that parallelism is not always the fastest processing method and can beat serial operations only if there is large enough data and multiple processor cores for parallel processing.

An individual programmer is responsible for finding out if a particular program will run best using parallelism. This is often a decision that depends on creating individual groups and objects that can get processed at the same time to resolve the overall computing solution.

Parallelism only occurs when a single task or a collection of functions can be subdivided within the memory allocation and processing. Each task may be split up into individual sub-tasks, which can then be completed in parallel by taking advantage of the multiple cores.

This process is different from concurrent tasks, which are mutually exclusive and can always be completed irrespective of each other. This means that most applications may not always be good for parallel working, but may include individual tasks that can be in terms of a concurrency model. An application running on Java may use these methods or have tasks that require iteration and can only run in the form of a serialized processing activity.

Modern GC collections allow working with applications that fully employ parallelism as well as concurrency. This ensures that they can work with all kinds of programming solutions. The benefits of parallelism are only applicable when a programmer specifically implements strategies to use the available multithread options.

The analysis is usually performed during each application coding and, therefore, the selection of the ideal parallel model depends on the individual application.

There are several examples of running different streams in either series or parallel. The Java runtime is responsible for creating the relevant sub-divisions, which are then carried out using aggregate operations. These operations iterate as many times as required to process the sub-streams and are then combined at the end to produce the end results.

This method ensures that you take great care of changing the default memory allocation system of JVM to ensure that it will run smoothly and at the quickest possible speed.

Streams can be executed in serial or in parallel. In parallel execution of streams, the Java runtime then partitions this stream into multiple sub-streams. These sub-streams then iterate over in parallel and combine the results together. Here is an example that shows how a parallel stream can run that calculates the average sale of all the customers who are 30 years old in a parallel computing activity:

```
double average = ageCal
.parallelStream()
.filter(c ->c.getAge() == Customer.Age.THIRTY)
.mapToInt(Customer::getSale)
.average()
.getAsDouble();
```

Parallel garbage collection is an excellent way of ensuring that the power of available hardware elements can be perfectly acknowledged and used by the JVM.

Why parallelism?

It may be a subject of interest to learn why parallelism is an important trend in the Java community. This is due to the current microprocessors being developed and promoted by top companies, such as Intel, IBM, and AMD. These processors are able to process multiple threads and have multiple physical cores as well. The availability of 64-bit JVMs now allows us to create and run huge heaps that were never possible on 32-bit machines. There are several advantages of using parallelism in Java since it has been available in Java 5 and the later versions.

Garbage problem is often created by a number of threads. A serial garbage collection removes the effect of one thread at a time that may create a strong bottleneck in a program with strong heap requirements. The `ParallelGC` method employs the ideal parallelism since it only works on collecting the young generation. It is available as the default method in most Java kits and will only give way to the new method of G1GC as the default garbage collector in the Java 9 update.

The parallel method takes the advantage of tracing objects in the young generation and copying them after the reclamation. Objects that are already old are promoted to the old generation. It requires the use of buffers to allow for the changing of position of program objects.

The `ParallelGC` method produces a stop-the-world effect during the collection step since it uses all the available threads. Remember that having this pause time means that the `ParallelGC` method may not always be the fastest method, but it usually is due to running over multiple threads at the same time.

Remember that turning to the `ParallelGC` method is a compromise where you are willing to increase the overall computing time of the application as long as you can reduce the size of the pauses that may occur due to the necessary garbage collection in the program.

The new G1 collector

The Java community is keen and excited about the Java 9 and its related packages and primary features. Garbage collection is an important Java function, and therefore, it is essential to discuss the new G1 collector that is being promoted in the new package. This takes away from the direction of the previous method of `ParallelGC`. We will refer to the new collector as the **Garbage First Garbage Collector** (**G1GC**) throughout the article.

It is a multithread-capable GC tool and has the ability to work concurrently on different processing threads. The G1GC collector is designed to work with application threads and reduce the pause times, which appear with the use of a garbage collection method.

G1GC is entirely different in terms of creating heap divisions. It does not create three big piles of heap. It creates a number of equal-sized heaps, which can work together. Different regions have their assigned roles, which also occurs in different GC systems.

The live data present in each region is properly tracked in the new method, and the G1GC clears the regions that have the most garbage first, whenever a collection is triggered. This process is also the responsible factor for naming the new GC.

Each collection of heap frees up the most space possible. The heap is also reduced through compacting, and this eliminates the presence of data fragments. The method also employs different metrics to calculate the performance and status of each region.

These metrics are used to calculate the time that will be required to collect the garbage. This essentially provides a basis for creating pause times and ensuring that the efficiency of the programming remains intact. The collector then attempts to collect maximum garbage in each attempt by using the available constraints.

A brief history

The new Java 9 G1GC default collector has been available since update 4 of Java 7, but it was not available for default use. This new method is able to split the processing of objects in multiple phases. Not all of these phases require the stopping of the processing. This results in faster processing overall and ensures that program threads remain short and can be recycled within different phases.

Garbage collection threads in G1GC have to work with application threads the entire time, which increases the maintenance overhead of the programming package. There is a need for synchronization in order to ensure that the memory model of Java remains operational.

There are additional memory barriers that are required for efficient functioning of different operations, due to this default garbage collection. These barriers will be implemented through Hotspot VM and will protect the memory. The calculations slow down with this collection method, reducing the work done in each cycle.

However, it offers protection from a long, single delay, which is not suitable for modern web applications, as they require consistency and well-defined program pauses to avoid crashing and client waiting.

Impact on programming

There will not be an immediate impact on current programmers. Most people do not set up their garbage collector using the command-line, and they will be forced to use the default collector tool. People who use manual GC methods do not have to be concerned about the new system since they can use the other available options.

People who love the `G1GC` method will be happy that it is now the default one, and they will stay away from explicit settings. There are 688 flags that are available in Java, and there are many programmers who really like to set up each flag for use in a complex program.

The main reason for pushing the G1GC collector is that it is extremely stable and ideal for all kinds of users. It is designed as a fit for all tools and moves the language towards modernization. However, most members of the Java community are naturally against large changes in the language structure and find that they are more comfortable with the traditional methods.

Some community members believe that it is too early to make G1GC the default garbage collection method in Java 9. The collector has just achieved stability, and therefore, it needs some time before reaching the maturity level required for making it a default method.

They argue that the right thing would have been to package this method, but only make it a default option in the next package of Java 10. Since it is a rough diamond, even expert community members are struggling to find ways to tune it to cater to specialized program needs. Some time is required for the natural progression of the method, as the Java community will be better able to embrace it.

Deep insight on G1GC

There is always the question of what are the key benefits of G1 that have made it a primary candidate to become the default garbage collection method. G1 is specially created to work on machines that have multiple processors and huge memories available for 64-bit heap sizing.

The `G1GC` method always attempts to achieve goals for pause time with high probability while still maintaining a very high throughput (GC efficiency) throughout the process of Java applications. This method combines parallelism with concurrency to achieve goals that may be too difficult to be attained with the previous default method of `ParallelGC`.

The main purpose of introducing the `G1GC` method is to make the pause times more predictable rather than trying to eliminate them. This method sets up the available heap in equal regions that represent a continuous virtual memory.

A global marking phase is carried out to check which objects are currently operational within the entire heap. The marking allows the collector to learn about the empty and occupied regions. This allows G1GC to first collect empty regions that are able to quickly provide large chunks of free space. This is an ideal situation for applications that run on a server and must always have access to huge memory for seamless operations.

The `G1GC` method uses a prediction model to ensure that it can achieve the required target of pause time. This prediction also returns information about the number of heap regions that need to be recollected within the target pause for GC.

The G1 method can pick up objects from multiple regions and place them within a single region. This step can have the double benefit of freeing up the available memory and compressing the stored information.

The `G1GC` method performs this process by using parallelism and working on all the available processors. This parallel approach increases the throughput while decreasing the pause time during garbage collection. Each garbage collection continuously reduces memory fragmentation, thus greatly improving the efficiency of the available heap.

The compaction of application achieved in the `G1GC` method is one benefit, which is not available in previous methods, such as `ParallelGC`. Previous collectors are not able to compact the data in this fashion and can at best perform a complete compaction, which can produce a significant pause time and hang up the application.

G1GC does not have fixed pause time parameters, as it does not work in real time. It uses the method of achieving high probability but does not offer certainty. It produces the predictability by using the data from the previous collections. This, in turn, gives an estimation of the regions that can be targeted in the available pause time.

G1GC attempts to calculate the time of garbage collection and then attempts to perform the collection in a manner that also tends to compact the objects in the available regions of the heap. This often ensures that the GC is performed within the user-defined pause time.

This means that the G1GC is a great solution for applications that use huge heap sizes. Modern applications require large memory and, therefore, are ideal for implementing G1GC that produces controllable GC latency. It allows the use of large memories that may be over 6 GB, while still offering pause times under half a second with good predictability.

Comparing G1 collector to ParallelGC

Many Java programmers do not know that there are four different garbage collectors that are available. Most professionals only employ the default garbage collection method in JVM, which used to be the `ParallelGC` method. Here, we will especially discuss `ParallelGC` and compare it with `G1GC`, which becomes the new default garbage collector in the Java 9 package.

This means that Java programmers will now have to pay extra attention when simply using the default GC method in their programs. The objectives of both methods are different, and this means that ordinary programs may not behave in the same manner due to this fundamental change. However, any programmer can still use the older default method, but the emphasis should remain on understanding the changing environment of garbage collection in JVM.

Common points

When we compare these two garbage collection methods, we find that there are many points of parity between them. Currently, all garbage collection methods in Java use generations. This means that both the `G1GC` and `ParallelGC` methods employ young and tenured generations during their GC marking schemes.

They both work on the concept that most objects have a short life and can be safely recycled quickly after their use. On the other hand, frequently used objects need to be identified so that they can be transferred to the tenured generation for a later garbage collection review.

The qualities of ParallelGC

The method `ParallelGC` has remained the default collector of JVM for a number of versions. This is due to the fact that it uses multiple threads at the same time. This, in turn, compresses the heap and ensures that it was possible to carry out garbage collection at reduced pause times.

However, like all other all garbage collectors, there is a downside to this benefit. Since it needs to run multiple GC threads, it will always stop the main application threads when carrying out the step of a full GC collection or even a minor collection.

`ParallelGC` is an excellent GC method for applications that are looking to optimize the CPU usage and can sustain moderate application pauses. This is true for all the applications that are hosted on individual computers and are often bound by the availability of fixed computing resources.

This means that this method becomes limited when creating applications for servers that host a live service for hundreds of clients. A single stoppage may disrupt the service and break the concept of providing clients seamless connectivity and functionality.

The qualities of G1GC

`G1GC` is a new method that first appeared in JDK 7 Update 4. It was specially designed to work with applications that use memory sizes of over 4 GB. This garbage collector focuses on the working of various threads in order to keep them in separate regions. It can create large heap regions of up to 32 MB.

This garbage collector is, therefore, designed to provide the functionality of removing regions that hold the most garbage elements.

The G1 collector also needs to stop the watch if the heap reduction change has already finished, but the application needs to use more memory. It offers the excellent advantage of compacting the available heap by transferring it according to the age of the objects and marking them out for generational exchange.

It performs better than the `ParallelGC` method when performing on-the-go heap changes. It also has the capacity to properly deal with large heap sizes. This ensures that this method can be used by programmers to create large applications that may run on a single machine. The isolation of different parts allows for better use of memory, which is the main improvement to be offered with every new Java development.

The main advantage of `G1GC` is the significant reduction of the stop-the-world pauses. It has a default value of 200 milliseconds, but it is common to find that it can reduce the pause time by four times when compared with the previous default method of `ParallelGC`.

Large heaps can slow down `ParallelGC`, which is where the new `G1GC` default method is able to deliver a higher performance. This method may put more load on the CPU, but it has the capacity to ensure that client-side applications do not experience large stoppages. The `G1` method is ideal for the new direction for JVM, where the package is looking to offer improved support to large-scale programs that are hosted on 64-bit virtual machines.

Concurrent mode failures

Understanding the concurrent mode in JVM is essential when looking to understand the failures that may occur. Concurrency is explained as a process in which Java attempts to carry out multiple functions at the same time. The issue with the concurrent mode is that it can fail if the program is not able to resource enough heap to carry out simultaneous functions. The failure of the concurrent mode results in the use of stop the world garbage collection, which takes a lot of time and truly eliminates the benefits of using a low pause collector, such as the G1GC. Understanding the failure is simple; understanding the mistakes that are causing concurrent mode failures is a lot more difficult.

The Java documentation says that concurrent collector occurs when a single or multiple collection thread attempts to run with the applicant threads at the same time. The goal of this garbage collection is to collect the tenured and the permanent generations before they are fully consumed, leaving no room for new program objects.

The collection is able to perform concurrent work; therefore, there is no need for an **stop-the-world (STW)** step.

 The term stop-the-world is used to define a process where GC execution is blocked for the applications by JVM. In this process, only GC threads are allowed to run and all other threads are ceased until the GC threads complete their intended tasks. Maintaining a low stop-the-world time is one of the important steps in GC tuning.

However, the collector requires the use of a longer stop if it is not able to complete the reclamation work before the tenured generation in the JVM fills up completely. There is also the need for a long pause if the available free heap space is not enough to carry out the next allocation marked by the collector.

A concurrent mode failure is defined by Oracle as the failure of carrying out the collection in a concurrent manner, without requiring a stop-the-world event. Such a situation demands a change in concurrent parameters that control heap sizes as well as the triggering of the concurrent threads of garbage collection.

The normal process of a concurrent garbage collection occurs when a collector keeps attempting to perform the collection of the tenured generation, but also faces the problem of completely using up the available heap. This, in turn, implies that there is no memory left for objects to be transported to the tenured generation from the young generation while the application is still running actively. Ideally, the collector needs to finish its concurrent operation **just-in-time (JIT)** before there is a need to clear up space from the older generations once again.

The problem occurs because concurrent garbage collection is a function of using the probability of when the tenured generation will be full by using the historical data available in a Java running program. Since the collector uses a prediction model, there is always a chance of going wrong, especially if the available heap is smaller to start with. Concurrent mode failure is a problem because it produces a long pause and stops the application, which goes against the whole concept of using a collector that employs concurrent garbage collection mechanism.

The main reason behind the failure is that the tenured generation becomes extremely large and contains too much live data. This means that there are not enough heap regions available in this old generation for supporting the allocation of the next object movements. This kind of problem appears when your Java application requires a lot of live objects but is not supported with enough heaps to reserve memory for both the application and the garbage collection threads.

Another way this problem may appear is when your historical data does not accurately represent the direction of your program. This occurs when your program quickly changes behavior, due to accommodating a particular need of a client, directly using an application hosted on a JVM. This implies that there is a greater chance of experiencing a concurrent mode failure, during the early stages of such a change, which will cause a noticeable pause. The collector will automatically improve if the new demands of the program remain consistent since it depends on the available historical data.

You can always reduce the chances of concurrent mode failures that happen due to the change in the way your application is running. However, tuning up your collector to cover against concurrent mode failure will result in grading down the overall performance of the garbage collection. This is a trade-off that provides stability over optimal performance. You can change the flag that contains the initial heap size of the tenured generation for starting concurrent collection. This will provide a steadier behavior and also increase the number of collections. This situation decreases the throughput of the collector but provides consistent pauses that will not cause a surprise. You may also set this initial heap size for collection to be zero, which will cause the fastest garbage collections, but this situation is not suited to providing ideal answers.

Another problem occurs when your program experiences variance in heap allocation. This variation may mean that your concurrent garbage collection is not able to end in time, but there is no need to make dramatic allocation changes. This problem is simply eliminated by adding some padding to the collection starting time. This ensures that there is extra time available for the collection, and STW instances are not required during the program.

The default value that was available in Java was to launch a collection when the tenured generation in the background reached 92 percent of its capacity. This problem is not significant in normal programs but appears as a threat when running high-memory programs, such as database search tools. Since such an application may require several GBs of memory, it is possible to easily arrive at concurrent mode failures due to lack of available memory. The right practice in this manner is to set up garbage collection when the heap availability of the tenured generation crosses 10 percent of the overall heap capacity.

Understanding memory errors

Concurrent collection mode is available as a separate option, and also forms part of the package in the G1GC, which uses several techniques to reduce pause times without affecting the efficiency of the garbage collection. An `OutOfMemoryError` exception occurs when over 98 percent of the time is already spent performing garbage collection, while only 2 percent of the heap is recollected from the operation.

This out-of-memory feature is important, since otherwise, a program will continue for longer periods without performing any useful garbage collection. This will result in causing long stop-the-watch pauses, especially on JVMs that have a small heap available to them.

Problems may occur when a program uses the available concurrent time to its absolute limit. This means that the program starts to lose its predictability and runs out of memory whenever there is a sudden need to use a greater percentage of the heap. This may also happen due to an explicit garbage collection requirement, which is made part of a Java program, before a major part of the application needs to produce large objects.

The concurrent collector uses a tracing mechanism. It is also an incremental collector since it focuses on first identifying all the objects present in the heap for garbage collection. Since this marking is done when the actual application threads are also running concurrently, there is a possibility that many objects may become unreachable when the garbage collection is finished.

This results in creating the problem of floating garbage, which usually depends on the number of reference updates, that are also termed application mutations. A greater size of the tenured generation often reduces the chance of experiencing a concurrent mode failure, since it ensures that there is space in the older generation for floating garbage, which should then be collected in the next GC cycle.

Concurrent collection also requires pausing the application. It produces two stops. The first one is used to mark objects that can be reached from the references on the application threads. This is also termed as the *initial pause*. The second pause comes after the tracing phase and is used by the collector to find objects missed during the tracing due to the updating of the references of objects. It is termed as the *remark pause*.

Summary

Java 9 is a great update and contains excellent opportunities for Java community members who are looking to create even larger programs and applications. Its garbage collection methods are geared towards providing consistent pause times, even at the expense of requiring more computational power. G1GC becomes the default garbage collection method and allows the full use of the capacity of the 64-bit JVMs to use large heap regions.

In the next chapter, you will learn about microbenchmarking and understand how to optimize the code with it. You will also learn about **Java Microbenchmark Harness (JMH)** and understand how to set up JMH. We will see some practical examples of using JMH in a real project.

6
Optimizing Code with Microbenchmarking

Java 9 is the latest development kit of the famous development platform. This new version from Oracle contains a lot of powerful updates. One of the perks is the ability to perform better microbenchmarking, which has additional benefits over the previous versions.

This chapter discusses the concept of microbenchmarking. It then describes its benefits and its presence in Java. This is followed up with a detailed discussion of the **Java Microbenchmark Harness (JMH)** toolkit. This excellent solution provides the Java community with everything that they need to improve their microbenchmarking in the new, Java Development Kit 9.

The points we will be exploring are as follows:

- Understanding the concept of microbenchmarking
- Learning about microbenchmarking in Java
- Learning about the **Java Microbenchmark Harness (JMH)**
- How to setup and build the JMH
- Learning about various benchmark modes like throughput measures and time-based measures
- Practical example of using the JMH in your application
- Why use mircobenchmarking
- Challenges associated with microbenchmarking
- Wrong solutions from microbenchmarking like wrong component use, wrong hierarchy, wrong memory use, and use of a specific environment
- Various benefits of using the JMH
- Understanding the limitations of JMH

The concept of microbenchmarking

The Java community has always adopted the creation of predictable and transparent program build practices. This is done to reduce the risk when developing software. Continuous delivery of strong code is only possible using the feedback obtained during the programming procedure. The first-to-know approach allows a programmer to understand the problems and then implement the solutions before the program is out for general testing.

All developers will need standardized tools and practices to get the necessary feedback to deliver strong code. There are already external tools that can be used to checkout the finalized code. What programmers need is the comparison of their techniques in real time, during the programming procedure. This is where the use of microbenchmarks has its importance.

However, microbenchmark techniques are not commonly used in the developer community. Why? Because most programmers do not know that they can be actively used to produce improvements in their current coding, program generation, and arithmetic techniques. Many new programmers struggle to understand and use microbenchmarks, as they are not informed about their use during their academic studies.

Microbenchmarks provide a detailed way to improve your code, if you are aware of how your algorithm works. It requires the use of Maven, although other software creation tools can also be used to create and employ microbenchmarks to optimize code during the initial stage.

Microbenchmarking refers to the use of small program routines, which are termed as microbenchmarks. These are tiny programs that are designed for measuring the performance of code sections. They are extremely efficient at testing out the ability of a particular coding section to perform in an ideal setting.

The code that is tested using these tools usually does not have a communication function with an I/O need. A microbenchmark often tests a particular, single function that lies within a complete program task. It is an excellent way of ensuring that you will get the ideal results, when you combine everything.

The results of microbenchmarking need to be taken with a lot of care. Small-scale optimization can be the hardest to perform, since various factors can alter the measured performance of small sections of code. A common problem that occurs is the problem of compiler functionality.

Microbenchmarks usually measure small code, which may run faster than the actual benchmark code. This produces poorly-informed results, which are of no actual use to a programmer. An empty loop is one example, which will always execute faster than the measuring time. This is due to the fact that the compiler does not create a machine code for an empty loop, which simply does nothing.

This type of testing is not able to replace the typical full-program benchmarks and profiling tests. They are ideally designed to keep checking that you are picking up the most optimized options from the small key elements of the overall code.

However, the right use of microbenchmarking can provide numerous benefits. It can optimize the program and ensure that all the elements run in a smooth, coordinated, and predictable manner.

The concept of microbenchmarks arrives from microprocessors. Early processors had a limited performance and could always use the benefits that are offered by an optimized code. Optimization is only possible when different coding schemes are tested in order to find out their performance parameters.

The microbenchmark is designed for software programmers as it allows them to test out how their code performs on typical processors and memory units. However, it can become difficult to design and use, since the code is processed usually on a virtual machine. The actual hardware components already have optimization functions, which makes it difficult to predict the results of software-based benchmark results.

Microbenchmarks are ideally designed to only test out core program routines that run a small part of a longer and continuous code. It also measures basic performance parameters, which may not be of importance in an application, which is running on a larger scale. However, it is useful for detecting how the program is using the available hardware and if there is a possibility of improving this use.

Microbenchmarks in Java

Microbenchmarking is an important way of improving the fine bits of code that programmers use to carry out much larger functions. We start off with a simple example, which signifies how a microbenchmark will perform in Java:

```
import java.util.ArrayList;
import java.util.LinkedList;
import java.util.List;

public class SimpleMicroBenchmark {
    public static Long buildTimeForArrayList = 01;
```

```java
    public static Long buildTimeForLinkedList = 0l;
    public static void main(String[] args) {
        System.out.println("Building an ArrayList with 10,000 elements" );
        System.out.println("--------build test----------" );
        List<Integer> arrayList = buildList("ArrayList",new
ArrayList<Integer>(), 10000 );
        List<Integer> linkedList = buildList("LinkedList",new
LinkedList<Integer>(), 10000 );
        System.out.println("ArrayList vs LinkedList Build time: " +
((double)buildTimeForArrayList/(double)buildTimeForLinkedList));
        System.out.println("--------end of build test----------" );

        System.out.println("--------iterate test----------" );
        Long arrayListIterate = iterateOverList(arrayList);
        Long linkedListIterate = iterateOverList(linkedList);
        System.out.println("arrayListIterate : " + arrayListIterate);
        System.out.println("linkedListIterate : " + linkedListIterate);
        System.out.println("ArrayList vs LinkedList Iterate time: " +
((double)arrayListIterate/(double)linkedListIterate));
        System.out.println("--------end of iterate test----------" );
    }

    private static List<Integer> buildList(String type, List<Integer> list,
Integer size){
        Long start = System.nanoTime();
        for(int i=0; i<10000; i++) {
            list.add(i);
        }
        Long end = System.nanoTime();
        Long diff = end-start;
        System.out.println("Build Time for " + type + " : " + diff);
        if(type.equals("ArrayList")){
            buildTimeForArrayList = diff;
        }else if(type.equals("LinkedList")){
            buildTimeForLinkedList = diff;
        }
        return list;
    }
    private static Long iterateOverList(List<Integer> list) {
        int counter = 0;
        Long start = System.nanoTime();
        for(int i=0; i<list.size(); i++) {
            counter += list.get(i);
        }
```

```
        Long end = System.nanoTime();
        return end-start;
    }

}
```

The previous code tests the speed of `ArrayList` versus `LinkedList` for building a list and iterating over it. This is just a simple example to check how a microbenchmark is able to test out different code elements and find a better optimization solution. The result of the previous algorithm is as follows:

```
Building an ArrayList with 10,000 elements
--------build test----------
Build Time for ArrayList : 1597451
Build Time for LinkedList : 1299940
ArrayList vs LinkedList Build time: 1.2288651783928488
--------end of build test----------
--------iterate test----------
arrayListIterate : 1329749
linkedListIterate : 52159245
ArrayList vs LinkedList Iterate time: 0.025494023159269272
--------end of iterate test----------
```

There are several advantages of using microbenchmarks in Java. Microbenchmarks in the new JDK 9 promise to improve program optimizations. This, in turn, should result in the creation of crisp programs that are able to deliver the right kind of results.

Microbenchmarks have been a part of Java for quite some time, but they are still difficult to create and actively use to produce the required results. The microbenchmark design has the ability to face problems, because it all depends on the programmers. Setting up the wrong parameters produces a wrong result.

Here is one example that we bring from IBM:

```
interface Incrementer {
void increment();
}

class LockIncrementer implements Incrementer {
private long counter = 0;
private Lock lock = new ReentrantLock();
public void increment() {
lock.lock();
    try {
      ++counter;
```

```
    } finally {
lock.unlock();
    }
  }
}

class SyncIncrementer implements Incrementer {
    private long counter = 0;
    public synchronized void increment() {
        ++counter;
  }
}

class SyncLockTest {
static long test(Incrementerincr) {
    long start = System.nanoTime();
for(long i = 0; i< 10000000L; i++)
incr.increment();
    return System.nanoTime() - start;
  }

public static void main(String[] args) {
    long synchTime = test(new SyncIncrementer());
    long lockTime = test(new LockIncrementer());
    System.out.printf("synchronized: %1$10d\n", synchTime);
    System.out.printf("Lock:         %1$10d\n", lockTime);
    System.out.printf("Lock/synchronized = %1$.3f",
        (double)lockTime/(double)synchTime);
  }
}
```

This is a code that checks two separate implementations of the interface. The executions occur 10 million times and are measured through the use of a counter. One uses a synchronization method, while the other employs a particular class. In this example, we are using the ReentrantLock method by using the following code:

```
private Lock lock = new ReentrantLock();
```

The ReentrantLock method has existed since Java 1.5 in the Java concurrency package. The ReentrantLock method has been used to create several classes like ConcurrentHashMap in the java.util.concurrent package. In order to make applications more responsive and scalable, ReentrantLock provides more control on lock acquisition. It enables us to get a lock with the capability to interrupt and, if in waiting for lock state, the ability to timeout. It improves upon the synchronized keyword functionality and allows more controlled locking.

This microbenchmark on the surface looks to work well, but it fails because it does not measure anything useful. The test performed in this match is not ideally designed for the particular function, and therefore, its results are simply not on par with the overall objective of comparing the performance.

The benchmark works by comparing instances when multiple threads are used on a defined class. However, the testing code shows that this situation never materializes, due to the presence of only a single thread, which is available here.

Microbenchmarks work well when they are placed properly with the other code. They are designed to work smartly, when employed with tools that are in the same form, as they will be in a finalized application code. This way, they work in the ideal manner. The Java Microbenchmark Harness works amazingly, if it is used in Maven with the right projects set up to test the coding situations.

Understanding the JMH

The **Java Microbenchmark Harness** (**JMH**) is an important harness and is employed in Java 9 to build all types of microbenchmarks. These benchmarks are able to analyze various functions and code sections that may work at different speeds.

The JMH allows coders to design benchmarks that can measure either faster code sections or the much slower and longer functions. It works as a harness for microbenchmarks that are prepared in Java or other languages that are being targeted for use in the JVM environment.

There are different ways of using JMH benchmarks. One approach is to use standalone projects in order to test out the individual code sections of your application. The benchmarks are able to produce the required results, only when they are properly initialized. Setting up the benchmarks in an individual project ensures that your main program is not disturbed in the testing phase.

There are also IDE environments that are available to test using microbenchmarks. However, it can be complex to set up the relevant comparisons and produce reliable results. The JMH requires the use of annotations to create synthetic code. There are various methods, such as the use of Maven, to enable the use of artificial code elements.

Although there are other choices available for benchmarking your Java code, the JMH holds an advantage since it provides lower brittleness and reduces the need for coupling different elements during software design.

It is also a light method of testing different parts of your code, and therefore it ideally allows JVM application developers to compare and find the best techniques for their improvised code design.

The JMH allows the use of the command line to carry out different Java benchmarks in the form of fixed archetypes. There are various IDEs as well that allow the use of the JMH toolkit library. The Maven plugin is often used to carry out various activities.

Microbenchmarks work well when they are implemented using specialized Java products. These products can be set up with Java development tools such as Maven. Integrated development environments can also use benchmarks, but the relevant libraries and tools need to be set up for this purpose.

One thing to keep in mind is that the JMH is not a full-scale testing library. It only works if you are able to work on individual benchmarks and create them for a particular use. The JMH benchmarks usually require the use of Java APIs.

Each project requires the building of a complete benchmark scenario, before the actual build starts. It is possible to include explicit concepts in the microbenchmark design, which is carried out using the JMH.

Setting up the JMH

The JMH requires the use of an automation tool to help it carry out the necessary comparisons. The Apache Maven is an important tool in this regard, as it allows the creation of new software by providing the parameters to describe the complete coding process. Maven is also excellent in describing the way the particular coding depends on various elements such as specific libraries and JMH options.

Maven allows the use of the JMH. The new Java 9 is coming out with the JMH already available to directly use in the JVM setting. The JMH helps in optimizing the code and helps the JVM to warm up and run the best coding paths. The JMH in the new version can still use the previous Java framework and work through defining dependencies and putting the comparison code in it.

The JMH is able to carry out various tests and produce values for average time, sample time, and throughput performance of different code elements. In fact, it also allows to carry out warm-up executions. These executions can happen over multiple times and ensure that the real testing is able to find out values that are closer to the actual program conditions.

The JMH can also perform benchmarking on the state of a code. The state helps to create code that provides privacy and protection from organized attacks to reduce the code functionality, such as a robot program attempting to guess the password of an application through the use of a dictionary.

Here is the example of the JMH running through a plugin. It uses a benchmark code and saves it in a proper manner. Once a folder is set up through this code, it is always possible to create and execute multiple benchmarks as required to produce a comparison or find out the performance parameters of certain code tasks:

```java
import org.openjdk.jmh.annotations.*;
import org.openjdk.jmh.runner.Runner;
import org.openjdk.jmh.runner.RunnerException;
import org.openjdk.jmh.runner.options.Options;
import org.openjdk.jmh.runner.options.OptionsBuilder;
import java.io.IOException;

public class MicroBenchmark {
public static void main(String... args) throws IOException, RunnerException
{
Options opt = new OptionsBuilder()
.include(MicroBenchmark.class.getSimpleName())
.forks(1)
.build();

new Runner(opt).run();
}
```

The JMH benchmarks can be set up once the application has the spacing for displaying the answers after different functions and objects have been compared. The microbenchmarking works by comparing the small processes that may occur in different parts of the program. This method is also ideal when it is used within a single benchmark design to compare the efficiency of objects, which may use parallel processing techniques.

The JMH project can be set up in Maven, in the following manner:

```
$ mvnarchetype:generate \
        -DinteractiveMode=false \
        -DarchetypeGroupId=org.openjdk.jmh \
        -DarchetypeArtifactId=jmh-java-benchmark-archetype \
        -DgroupId=org.sample \
        -DartifactId=test \
        -Dversion=1.0
```

The JMH can also employ a benchmark on other languages that are employed in the JVM. The use of archetypes is implemented to apply benchmarks in this case. The benchmarks then return the values in milli, micro, and nano seconds, according to the operational performance of the project objects. A benchmark may be run in the following manner:

```
$ java -jar target/benchmarks.jar
```

The ideal way to use these options is by setting up the subprojects and using the process of testing independent modules to achieve the required functionality.

The JMH can also be set up using IDEs. These IDEs allow the creation of a Maven project, which then provides the same functionality as that of a command-line program. There is also the option of using bleeding edge microbenchmarking. This can be set up using specific tools.

Building up in the JMH

Creating strong microbenchmarks is not easy. It takes time and effort to create the right kind of tools that help in creating the right application. The important thing is to understand, since most processors and JVMs have their own exterior optimization tools, it can be difficult to actually benchmark the performance of a code element in complete isolation to the rest of the program or the processing resources.

Microbenchmarks that are poorly designed fail to perform their actual task, which is to compare different code and produce a winning answer. The JMH provides all the options, especially in the new JVM 9, but the ideal use depends on the abilities of the programmer to identify instances where they need to compare code and where they can let the microprocessor and the JVM use their own optimization scheme.

The right microbenchmark in the JMH is the one that does not affect the optimization already present in the hardware and is able to produce active results based on the actual performance of the code bits during the processing of the actual Java objects and code parts. The whole purpose of the JMH is to provide this specific functionality.

The JMH works well when it is properly initialized and allows the program to only reach the testing phase when it is running in a normal, well-coordinated manner. The JMH is perfect for improving program sections, when it performs some iterations of the code, and then starts to note down the microbenchmark times that are required for the particular testing project.

You should also use the printing function for the compiler. This ensures that your processor is not performing other work while running the benchmark. This is essential, since multiple functions may ruin your results, by filling it up with time used by other application threads.

Efficient programmers understand that there is a difference between the output received when using either a client or the server-based JVM settings. Initialization is also the key element when creating and running microbenchmarks. It is essential to allow the initialization to set in, because that is going to happen during normal software application use.

Microbenchmarks work well, when they are used with the learning of the internal optimization procedures. It needs to happen in a manner where the results are exclusive and are able to produce the most efficient picture of how different parts of a software code are performing in a realistic application use condition.

Benchmark modes in the JMH

There are different benchmark modes that are available in the JMH to perform the much-required comparison of code items. However, all microbenchmarks are ideally defined as two main measuring instruments. In the following sections, we explain both categories in greater detail.

Throughput measure

The first is the throughput measure. It represents the number of functions that can be completed within a single unit of time. This means that it effectively measures the maximum load that a test can handle and produces the results in terms of successful and failed object operations.

The JMH is great in this regard, as it holds the collection of these operations. It occurs with the help of object creation, which is an important tool commonly employed in Java-based code. The microbenchmarks designed for this measure are able to work within a particular method, or they can also be used in standalone, pretest phase projects to find out the programming efficiency.

The throughput microbenchmark results are understood by the numerical value of the output. A larger value depicts that the operations are running at a fast pace. However, the results are only as good as their comparison with various techniques. The results also have to be mixed with other tools, since testing may not allow the takeover of the internal optimizations that are available in processors and the JVM itself.

Time-based measures

Time-based microbenchmarks work as the opposing counter to throughput measurements. These measures test out the time it takes for the required operation. This is useful if you need to test out the performance of different code samples that produce the same output. The time measure is essential in making the final choice to implement in the finished application product.

There are several measures that involve time-based statistical results. Here, we present the different measures that come under this category. The first is the use of average time, which represents the average time it takes for one iteration to complete.

The JMH also produces a Score Error report with the output. This error is presented at 50 percent confidence level and is designed to show the deviation of the out results from the average time calculated by the microbenchmark. A lower result of the Score Error indicates that a particular code section is consistently returning a low average runtime of the JVM processing operation.

The JMH also presents the microbenchmark that outputs Sample Time. It is like the average processing time and implements the use of loading the processor to identify the failures. The JMH attempts to produce failure percentages. It is designed for programmers who want to find out the level of failures that may occur in their program processing time and throughput results.

The `SampleTime` benchmark allows programmers to find out the extent of load that their particular coding can produce on the processor and design the other functions in a coordinated manner to produce the best results. The length of time taken during multiple iterations provides the information required to program efficiently on a consistent scale.

There is also the `SingleShotTime` microbenchmark. This is not commonly used since it only runs a single iteration of the compared code items. This provides a cold testing method, but one which is difficult to use without the relevant tools. It is a parameter, which may be used for testing elements in a swift manner. It should only be used for making simpler testing decisions.

A lower value signifies that the code operates at a quicker speed during the single iteration. It is great for cold testing, since there are no multiple iterations, which may allow the processor to optimize the test or perform memory cache transfers for quick code transfers.

Applying the JMH in Java projects

The JMH can be easily used to add various tests within the code. This means that there is no additional overhead and the actual code does not need to be repeated in a separate, standalone project. The JMH tools used are easily separated from the final code using the test scope, which is available for creating a buffer between tools and the application code.

Each JMH functionality requires the use of dependencies. These dependencies are essential for providing the functionality that most microbenchmarks will require in order to produce the required results.

It is easy to create a harness that you can use with multiple Java projects. These harnesses may contain typical microbenchmark tests, which you attempt to use for establishing standardized code optimization practices.

The JMH recommends the use of packaging benchmark tests. This can happen by using a transportation JAR, or plugins that are designed for producing performance optimization options. A test harness is created by configuring a particular Java class. This creation allows the use of the object in different settings once it has already been used for a particular Java program.

The properties for your benchmarks can also be specifically created and saved in the form of configuration properties. The JMH also provides programmers with an option to produce an output of these results. They can also be used for setting up JSON. The results are excellent for creating integrated optimization solutions and allow you to reach the ideal historical learning curves.

The specific coding then works as the harness point and is used in Maven, which is the ideal software development tool in this regard. The class creation allows the microbenchmark to run in the real-time environment. The normal program functions such as reading file entries, creating logs, and the allocation of external resources, all occur during the testing phase.

This means that you can better control your microbenchmark. You can also include certain dependencies while leaving the others to isolate the main code and get results with improved confidence levels.

Here is a code application that shows the setting up of benchmarks and relevant classes for creating tools that can be used multiple times:

```
public void setup() {
IngredientUsedjalepenoUsed = new IngredientUsed(new Ingredient("Jalepeno",
"Spicy Pepper"), MeasurementType.ITEM, 1);
IngredientUsedcheeseUsed = new IngredientUsed(new Ingredient("Cheese",
"Creamy Cheese"), MeasurementType.OUNCE, 4);
        recipe = RecipeTestUtil.createRecipe("My Food", "Spicy foods with
few ingredients", ImmutableList.of(jalepenoUsed, cheeseUsed));
        service = new RecipeService(new ObjectMapper());
protoRecipe = service.recipeAsProto(recipe).toByteArray();
recipeAsJSON= service.recipeAsJSON(recipe);
    }
    @Benchmark
    public Messages.Recipeserialize_recipe_object_to_protobuf() {
        return service.recipeAsProto(recipe);
    }
    @Benchmark
    public String serialize_recipe_object_to_JSON() {
        return service.recipeAsJSON(recipe);
    }
    @Benchmark
    public Recipe deserialize_protobuf_to_recipe_object() {
        return service.getRecipe(protoRecipe);
    }
}
```

The best way of going about these benchmarks is to create a file in Maven, which stores future use files for them. The creation of classes and specific paths allow the microbenchmark tests to run in parallel. However, you may find that it is not the best approach to use when you are testing code brevity and its performance in terms of using the available memory in the JVM.

What is Maven?

Throughout this book, we have been talking about Maven, which is simply defined as a tool that allows for software development in different environments. The name of this particular tool is taken from Yiddish and translates as knowledge accumulator. It was started in order to simplify complex Java builds.

Maven has now turned into the top Java software preparation tool. It allows defining a project and publishing the information about it in a useful manner. It allows the creation of **Java Archives (JARs)** as well as their sharing over different Java projects.

Maven provides support and structure to other tools and libraries such as the JMH. Other harnesses and programming languages can be easily integrated with the core JVM running a program for a systematic software solution. It provides standardization as well as the ability to divide work in a software project. It also serves as an excellent testing and implementation platform for Java projects.

Maven helps Java programmers on the daily management of software projects. Since it is a development tool, Maven focuses on providing the backend support, which is required for functions such as microbenchmarks, comparisons, and other code optimizations.

The main objective of Maven remains the provision of a complete development environment to a Java programmer. It provides this functionality by simplifying the Java build process and providing uniformity on multiple projects. It also serves as an information tool and provides continuous information about the different elements of a Java-based project.

Maven also provides the ideal guidelines for developing software. Since it offers transparent migrations to new Java features, it serves as an excellent platform for employing different Java harnesses in the main software project on the tool.

It eases the software building process by providing shielding from difficult details of programming and providing a set of tools, such as using the JMH for creating the relevant microbenchmarks to ensure the best code optimization.

Maven allows programmers to create a **Project Object Model** (**POM**). A programmer can set up a number of tools, such as the JMH, when building projects using the uniform system present in Maven. Maven projects need to be learned just once, and then you can use different tools, harnesses, and code optimizers, all working around your main Java software coding project.

Maven is also perfect, since it allows for the creation of log documentation and provides sources that are ideally cross referenced. It creates and handles dependencies, which means that you are able to set up different JMH options by building side testing projects that provide code optimization as you go along, preparing the complete software. It also allows the addition of information by using the POM to create additional information prepared from the plugins employed during a particular build.

Maven helps the use of current Java principles, and also provides a buildup guide toward new arrivals, such as the JDK 9, in the Java community. The specification and execution of tests can be carried out in this environment, and the results of tools such as the JMH can then be used to take prioritizing decisions.

The ideal way of testing code is to create a parallel source tree, which keeps the original project separate, but is able to process and test the code in the same way. The test cases can then perform the required comparisons and benchmarks that will essentially allow the programmer to understand the operational differences of using different programming techniques and functions.

The test cases are ideal for using Java harnesses and comparisons to find the ideal code optimizations that improve the main code for a particular software project. It also allows you to keep preparing your Java project; therefore, testing occurs on a parallel level. In fact, you can often perform multiple testing and optimizations by running the program on multicore processors.

Maven lets you set up a proper directory structure, which helps the programmer code in other environments, but still face no issues in allocating files and other data objects.

Maven users can also switch up to new features once a new version comes out, since automatic installation updates take care of program optimization needs. The programmers can easily update plugins such as the JMH and set up more powerful benchmarks to achieve the desired results.

Many Java programmers are not sure about the power of Maven. They believe that it is a simple documentation tool and one where you can download your program dependencies. They also think that it is simply a tool that provides the addition of small Java scripts, which can then be directly used.

However, Maven has a much larger functionality set. It provides these standard functions, but it goes beyond to create test projects and help you set up the right microbenchmarks. A key feature of Maven is to allow builds that are able to progress smoothly on all fronts.

One thing to remember is that Maven decidedly favors structured Java program development. It is designed to build dependencies for creating microbenchmarks. The right use of Maven testing and development projects ensures that you avoid using bad code and optimize program objects and functions, while not wasting any time in reworking your whole program after each microbenchmark test.

Installing Maven to start working on dependencies and benchmark testing is relatively simple. It requires the basic version of Java, over which it creates its own development structure. The installation instructions are simple and facilitate a successful installation. Typing the `mvn --version` command returns the details of the Maven version, which is installed in your Java directory.

Creating a project is easy in Maven, as you simply have to create a directory for the shell structure. A simple command directly inputted through the command line is able to generate a project and start working on producing your Java code.

Maven works by creating an archetype structure based on the dependencies that maybe required in your Java project. You may use some options available in the software development tool; therefore, it is ideal to only learn about the parts that you start to build up. Maven is great at allowing you to test out your code at any instant, by creating separate programs that use the same code, but do not put burden the actual software construction. The Maven tool also allows you to directly generate a Java-powered website by converting your code into a web application.

Maven is truly a software that allows you to fully employ the power of the Java Microbenchmark Harness. It also allows you to set up benchmarking practices that you can then use in all of your Java-based programs and application designs.

Why use microbenchmarking?

There is always a question as to when is the right time to use a microbenchmarking experiment. This practice is rarely used. However, with Java 9 providing the JMH option without the need for installing other tools, it becomes an excellent and efficiently-available tool.

The debate about the rightful use of microbenchmarking stems from the fact that optimizing a code before it is actually completed and used for a particular task takes away its impact in a commercial environment.

If you keep testing every bit of code that you write as a programmer, then the whole process becomes extremely slow and difficult to follow in a dedicated and shortened timeline. Most programmers believe that the attempt to optimize code without finishing functionality results in a poorly developed situation.

Microbenchmarking continues to be a great tool, when it is used in the right context and form. Modern programs run on heavy servers, which have the ability to use multiple machines and sometimes almost unlimited memory. This means that it is not important to reduce the memory and processing requirements of a code section.

What is important is that the code needs to run efficiently and should not cause unnecessary pauses. This may require some form of microbenchmarking, but this should always occur once a particular code out of the complete application module is already identified as a slow and problematic element.

The method of employing the JMH will then be able to provide real-time solutions that can be implemented to carefully improve certain program aspects. If a programmer can attach the value of strong microbenchmarking in the form of improved revenue and performance in a JVM application, only then does this method need to be used in a strong manner.

There are three main reasons for employing microbenchmarking using the JMH, especially in the new Java 9 update. Let's carefully explain these reasons and their underlying benefits.

The first reason is to gain information about the microbenchmarking process and its impact in creating efficient code. This is an important reason, since there is strong competition in the market to create applications that are faster and able to effectively employ the available resources.

All programmers need to learn about the JMH that they will receive in JVM 9. This will enable them to use the available testing tools to reach the best programming conclusion for every task. The main purpose of this article is also to educate the programmers so that they can become aware of what's available in JVM 9 and help out the Java community.

The second reason is to test out various improvements in your current Java application or a particular code. This is the ideal way to use microbenchmarking. For example, if you have a working code, but you want to compare different options in order to improve how the code functions to produce the response.

This process always follows the identification of the code segment, which is causing problems with the complete program design. Microbenchmarking is able to check individual code elements and is ideally suited to make improvements in the end, when the design is already finalized, but there is strong room for improvement.

The third reason for using JMH tools is to identify the code that has been troubling your application. If you are not receiving the performance parameters that you sought, it is time to look into the matter by strongly dissecting your application.

Microbenchmarking can be difficult to use when inspecting large applications. The ideal way to use it remains to create modular programming and test it extensively. The JMH microbenchmarking can then be used to identify the coding practices that may be slowing down the application or requiring extra memory through repetition of objects and program elements.

Microbenchmarking remains an ideal method for optimizing your finished code. It is ideal for fine-tuning the smaller program elements, such as statistical and algebraic calculations that may control the way your actual program makes its important decisions for loading different objects.

The JMH is easy to add to your Java-based projects, especially when using the Maven platform. It benefits from the use of a historical ledger. Your benchmarks are available in a coordinated environment, where they are able to provide systematic results that you may employ on a consistent basis.

Adding a particular JMH is a great way of finding improvements in your Java-based coding solutions. The use of the JMH allows you to create a continuous feedback mechanism, automate initial testing, and ensure repeatability in all your code tests. The use of the JMH will surely improve the final solution that you create in terms of having uniform code that performs according to the best possible scenarios.

The challenges associated with microbenchmarks

There are several problems that may occur while using microbenchmarks. Here, we explain these problems and then present the benefits that you gain, when you switch to using the JMH. The JMH is specially designed to provide the best answers for these typical problems.

The first problem is that of the absence of a warm-up phase. Normal benchmarking may suffer from this problem. The Java interpreter is able to work out that all requests should be compiled just in time, which goes against the warm-up principle.

This problem is usually resolved by running the benchmark code several times before actually taking a measurement. This wastes time, since no important activity has taken place during the process. The time required for compilation can be checked by typing `-XX:+PrintCompilation`. This returns the complete chart of the compiler activity, letting you know the details of other compiling activities. There is a solution to this problem, as suggested in the next section. Once the warm-up phase is complete, there should be no activity experienced on the compiler.

Dead code elimination is also an important problem and may return extremely low benchmark times. This occurs due to the internal code optimization process, which is present in every Java compiler. If the compiler finds that a benchmark code contains iterations that are empty and do not provide a functionality, it entirely removes the code from the final program and runs it as a single, consistent command to the processor.

The program tester may be surprised by the astonishing benchmark results, but they are simply wrongly portrayed and do not provide any real insight into how the code will actually perform in a real-time environment. The new JDK 9 is extremely powerful, and may detect the code, which may be smartly optimized by the new, more powerful Java compiler and the 64-bit JVM.

It is still theoretically possible to create a measuring loop that actually does nothing. The compiler may skip it altogether when returning a machine code. However, the JMH may provide the necessary answers to resolve this problem.

The microbenchmarks may also suffer from causing deoptimization. This occurs because the Java compiler makes the required assumptions when measuring the benchmark values that are required in a harnessed program. The compiler reads the currently available classes in the memory and accordingly translates the program for effective use.

Once there is a need to run a new class, which is required for a benchmark measure, the Java compiler has to break its original optimization cycle and use another method, which is required for producing the output of the microbenchmark in the required manner.

Deoptimization, when not noted down, can change the values that you get as a result of setting up a microbenchmark. However, the use of warm-up practices in any manner ensures that you can get away with this problem. Remember, each benchmark can produce different effects on the running of different compiler code optimizations.

This problem can be resolved by using separate candidates and dependencies for each microbenchmark tested in Java. It can also be remedied by using a software development tool, such as the Apache Maven, and ensuring that you can set up different testing projects that employ the same coding elements in their essence.

Another problem is that of false sharing. This is a problem that occurs when using microbenchmarks, which are spread out over multiple threads. Since the objects will continue to load several times to cater to all the threads, there is a chance that additional information may be shared, therefore, increasing the time required for carrying out the function in a systematic manner.

Wrong solutions from microbenchmarks

There is always a chance that your microbenchmark is returning a poorly validated answer and not helping you achieve the ideal results. This may occur due to systematic reasons, where your input may not have caused the actual problem. Understanding these issues will help you avoid them in your microbenchmark testing and ensure that you get the best results from comparison and optimization tools.

Wrong component use

One of the situations is when the microbenchmark is executed by one writer, while the real application employs several writers. Each program writer has a particular use style, which means that the same component does not behave in the same manner within a program.

In fact, microbenchmarks are never planned to be implemented in this manner. They are designed to provide optimization solutions to the programmer who is responsible for creating the finalized version. The use with multiple programmers will always result in a misleading situation.

Wrong hierarchy

Setting up the correct hierarchy is the essential element in all kinds of Java programming. A microbenchmark may provide the wrong values if it is not able to work on the right hierarchal structures. This means that all the classes and subclasses should be carefully coordinated and work in the same manner as intended by the actual software developer.

The validity of a microbenchmark changes completely since the class structure describes how the functions will get called up. You will be familiar with this directional work, if you have previously worked in the C versions.

The problem arises when there is a misdirection in programming elements. One class may include various subclasses that get loaded up, only to remain in the garbage throughout the function performed for the benchmark parameters.

The compiler performs monomorphic methods and ensures that it employs direct class use as much as possible. It removes class mentions that are not going to affect the outcome of a program code.

However, the classes may actually be significant during the normal use of that code that happens in a real-time situation where all subclasses may be active and need to be recalled during the processing of the particular coding section.

Wrong memory use

One of the common problems that may occur during a microbenchmark operation is the wrong use of the available memory. The problem occurs especially when testing out small code elements. These elements directly load into the fastest L1 cache, which ensures that the program immediately reaches the CPU on a preferential basis.

However, when the same code performs in a situation where the dataset contained within program objects is larger than the size of the L1 cache, the actual program runs much slower due to using the conventional memory. This means that the microbenchmark results will not depict the original program situation and optimization would not be the best solution.

Use of a specific environment

Sometimes, all situations remaining similar, the microbenchmark fails to perform since there is a significant change in the hardware parameters that are supporting the JVM. One issue may be the difference in the JVM version, as new features come out all the time. The JVM versions have different optimization functions and therefore, may produce different results when running different types of code.

The benefits of using the JMH

The JMH works as an open project that you may run in any JDK environment. It is designed to provide you with several library options of using different microbenchmarks. These benchmarks can measure throughput as well as the processing time performance of the various functions and code elements.

There are several benefits of using this approach of optimizing the code on a micro level. Some experts are not sure if microbenchmarks provide the right benefits, but careful use in important code sections is certainly beneficial.

One benefit that you receive as a programmer is the understanding of how your code is using the available machine resources. You get the answers of how the memory is storing your objects and how they are being lined up for processing through the right setup of microbenchmarks.

Microbenchmarks are also great at creating performance documentation for important code elements. You can set up customized harnesses in your programs by creating testing and comparison projects in a building environment, such as Maven. This gives you a chance to present a complete testing document.

You do not necessarily have to change your code after each optimization attempt. However, even a brief look at your testing records will allow you to understand the overall picture of your software design and pick out elements that may be taking down the whole project, due to a small code, which lies out of synchronization with the rest of the program.

Microbenchmarks are also ideal for library creators. If you want to add new functionality for the Java community and are working to provide solutions that others may use without complex Java working knowledge, then you need to ensure that your code if fully optimized and works on the micro scale to employ the available resources in an ideal manner.

The JMH also provides you with different winning strategies. You can work on a project or create your own testing projects and attach benchmark harnesses to them. This allows you to understand how your code can be intrinsically improved in a number of different ways. Here is a benchmark example with the code explained as follows:

```
@State(Scope.Thread)
public class CopyOnArrayListBenchmark {
    private List<String> benchMarkingList;
    @Setting
    public void setting() {
        benchMarkingList = new CopyOnWriteArrayList<String>();
    }

    @Benchmark
    public void benchMarkArrayListAddStrings(Blackhole blackhole) {
        blackhole.consume(benchMarkingList.add("foo"));
    }
    public static void main(String[] args) throws RunnerException {
        Options options = new OptionsBuilder()
                .warmupIterations(5) //
                .measurementIterations(5)
                .mode(Mode.AverageTime)
                .forks(1)
                .threads(5)
                .include(CopyOnArrayListBenchmark.class.getSimpleName())
                .timeUnit(TimeUnit.MILLISECONDS)
                .build();
        new Runner(options).run();
    }
}
```

This code creates a benchmark using the JMH and provides the benefit of avoiding dead code. This code is caused by compiler-based optimizations. The JMH contains the tools, which are necessary to remove the challenge that a benchmark faces during its testing.

The JMH also protects your program from false sharing. This is the instance where an object and memory area is made available to a part of the program, although it is unnecessary and not used by that particular code.

The JMI I also allows code testers to create forking. It allows empowering of the benchmark and ensuring that the code is able to run in a default manner. The creation of multiple forks divides the program code into small bits and ensures that the compiler does not perform its own optimization on the code.

Initialization can often change testing results. The JMH provides the initialization through the setting annotation in the previous example. This is one function that disconnects your microbenchmark from the normal processor operations and therefore, cuts away the initialization time, which may appear in your tests.

The JMH creates the ideal microbenchmarks, and therefore, it especially ensures that you can warm up the processor before bringing in your code for comparison and comparing tests. You will find that the same benchmark may provide different results based on the number of times that they are run.

This issue occurs when the internal optimization kicks in and alters the way the code is run, although you do not want it optimized, since you are looking for problematic areas. The JMH allows the use of loops, which protect to your benchmarks.

This situation ensures that you can get the best possible results. You can directly mark how many times the warm-up should happen and the JMH will perform the necessary function for you. It means that your benchmarks are easier to run and return the most relevant time intervals and throughputs.

The JMH provides the advantage of running the same measurement several times, by directly setting up the required iterations. This means that programmers do not have to run a test as a loop, which may take away the actual benefit of carrying out a microbenchmark test in the first place.

Programmers can create specialized tests that use multiple threads for improved functionality, but it is a difficult process. The right way to go about it in a normal manner would be to look into how the program functions are running in a particular virtual machine, and then set up barriers that initiate and consistently provide multithread functionality.

The JMH provides the best answer by directly allowing you to run optimization tests by selecting the number of threats that you want your test to use. This is easier, more direct, and provides the right benefits for all Java community members.

The JMH also allows the maintenance of the system state during benchmark processing. This is essential when you are aiming to run a microbenchmark that measures the performance of a specific element. The JMH facility truly helps in setting up the right benchmark that provides useful information.

The JMH offers an important benefit. This is the availability of using a set of parameters with a range of values. This allows you to use conditions that may appear differently during an actual program run. The idea of a single harness on a test project providing answers to all situations saves time and gives the Java community the power to carry out multiple code optimizations in a short time.

When any program joins its space for processing on a CPU, it follows a continuity process and remains the same in microbenchmark projects as well. The use of Blackhole in the JMH allows the same functionality by burning some CPU cycles and creating the same conditions that you may actually find in a normal JVM running on a common CPU.

This provides the advantage of achieving microbenchmark results that are as close to the actual program use as possible. The JMH is extremely functional in this regard and presents the ideal code comparison results.

The JMH also provides multiple benchmark options. You can check the average times, the time for one iteration, as well as the throughput results for a particular section of your Java-based program code. This ensures that you are able to find the relevant information that you are eagerly looking for, as a software developer.

The JMH also allows you to use a garbage collection profiler or another method in order to check out the memory profile of your program. These profilers allow you to get deep information about your program code, which lets you set up more powerful code through consistent optimizations.

The JMH allows you get a good idea of which of your code sections are taking the most amount of time during Java garbage collections. This allows you to fully optimize your code and produce an application, which is able to create a balance between strong throughput efficiency and reduced pause times through the intrinsically optimized structure of your Java code.

These advantages will allow you to better understand why it is still beneficial to employ a microbenchmarking mechanism in order to optimize your Java code. These optimizations become more important with new versions coming out, which provide additional functionality through the use of powerful benchmarking protocols offered in the JMH.

Understanding the limitations of the JMH

Even the best tools can fail to provide you a solution which is ultimate and free from the problems that are associated with setting up microbenchmarks. The same is the issue when using microbenchmarks in Java through the use of the JMH. Remember, a benchmark is an experiment, which typically finds out the time and throughput of the machine in order to find out the functional benefits of using a particular code.

The use of a harness usually eliminates most of the problems. However, the basic principle behind the use of a microbenchmark remains the same. We cannot directly measure how a particular code performs within the CPU and the Java virtual machine. However, we can measure how much time and memory resources the code used during its processing. This means that these values must relate to how the code would have compiled and executed.

The right microbenchmark, therefore, can be only applied through a harness that provides the required controls to remove other variables. Although the JMH is excellent in this regard, it can only work if there are the right baseline measurements in order to produce meaningful results.

Understand that microbenchmarking is simply an experiment that allows programmers to better understand the power of the JMH and then use it accordingly to achieve programming and testing success.

Heisenberg's principle of uncertainty gets involved and makes it difficult to use the available microbenchmarks in the JMH. This principle states that it is difficult to measure multiple physical values at the same confidence level. This means that if you want to measure a particular operation, you would only want the machine to run and nothing else.

However, the Java compiler is smart and optimizes processes that do not actually perform a useful function. This reduces the time, which is required to run the empty operation, and therefore, it provides the wrong results. The right JMH operation is to find a balance between running an empty code and one with too many additional details. This means that it is essential to avoid dead code elimination that we have already described in this article.

The problem appears because the JIT optimizes each code according to its particular requirements. This means that a code during testing will not be optimized in the same manner as it would be during the actual execution of the program on a JVM. There are also synchronizations that occur when the code runs in the form of the finished application. This means that microbenchmarking is essentially limited and should only be used carefully to improve difficult code choices, after the initial coding process.

Summary

The JMH is a powerful harness and is truly capable of creating and running several types of microbenchmarks. The important point to remember is that JDK 9 is going to be the most powerful version of the famous virtual machine and will require the use of the most optimized code. microbenchmarks have been present in Java and other languages. They provide the time it needs to run a particular code as well as the throughput performance.

This information is useful in several instances, but it can simply present faulty information in the case of the compiler performing the optimizations, and eliminating the dead code, which it finds within the loops that are present in the created microbenchmark.

The JMH will now be included with the Java 9 package, and therefore, programmers should now attempt to actively use it as long as they are careful that it does not measure useless context and program objects.

Since the JMH will be present in the package, programmers need to understand its usefulness and should attempt to use it wherever it may offer relevant benefits. Another important tool is a development environment, such as Maven, which allows the use of harnesses and other relevant processes that are required for creating Java development projects.

We describe that microbenchmarks are fraught with the danger of optimizing code where it is unnecessary to do so. However, their use is justified if these projects are created in a Maven environment, while the work is carried out to further expand the software design.

When used in the right manner, these microbenchmarks are able to identify the flaws that appear in small sections of the code. A good way to use a Java microbenchmark is when a problem is already identified in a particular code section and further analysis is required of the individual code elements to find the culprit and replace it with a better code.

In the next chapter, we will learn about JSON generation. We will cover topics like the history of JSON, types in JSON for object modeling, types in JSON for streaming API, tree models, and so on. We will also see how to convert CSV and Excel to JSON, along with understanding value trees.

7

Speeding Up JSON Generation

One of the most essential elements in today's application development is the use of **JavaScript Object Notation (JSON)**. It is a lightweight yet powerful tool used for preparing the most efficient Java **Application Programming Interfaces (APIs)**.

JSON brings the ability to create several events, object trees, and information generators. It is a tool that allows you to create the best active APIs and take advantage of the information that is actively present on the internet, since it is capable of receiving an input stream of different data types and then parsing and creating the required value trees.

In this chapter, we will shed light on the JSON generation controls and discuss how JSON allows Java community members to create RESTful APIs. We will present various elements of the `javax.json` package, which include creating events, input and output streams, value trees, and JSON generators.

Following are the points we will cover in detail:

- What is JSON and basic syntax
- Brief history of JSON
- Different types in JSON for object modeling
- Different types in JSON for streaming API
- How to generate JSON
- Learn about `Javax.json`
- What are events and how do they work
- Learn about JSON tree and streams
- Understand tree models
- See how to convert CSV to JSON and Excel to JSON
- Learn about value trees

A transparent understanding of JSON in Java

JSON processing is the use of portable APIs in terms of creating JSON instances that are able to parse information, as well as generate data objects by reading them off from a number of sources, including internet searches in a live manner.

JSON is extremely capable because it is swift, occupies little space, and is able to perform data exchange, regardless of the programming language barrier. It is also easy to understand and provides an excellent mode of common understanding for both the programming and the virtual machine.

There are different values that JSON can generate, but it is important to understand that all JSON instances use two distinct structures of objects and arrays. An object is created whenever there is a need to create names and values that are not present in an orderly manner. The second type is the array. The arrays can have any set of values that are ordered.

This means that JSON creates a format that allows the handling of all the known data types, such as null value, numbers, strings, and Boolean values (true/false). These values fall under the two structures of objects and arrays in a specific manner. Since it is a collection of ordered or unordered information, it ideally creates, stores, and transfers data information in a number of program settings.

Here, we present an example that describes how JSON is able to fully describe a client using an object-based infrastructure. JSON employs string values, numbers, arrays, and in fact, another object value within this personal definition to create a complete record, which can then be transported out to a number of programming and record-keeping environments.

Let's see how to generate the previous output using the `javax.json` package. The following example will help you to generate a JSON array of a client's object.

```
import java.util.*;
import javax.json.Json;
import javax.json.stream.*;

public class JSONGenerator {

    public static void main(String[] args) {

        Map<String, Object> properties = new HashMap<String, Object>(1);
        properties.put(JsonGenerator.PRETTY_PRINTING, true);
        JsonGeneratorFactory jsonGeneratorFactory =
```

```
Json.createGeneratorFactory(properties);
        JsonGenerator jsonGenerator =
jsonGeneratorFactory.createGenerator(System.out);

        jsonGenerator.writeStartObject();
        jsonGenerator.writeStartArray("clients");
        Client client = buildClientObject();
        createCustomerJSON(jsonGenerator, client);
        jsonGenerator.writeEnd();
        jsonGenerator.close();
    }
    private static Client buildClientObject(){
        Client client = new Client();
        Address address = new Address();
        PhoneNumber phoneNumber = new PhoneNumber();
        client.setName("Mayur Ramgir");
        client.setCompanyName("Zonopact, Inc.");
        client.setContacted(true);
        address.setStreet("867 Boylston Street");
        address.setCity("Boston");
        address.setState("MA");
        address.setCountry("USA");
        phoneNumber.setNumber("855-966-6722");
        phoneNumber.setExtension("111");
        phoneNumber.setMobile("111-111-1111");
        client.setAddress(address);
        client.setPhoneNumber(phoneNumber);
        return client;
    }
    private static JsonGenerator createCustomerJSON(JsonGenerator
jsonGenerator, Client client){
        jsonGenerator.writeStartObject();
            jsonGenerator.write("name", client.getName());
            jsonGenerator.write("company", client.getCompanyName());
                jsonGenerator.writeStartObject("address");
                jsonGenerator.write("street",
client.getAddress().getStreet());
                jsonGenerator.writeNull("street2");
                jsonGenerator.write("city", client.getAddress().getCity());
                jsonGenerator.write("state",
client.getAddress().getState());
                jsonGenerator.write("contacted", true);
                jsonGenerator.writeEnd();
                jsonGenerator.writeStartArray("phone-numbers");
                    jsonGenerator.writeStartObject();
                    jsonGenerator.write("number",
client.getPhoneNumber().getNumber());
                    jsonGenerator.write("extension",
```

```
                client.getPhoneNumber().getExtension());
                        jsonGenerator.writeEnd();
                        jsonGenerator.writeStartObject();
                        jsonGenerator.write("mobile",
        client.getPhoneNumber().getMobile());
                        jsonGenerator.writeEnd();
                    jsonGenerator.writeEnd();
                jsonGenerator.writeEnd();
            jsonGenerator.writeEnd();
            return jsonGenerator;
        }
    }
```

The previous code is dependent on `Client.java`, `Address.java`, and `PhoneNumber.java`. The following code is for `Client.java`:

```
public class Client{
        private String name;
        private String companyName;
        private String email;
        private Address address;
        private PhoneNumber phoneNumber;
        private Boolean contacted;
        public Address getAddress() {
            return address;
        }
        public void setAddress(Address address) {
            this.address = address;
        }
        public PhoneNumber getPhoneNumber() {
            return phoneNumber;
        }
        public void setPhoneNumber(PhoneNumber phoneNumber) {
            this.phoneNumber = phoneNumber;
        }
        public String getName(){
            return name;
        }
        public void setName(String name){
            this.name = name;
        }
        public String getCompanyName(){
            return companyName;
        }
        public void setCompanyName(String companyName){
            this.companyName = companyName;
        }
        public String getEmail(){
```

```
            return email;
        }
        public void setEmail(String email){
            this.name = email;
        }
        public Boolean getContacted() {
            return contacted;
        }
        public void setContacted(Boolean contacted) {
            this.contacted = contacted;
        }
    }
```

The following code is for `Address.java`:

```
public class Address{
    private String street;
    private String street2;
    private String city;
    private String state;
    private String country;
    public String getStreet() {
        return street;
    }
    public void setStreet(String street) {
        this.street = street;
    }
    public String getStreet2() {
        return street2;
    }
    public void setStreet2(String street2) {
        this.street2 = street2;
    }
    public String getCity() {
        return city;
    }
    public void setCity(String city) {
        this.city = city;
    }
    public String getState() {
        return state;
    }
    public void setState(String state) {
        this.state = state;
    }
    public String getCountry() {
        return country;
    }
```

```
        public void setCountry(String country) {
            this.country = country;
        }
}
```

The following code is for PhoneNumber.java:

```
public class PhoneNumber{
    private String number;
    private String extension;
    private String mobile;
    public String getNumber() {
        return number;
    }
    public void setNumber(String number) {
        this.number = number;
    }
    public String getExtension() {
        return extension;
    }
    public void setExtension(String extension) {
        this.extension = extension;
    }
    public String getMobile() {
        return mobile;
    }
    public void setMobile(String mobile) {
        this.mobile = mobile;
    }
}
```

The previous code produces the following result, a nicely structured JSON output:

```
{
    "clients": [
        {
            "name": "Mayur Ramgir",
            "company": "Zonopact, Inc.",
            "address": {
                "street": "867 Boylston Street",
                "street2": null,
                "city": "Boston",
                "state": "MA",
                "contacted": true
            },
            "phone-numbers": [
                {
                    "number": "855-966-6722",
                    "extension": "111"
                },
                {
                    "mobile": "111-111-1111"
                }
            ]
        }
    ]
}
```

This is an excellent example and provides an information format that goes well in preparing databases and web services that need to ask and maintain information about people and events. Most interactive websites use JSON structures as the default data exchange websites in order to work with other RESTful online services.

JSON allows the creation of objects and arrays that are also ideal for parsing information in a systematic manner. The information can be broken down into a number of relevant categories, and each one can then be processed according to the particular requirements of an API. It is often great for producing streaming APIs that need to read and process information in real time.

A JSON generation is helpful because it employs a tree structure that clearly depicts the saved data in the memory. This tree is easy to navigate, and therefore, it is available for generating and empowering queries. It provides a flexible tool to an application developer, since random access is available to any content/data type present in a JSON object.

This process requires the use of more memory since the object details are individually saved up within the memory. The streaming model is extremely effective in this regard, because it efficiently saves the available memory resources and provides a unique solution.

A streaming API is also available with JSON. It uses streaming, but provides its complete control of parsing and generations to the programmer. JSON offers this functionality by using an event-based parser, which we will further discuss ahead. An application developer can simply ask to generate the next event, which means that there is no need to use a callback process.

JSON structures provide a procedural control. The parser events can be either used or discarded, according to a set of rules and JSON object values. The streaming model is perfect for performing local processing when there is no need to randomly access a portion of the JSON data. This method also provides properly formed JSON objects and arrays for streaming out to any function or program. It works by writing a single event at a time.

A JSON object ideally provides a mapping functionality and ensures that you can save up an unordered collection of data objects. The types are represented by `JsonObject` and `JsonArray`. The array contains any data types that may be ordered in a set of arrays.

A brief history of JSON and examples

Understanding the history of JSON is essential in terms of identifying why it is the top format used in the online world for transferring information online. The JSON generation is now the top method and is almost unanimously used for data transfers in place of the older XML format.

It generates a text file format, which allows it to easily work with an automated program, as well as provide information on manual queries. It is truly a lightweight tool in this regard, which makes it easier to use and convert to different formats and online platforms.

We understand that JSON is a means to exchange data in an orderly manner and allow it to use different databases, such as SQL, which can be supported through a Java program. A JSON-generational tool also allows the importing and exporting of data from proprietary web applications that have otherwise closed codes and are not open to other programs.

It was first derived from the traditional JavaScript and was specially designed to obtain and store objects and arrays that were needed in a specific order or tree-like structure, such as data with regards to a typical information module or register.

Although the JSON method is evolved from Java, it has the ability to parse data from all programming languages that are employed for application development. The data returned and sent is independent of the languages in question, which makes it a perfect method for data communication in a controlled and automated manner.

JSON can deliver the value pairs that are ideal for generating lists, dictionaries, and associated structures. These pairs are ideally constructed as objects, especially in JavaScripts. It is able to generate a hash table or prepare a list of items that can then be realized as keys for the different phenomenon.

JSON can also generate an order list of data values. Since all values are of the same type, most programming languages such as Java are able to collect them as an array or a sequence.

JSON is extremely simple, which means that there has never been a requirement for changing its syntax. If we look in its history, we find that it is powerful and lightweight at the same time, because many people took part in empowering the method that we now term as JSON. Although *Douglas Crockford*, famous for his Atari work, coined the term, he expressed that many programmers found that the object literals present in Java are ideal for creating a data object transfer system.

Crockford describes that several people started to use the method, but did not give it a name. The name appeared later on in the early 2000s when AJAX became more commonly available. However, he was responsible for popularizing this method, since it was ideal for data collection, storage, and parsing whether using XML or JavaScript. In fact, modern JDK solutions made it easier to employ the method and increased the available functionality.

The name JSON received popularity in 2005 when application developers started to really target the mobile industry, where it was essential to introduce a data exchange method for seamless functionality. The JSON object-oriented functionality became an instant winner, because it offered cross-platform functionality through a lightweight tool that could be employed in any machine.

JSON is easy to understand and its popularity depends on the way it is able to construct data in terms of an object tree in Java. The use of applications that run on a single page, provides the ability to transfer the information in a single go.

JSON also received popularity since it uses minimalistic network resources when receiving and sending data over different online channels, especially ones that are based on Java applications. JSON was also backed by the Java community, which felt that XML was not the right method to use, since it was not designed to favor individual programmers. Rather it gave power to large companies that complicated the technologies required to run the most advanced data applications.

Currently, the top internet brands that we see were all made by individual entrepreneurs who worked hard at finding innovative methods to change the previous culture of complexity. JSON data brought the tools that were required to simplify the handling of large data structures and made it possible to create web applications that can handle large amounts of data while still keeping their flexibility and agility.

A great example in this regard is that of Google which defeated a very strong rival in terms of Yahoo. Google used simpler structures and made sure that it created a faster format that helped people search faster, rather than creating a heavy structure with complex tools.

Although modern apps may employ Excel and CSV data formats, JSON remains a popular option, since all the current programming languages are capable of parsing JSON generation and creating the required data objects and arrays through swift processing. It remains the industry standard, which allows for quickly switching between different platforms, even different virtual machines.

JSON remains an active option and will remain so in the new world of cloud computing. With the need of data increasing on a daily basis, only JSON has the ability to provide power to the new generation of APIs, which are in need of solid support.

JSON also has the ability to grease the wheels of an open online network. It can provide data to all formats, languages, and online machines. It can truly serve as the tool that creates the data storage, which is essential for empowering programs that are generated using different tools and operate on different machines.

Understanding JSON generation

JSON generation is required if you are looking to test your API or see how JavaScript is able to process a particular set of data. JSON generation has the capacity to either capture the live data from a source, or it may also be set up using a random generator that provides object values, without having to do the actual data heavy lifting.

JSON generation is lightweight and easily able to produce large chunks of information. It also allows the setting up of unique identifiers and index values, which can be used to store distinct sets of information. Next, we will discuss some of the JSON options that we get in the `Javax.json` package.

What is Javax.json?

The `Javax.json` package is a collection of all the utilities that are available for use in Java environments to process JSON. It includes facilities such as getting immutable objects or event streams by parsing input streams, feeding output streams with these immutable objects or event streams, building immutable objects using builders, and navigating immutable objects.

Here, we will discuss some of the most important items that are included in this package. These are the objects that are important in terms of using a JSON generation and controlled data transfers.

- `javax.json.JsonReader`: This interface provides methods to create the `JsonObject` instance by reading a JSON object or an array. The `JsonReader` instance can be created from a factory method `JsonReaderFactory` or the `Json` class.
- `javax.json.JsonWriter`: This interface provides methods to allows you to insert a JSON object to an output stream.
- `javax.json.stream.JsonParser`: This interface provides a parsing facility to read a JSON object via a stream.
- `javax.json.stream.JsonGenerator`: This interface provides the facility to write a JSON object to an output source via a stream.
- `javax.json.Json`: Creates JSON objects with this factory class.
- `javax.json.JsonObject`: This denotes an immutable JSON object value.

This `javax.json` package provides two APIs, an object model and streaming model to parse, generate, transform, and query JSON.

JSON object model

The object model API allows random access by specifying a tree-like structure in memory. Once the tree is structured, a specific element can be retrieved by navigating through nodes. This functionality makes this model more flexible however, it requires more memory. Hence, it's not that efficient compare to the streaming model.

JSON stream

The streaming API as you may have guessed by now, parses and generates JSON in a streaming manner. This API is not suitable for random access as it works on events. It processes one event at a time and instead of parsing it in a callback event, it gives control to the application developers where a developer can pull the event and decide if he or she wants to parse it or not.

A JSON stream is part of the `javax.json` package. It works as an API and is able to perform the generation of the JSON whenever required by the program. A stream is also required to provide a parsing option. There are two different interfaces that are available for the streams that are generated by the stream API. The first one consists of `JsonParser`, which is a facility that contains methods that allow the parsing of the JSON generation, which the results are available for being streamed to an output mechanism. The second interface is `JsonGenerator`, that provides methods to write JSON, which is streamed to an output mechanism.

Once the generator is used, the interface allows the JSON factory to set up individual instances that create JSON generational values. The location command allows the coders to set up the location information, which shows that a JSON event is available through an input source to the program. `JsonParser` can also be used in this capacity since it provides streaming access to the JSON data in a read-only mode and is perfect for use in programs where speed is of the essence.

The factory also exists for generating parsing instances. It works with its own event recognizer and is able to produce exceptions for both the generation and the parsing methods. There are several streaming APIs that can make use of the JSON data facility. The idea behind each use remains the presence of a high-performance streaming method, which is able to provide you with details of the JSON data available in a program or a Java-based application.

What are events?

An event has extreme significance in JavaScript. It can be identified as an object, which is created when the **graphical user interface** (**GUI**) experiences a particular change, such as the pressing of a button. When a user performs an action, an event is triggered, which can be attached to either gathering data or transmitting it out, using the JSON generation functionality.

The triggering of events is often used as the method for creating new objects within the live application. The behavior is controlled by the Event Handling mode of Java and is often included in the relevant Java libraries.

The triggering of an event remains pointless, unless an event listener is installed. A JSON object or an array is great in this regard, since it is able to store the set of data that may occur as a result of the event triggering.

How does an event work?

An event is handled by two elements. The first is the event source. This is actually an object that is created when an event is triggered. There are several types of event sources that are present in Java. A JSON generation can be initialized when an event source is detected according to the right trigger event.

The second is the event listener. This is an object, which actually looks for a particular event and then processes the required actions after the event has been established. This means that even listeners are required for carrying out any activities after the detection of a trigger.

There are different events that require their particular listeners. A common event is `ActionEvent`. This is an event that is triggered when the user clicks a button or selects an item from a list. An object is created in this regard that contains information regarding the source of the information as well as records the user action that actually triggered the event.

When the object is created, it is passed to the corresponding method through a command:

```
void actionPerf (ActionEvent a)
```

This generates a call to the method, which is then executed to produce an appropriate GUI response. This response may be the opening of a dialog or the triggering of a functionality, such as a file download. There are several actions that can be made available to the application users in a GUI-based solution.

Here, we will discuss other common events as well. `ContainerEvent` is another common event that occurs with the GUI structure of an application. This may occur when a user modifies an object present in the interface. It is easy to listen to using the `ContainerListener` event listener.

`KeyEvent` is another one that is triggered with the pressing of a key and is learned through the `KeyListener` event. `WindowEvent` is triggered when a window is altered and is also listened by a similarly named listener. `MouseEvent` is the one that is generated through the actions of a computer mouse button operation.

These listeners are easily able to interact with each other. This means that a single listener is able to read multiple events as long as they are of the same type. In actual programming, this means that a single listener is placed to handle all events of a particular event type.

On the other hand, a single event may trigger multiple listeners if the event matches the characteristics that are mentioned within the details for the listening command. It is up to the particular program design, although it is common to create different types of listeners to correspond to the different types of events.

Now let's explore these two types, object modeling and streaming, in more details. Here we will see various types for each API.

Types in JSON for object modeling

There are different interfaces that are available when setting up object-based APIs through JSON. The first is the static method created by using the class `Json`. It sets up any method, including factory objects and build structures.

The `JsonGenerator` class allows us to write a single value at one time, when using JSON data to record a stream of information.

The `JsonReader` class reads a data element and then creates an object in the memory for all relevant information.

The `JsonObjectBuilder` and `JsonArrayBuilder` classes create JSON objects and arrays in the memory by producing the required values from the Java code.

The `JsonWriter` class allows us to write an object saved in the memory to an output stream. There are four subclasses of the class `JsonValue`. These are namely `JsonArray`, `JsonNumber`, `JsonObject`, and `JsonString`, with each one representing the relevant data type.

These options are excellent at creating objects from input streams as well as sending objects for output. This functionality is excellent when searching vast databases on the internet, such as social media websites, where it may be important to go and look for a particular term. The JSON generation can also provide power to a resource management system, since it is able to generate and send systemized information objects.

Types in JSON for streaming API

The streaming functionality of JSON is the same as the one found in other website-generation languages such as XML. The interfaces that empower the streaming side include `JsonParser` and `JsonGenerator`.

The `JsonParser` class contains the methods that are required to parse the data that is being received through the streaming model. `JsonGenerator`, on the other hand, contains the methods that allow programs to use this JSON data and send it out to an output. Here, we will discuss the main interface options available in this method.

The `JsonParser` class provides read-only access to the data, which is what is required for a parsing programming model that only needs to pull the data out. The application runs the calling methods in this mode and controls the parsing, since it is only done to achieve the needs of the particular application. The JSON data can be obtained from the current state, or the parser can be forwarded to the next interface instance.

The `JsonGenerator` class is perfect for writing data to a stream, which may be required to run a particular Java-based application. The generator usually writes down in pairs by placing values that may either be present in an object or an array.

The streaming API is perfect for using JSON since it works on a low level and is ideal for processing large amounts of data, which can be delivered by an actively streaming JSON data setup. The streaming applications can be used to carry out the same functionality as that done by object modeling, and the main difference lies between the way the data is stored and transmitted between the input and the output data streams.

This code describes how this functionality can be achieved for searching up our `Clients.json` file and printing particular ones, through JSON parsing functionality:

```
import java.io.FileInputStream;
import javax.json.Json;
import javax.json.stream.JsonParser;
import javax.json.stream.JsonParser.Event;

public class JSONStream {

    public static void main(String[] args) throws Exception  {
        try {
            FileInputStream json = new
FileInputStream("/Users/MayurRamgir/clients.json");
            JsonParser jsonParser = Json.createParser(json);
            Event event = null;
            System.out.println("------------Address----------");
            event = parseElement(event, jsonParser, "address");
            printData(event, jsonParser);
        }catch(Exception e){
            // Handle the exception logic here
        }
    }
    private static Event parseElement(Event event, JsonParser jsonParser,
```

```
String element) {
      while(jsonParser.hasNext()) {
          event = jsonParser.next();
          if(event == Event.KEY_NAME &&
element.equals(jsonParser.getString())) {
              event = jsonParser.next();
              break;
          }
      }
      return event;
  }

  private static void printData(Event event, JsonParser jsonParser){
      while(event != Event.END_OBJECT) {
          switch(event) {
              case KEY_NAME: {
                  System.out.print(jsonParser.getString());
                  System.out.print(" = ");
                  break;
              }
              case VALUE_FALSE: {
                  System.out.println(false);
                  break;
              }
              case VALUE_NULL: {
                  System.out.println("null");
                  break;
              }
              case VALUE_NUMBER: {
                  if(jsonParser.isIntegralNumber()) {
                      System.out.println(jsonParser.getInt());
                  } else {
                      System.out.println(jsonParser.getBigDecimal());
                  }
                break;
              }
              case VALUE_STRING: {
                  System.out.println(jsonParser.getString());
                  break;
              }
              case VALUE_TRUE: {
                  System.out.println(true);
                  break;
              }
              default: {
              }
          }
          event = jsonParser.next();
```

```
            }
        }
    }
```

The previous code produces the following result:

```
-----------Address----------
street = 867 Boylston Street
street2 = null
city = Boston
state = MA
contacted = true
```

You can also use an online resource to get a JSON stream. For that you can use the following code block:

```
URL url = new URL("https://<URL>/<filename>.json");
  InputStream is = url.openStream();
```

This provides the required functionality and describes how JSON processing has its application in a variety of data processing and parsing environments. The Java APIs can use JSON in order to parse the incoming data, as well as for writing the data of a particular stream of data as activated by the triggering of an event.

The JSON method is also able to navigate objects around, and it is also perfect for building object structures and other classes. It is excellent for providing functionality for APIs that need to manipulate data. Here, we will continue to shed light on other important topics that are related to the JSON generation.

JSON trees

In this section, we will explore another yet important library, called Jackson, for JSON processing for Java. It not only provides basic JSON-processing functionality but also provides data processing tools to create POJOs from JSON and JSON from POJO.

 You can learn more about this project by visiting `https://github.com/FasterXML/jackson` and `https://github.com/FasterXML/jackson-core`.

Jackson library enables Java to structure JSON in a tree mode by using nodes and setting up structures to convert the available JSON information into the Java tree models. It is similar to converting data fields in a coordinated manner in other languages as well. An example code in this regard is given here, which shows JSON code being extracted to become a Java tree structure:

```java
import java.io.File;
import java.io.IOException;

import com.fasterxml.jackson.core.JsonGenerationException;
import com.fasterxml.jackson.databind.JsonMappingException;
import com.fasterxml.jackson.databind.JsonNode;
import com.fasterxml.jackson.databind.ObjectMapper;

public class JSONTreeExample {

    public static void main(String[] args) {

        try {

            ObjectMapper mapper = new ObjectMapper();

            JsonNode root = mapper.readTree(new
File("/Users/MayurRamgir/clients.json"));

            JsonNode clientsNode = root.path("clients");
            if (clientsNode.isArray()) {
                for (JsonNode clientNode : clientsNode) {
                    String name = clientNode.path("name").asText();
                    String company = clientNode.path("company").asText();
                    JsonNode addressNode = clientNode.path("address");
                    String street = addressNode.path("street").asText();
                    String city = addressNode.path("city").asText();
                    String state = addressNode.path("state").asText();
                    System.out.println("name : " + name);
                    System.out.println("company name : " + company);
                    System.out.println("street : " + street);
                    System.out.println("city : " + city);
                    System.out.println("state : " + state);
                    JsonNode phoneNumbersNodes = clientNode.path("phone-
numbers");
                    if (phoneNumbersNodes.isArray()) {
                        for (JsonNode phoneNode : phoneNumbersNodes) {
                            if (!phoneNode.path("number").isMissingNode())
{
                                String phoneNumber =
phoneNode.path("number").asText();
```

```
                                String extension =
phoneNode.path("extension").asText();
                                System.out.println("phone number : " +
phoneNumber);
                                System.out.println("extension : " +
extension);
                            }
                            if (!phoneNode.path("mobile").isMissingNode())
{
                                String mobile =
phoneNode.path("mobile").asText();
                                System.out.println("mobile : " + mobile);
                            }
                        }
                    }
                }
            }

        } catch (JsonGenerationException e) {
            e.printStackTrace();
        } catch (JsonMappingException e) {
            e.printStackTrace();
        } catch (IOException e) {
            e.printStackTrace();
        }
    }

}
```

The previous code will produce the following result:

```
name : Mayur Ramgir
company name : Zonopact, Inc.
street : 867 Boylston Street
city : Boston
state : MA
phone number : 855-966-6722
extension : 111
mobile : 111-111-1111
```

Please note isMissingNode--it is able to point out a missing node rather than providing a null value for generating the tree.

With this use complete, now we will turn our attention to describing the Java tree. It is important to first describe the way it is used, since it helps a great deal in understanding how the tree is defined and set up for operations.

The tree is created with the `JTree` class that allows programmers to use and display data arranged in a hierarchical order. The actual objects that are created by the tree do not contain the information, rather they allow you access to a view of the relevant data.

Each row of the data is presented in the tree information in the form of one data element and creates an instance in the form of a data node. Each Java tree has a characteristic root of the node, and all the nodes descend accordingly in a connected and well-informed manner.

Let's understand the tree structure that shows the data in a vertical manner. Each row works as a node and only contains a singular data item, which is termed as the node. The root node is the one that works just like the directory works in a file information system, where all roots descend from a single entity.

However, there can be branch nodes that have multiple entries, which can be termed as daughter entries. These branch nodes can be viewed in an expanded as well as collapsed form. Usually, the GUI will allow the viewing and changing of these items by clicking them. A Java-based program is able to observe the state of these trees and then use them accordingly. Specific nodes can also be identified in the program and then used to describe events using `TreeExpansionListener`, which can be easily programmed.

A specific node is ideally defined as the one that is part of an object that contains its details and that of all its ancestors. It can also be identified using the display row that allows the information of both collapsed and expanded nodes. There are also hidden nodes, which lie under an ancestor that is currently in a collapsed manner.

A simple code generates a `JTree` as an object and places it in the scroll panel in the JDK. Here is a relevant example extracted from Oracle's documents:

```
//Instance variables are declared here:

private JTree tree;

...

public TreeDemo() {

    ...

    DefaultMutableTreeNode top =

        new DefaultMutableTreeNode("The Java Series");
```

```
        createNodes(top);

        tree = new JTree(top);

        . . .

        JScrollPane treeView = new JScrollPane(tree);

        . . .

    }
```

This code generates an instance of a tree, and the instance then serves as the root node for this particular tree. The code then keeps on growing the tree by adding the rest of the nodes. It creates the overall tree and also passes the root node as a declaration argument to the JTree constructor. The tree is also placed in a scroll panel. This is a common method since the available space is too small to house the complete tree structure.

The tree is created to use the various user objects that may point to data that belongs to a tree through a node. The object created by the user can work as a string and be defined in a customized manner. The Java tree is designed to render each node by using the values that it receives through the toString function. However, Java allows the overriding of values in order to map the object in a specific manner.

The JTree constructor is able to create and specify special TreeNode structures as arguments. You can use these tree structures to examine data objects and increase productivity by ensuring that your program allows structured access to the information that it stores, perhaps directly from a JSON source that returns perfect data for tree storage.

Java is able to set up the tree using various icon displays as defined by the relevant code. It generally uses the available motifs present on the host system. Folder-like symbols commonly appear, but the display that will normally present itself is the one that depends on whether the node is a leaf, a branch, or any other level in the chain of node roots.

Trees also provide the programmer with the option of creating a particular data model. This may be the one that is suitably designed to perform a particular function. The creation of an interface ensures that any object can be used to specify a tree node.

If you set up a tree with the right number of nodes, you are all set for obtaining JSON data from a number of sources. This can be done through parsing as well by reading streams of JSON data from online sources.

The list of the available nodes is extracted in this regard, and it is set up to match the JSON generational data. The important point here is to set up the properties in a manner that they become the tree nodes. This provides the structural background that is then used to obtain, store, and use the generational data in the form of a tree structure.

Sub-nodes can be easily defined by creating them as children of the original nodes that lie above them. Parsing is another option to take when implementing a balance in Java trees in order to obtain information from the existing JSON structures.

Understanding the tree model

There are many JSON processing tools that can be used to create a tree structure and then use it for a multitude of tasks. Many programmers are not comfortable with using the tree model since they find it harder to set up these structures and prefer using other ways available to process a JSON generation.

It takes time and effort to create the efficient tree structures. However, once established, they can make the effort of obtaining information from data streams a breeze, and in fact, programmers will be amazed at how swift, coherent, and functional a tree model can become with adequate training and setting effort.

Many programmers are afraid of the tree model, because they find it difficult to use tree models in other network programming languages such as the XML. However, the new Java models use the experience of these troublesome languages and produce a much better approach towards providing a tree model structure. This means that the modern JSON structures and their dealing with a tree approach are much better than older hierarchical structures that lacked deep support and organizational structure.

There are various tools, such as Jackson, that make it easier to employ JSON trees that are powered by creating the `JsonNode`-based design. This design has the structural support that allows the conversion of data elements between different models and software tools. It also ensures that the programmer can combine different approaches and achieve design excellence when creating tools for efficient memory structures and data types.

The conversion between different data objects through a tree structure ensures that you can employ a broad strategy, where you do not have to worry about the individual gains that you would make with just a single one. A single strategy is beneficial for a particular purpose, but it may fail to provide the memory efficiency required for complex programs that can do well using the strengths of multiple data object models.

The tree model provides power in a controlled manner and is perfect when used in specific data-processing steps. It also helps when programmers are creating prototypes. They want efficient and swift data objects that are easily transferable and can parse and extract data from every available source during the testing and documentation phase.

A JSON tree is set up by using a simple node object. This object allows the creation of a logical tree, which can then be employed in a number of ways. The basic interface once set up is designed to work as an `ObjectNode` and is perfectly suited to carrying out the relevant operations through the defined node.

There are three operations that you can then perform in the tree model. The first is the parsing of data from an active JSON source. This can easily happen by connecting a node by reading the data for the tree objects.

You can also convert a POJO source by using and setting up a tree structure. This is simply a space case scenario, where the object mapper is able to read and convert the value in the right form.

The tree structure can also operate from scratch since the mapper is able to directly generate the required objects and their nodes.

The right choice is the one that is perfect according to the programmer's unique requirements. Whether you use a new tree or alter a JSON structure, it is up to you to set up your program so that you can comfortably gather streaming information in a structural and coordinated manner.

Converting CSV to JSON

Comma Separated Values (**CSVs**) is an ideal method for storing data in a tabular form. CSV files can be easily moved in and out of several data-processing software tools, such as Microsoft Excel. It is simple and perfect for a quick transfer in a number of environments.

However, JSON is present all around the web, and there is often a requirement to convert the CSV data to JSON in order to use it in a different programming and data-processing environment. Any JSON conversion can occur by using two modes of standard or minimal conversion.

A simple table can be read using table annotations that point to individual values. This is an easy-to-read model where column titles and cell values can be directly referred using Unicode character sets. Normalization may also apply when converting string values to JSON data, which can then be parsed in real time.

The minimal mode is easy to use. Simply start with creating and entering an empty array to a JSON output. This is to create the value pairs that have to be associated with the cell values that will then be entered into the array thus created in JSON.

The next step is that the subsequent tables should be referenced in a sequential error. It is essential to create proper table groups when converting multiple data elements. The output annotation must stop to ensure that the table is locked in place.

Then, there is a need for processing each row in a sequential order. This should happen starting from the first sequence of the objects to the *nth* sequence. Each one should correspond to one row of the data in CSV, therefore generating JSON objects that are aligned in the same manner as the original data.

The annotation present describes the subject that is present in each cell of the row that is selected during the transfer. If there is no annotation, then the default subject will be selected for converting the row.

Nested objects can also be processed by using a number of object creations. This often generates the required number of root objects where each root provides a reference to a single nest. One row may also hold multiple objects that are related. The URL annotation in this case will match up with the annotations that are entered within the same row object elements. This method usually curtails adding multiple sequences in each root object, by starting from the first and going to the m element.

The standard mode can be used to convert groups of tables that are already set up according to a rule and identifier. This process starts with inserting an empty object first in the JSON output. This is associated with controlling the entry of the whole group of tables.

The name value pair for the object will follow the name that is presented in the identifier of the CSV table. This will occur in this manner:

```
name @id value IG
```

Other notes and annotations that are given from the tables will be converted to the object made in the JSON generation by following the transfer rules that govern the JSON model. Once this is done, it can be followed up by directly entering the complete tables into the newly created object. This will allow for a swift conversion, which can be used in any CSV environment for quick data transfer.

Converting Excel to JSON

Converting Excel data to JSON is an activity that programmers need to perform when producing a conformity in a Java application. The right conversion requires the correct reading of the headers of rows and columns and then creating the required array structure for saving data in terms of JSON structures.

The best way to do this is to create a list of the items, and then work out a transfer to a JSON data form. This happens when you create a class in a software tool such as POJO and keep using relevant array structures to save the information that you have in terms of the rows and columns of a spreadsheet.

One way to perform the function of reading data from the different cells of a spreadsheet and putting it into a relevant JSON array is in the following manner:

```java
import java.io.FileInputStream;
import java.io.FileNotFoundException;
import java.io.IOException;
import java.io.InputStream;
import java.util.HashMap;
import java.util.Iterator;
import java.util.Map;

import org.apache.poi.EncryptedDocumentException;
import org.apache.poi.openxml4j.exceptions.InvalidFormatException;
import org.apache.poi.ss.usermodel.Cell;
import org.apache.poi.ss.usermodel.Row;
import org.apache.poi.ss.usermodel.Sheet;
import org.apache.poi.ss.usermodel.Workbook;
import org.apache.poi.ss.usermodel.WorkbookFactory;
import javax.json.*;
import javax.json.stream.JsonGenerator;
import javax.json.stream.JsonGeneratorFactory;

public class JSONExcelToJson {
    public static void main(String[] args) {
        Map<String, Object> properties = new HashMap<String, Object>(1);
        properties.put(JsonGenerator.PRETTY_PRINTING, true);
        JsonGeneratorFactory jsonGeneratorFactory =
Json.createGeneratorFactory(properties);
        JsonGenerator jsonGenerator =
jsonGeneratorFactory.createGenerator(System.out);

        InputStream inp;
        try {
            inp = new FileInputStream("/Users/MayurRamgir/workbook.xlsx");
```

```
        Workbook workbook = WorkbookFactory.create(inp);

        // Start with obtaining the first sheet of the workbook.
        Sheet sheet = workbook.getSheetAt(0);

        jsonGenerator.writeStartObject();

        for (Iterator<Row> rowsIT = sheet.rowIterator();
rowsIT.hasNext();) {
            Row row = rowsIT.next();
            for (Iterator<Cell> cellsIT = row.cellIterator();
cellsIT.hasNext();) {
                Cell cell = cellsIT.next();
                jsonGenerator.write("name",cell.getStringCellValue());
            }
        }
        jsonGenerator.writeEnd();
        jsonGenerator.close();

    } catch (FileNotFoundException e) {
        // TODO Auto-generated catch block
        e.printStackTrace();
    } catch (EncryptedDocumentException e) {
        // TODO Auto-generated catch block
        e.printStackTrace();
    } catch (InvalidFormatException e) {
        // TODO Auto-generated catch block
        e.printStackTrace();
    } catch (IOException e) {
        // TODO Auto-generated catch block
        e.printStackTrace();
    }

  }
}
```

The following is the image of the Excel file used in the previous code:

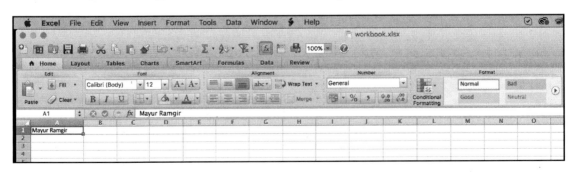

The previous code with the excel file produces the following result:

```
{
    "name": "Mayur Ramgir"
}
```

This code will read the values in the spreadsheet cells, create a relevant JSON array, and save the information in an orderly and structured manner for exporting the data to a relevant data form. Once data objects are transferred to the JSON generation, the JSON library can then be used to transfer them to Java and perform the required operations on the information elements. The same structure needs to be created for reading the JSON and then processing it for the required application objective.

There are some common errors that programmers can make when working spreadsheets to JSON objects. One common error is failing to account for the need to initialize JSON objects for every new row of the spreadsheet. Failure to do this may produce null values and only save the last row that is read, since the object is replaced each time the iteration is performed for a new data row.

One way to keep a record of the ideal row transfers is if you print out the data present in the rows that are being sent in the JSON array object. This output will describe how the data is being read and whether it is being overwritten with every iteration in the code.

Understanding value trees

Understanding the value trees requires the understanding of how a tree structure is set up in Java. It is best described as a structure that does not use a linear representation of the data objects. The objects follow a hierarchical system where they are connected to each other in both a parallel and perpendicular manner.

The data present in a tree, such as the one created with a JSON structure, does not have the linear organization found in a simple array. The data elements that are present in a tree structure are usually saved in the form of nodes. There is a node at the tip of the structure, which is termed as the root node of the tree.

This tree structure is perfect when a linear presentation is simply not possible. This happens when there is a need to create a family of specific data elements. Java is able to deal with these trees since there are two classes in its utility set that are designed to take care of tree-based, non-linear data. The two classes are `TreeMap` and `TreeSet`. Programmers may use these classes and create objects in them according to the data elements that they have for processing.

The JTree classes are simply the special cases of using the tree data structure. They are implementations that follow the setting up of unique elements in the form of tree nodes that generate from a single root node.

In a simple manner, a Java tree is defined as a set of elements that is filled with values. There is always one element that acts as the node, while all other elements make up sub-groups that are better termed as sub-trees, just like the subsets defined in the set theory. These elements may contain further partitions and smaller nodes that can be defined as the subsets of these subsets.

Family structures are the best in terms of understanding the tree structures. Here, we enter a family structure and then describe how it can be used to describe the typical trees that are present in the Java utility set in two different capacities.

This a typical family tree where Tom, the grandfather, sits on the top of the tree in the form of the root node. There are two nodes of William and Hansen that lie beneath him. They can be termed as the subdirectory structures. Both subdirectories have two separate values. These ending values are often termed as the leaves of the data tree structure, since they often contain the actual data information.

This data structure allows every person to understand the relationships between the different nodes. It allows us to find out that Andy and Tim are cousins, while William and Hansen are brothers. One of the most common tree structures that is often employed in Java is the use of a binary tree. A binary tree is the one that only allows for two values to be generated out of every node.

This tree structure is divided in terms of the right-hand side and the left-hand side sub-trees. The binary structure is easy to understand and is often valuable in a number of data applications. There are different ways to implement binary structures, and the programmers must choose a method that allows for swift recalling of the data from the structure.

There are several types of these trees that are used in programming. A common type is a red-black tree employed when creating Java-tree based APIs that are able to use this particular data structure. This structure is ideal for creating swift APIs because it operates the fastest even when the required data is present at the bottom of the longest nodal structure.

This tree structure is special since it uses the extra information of color with every node. The root is always black while every leaf (the ending nodes) are also always black. The nodes in between are red color, and therefore, all parent nodes must have black children.

The presence of these rules means that these data structures are coherent and can be easily checked for consistency. These properties need to be followed up in every instance, especially when creating new nodes or deleting the old ones due to a change in the data structure.

The Java API library contains the tools that do not require you to focus on working on low-level machine decisions. The APIs already have the logic implemented, and the program simply needs to import the package and use the two classes in `Java.json` that we mentioned earlier.

The first type is defined as a set and uses the mathematical structure where distinct elements are used to display the information present in the subsets. It uses the abstraction model available in the set theory.

The second type uses a mapping system, where every collection of data elements contains a unique key termed as the value pair. Since each key only points out to one value, there is no issue of any duplication. A value may be duplicated if required, but the key remains distinct and allows for use in the form of map pointers.

A binary tree structure created using these Java classes is excellent for searching the values in different nodes. There is always a particular pointer that connects with the sub-trees either in the form of subsets or a range of mapping values that point to the data leaves in the tree structure.

Pointers can also be changed, while different searching patterns can be introduced in order to produce the maximum speed during the searching of the relevant strings in the tree-based data structure.

Remember that creating an intricate tree structure may not be the best way to implement the data elements in terms of speed. However, this does not decrease the value of the tree structure, since it provides functionality that cannot be matched by other methods. The presence of rules allows the smart creation of maps and hash setups that can then point to the relevant data sets. This is important when designing applications that employ JSON generations and transfer data elements between different Java-based applications.

The benefits of using JSON

There are several benefits of using JSON when you are creating large-scale applications that are based on Java. These are the applications that often require the parsing of data from different sources. If your application needs to access cloud data and often create information that needs to be shared, the best way to go about it is to use the relevant JSON objects.

Another amazing thing about the JSON structure is that it finds support in all modern programming languages. This means that it adds productivity and the reflexes that you need in your application when the times modernize and your data structures need to stay relevant for the years to come. Using JSON ensures that you would have the relevant support regardless of dealing with any application of choice.

Another benefit is when creating mobile applications. Mobile phones are limited by the available memory and computing power. They need to use data objects and classes that are swift and able to quickly transfer data from one source to another. JSON is fast and does all the required operations without putting any load on the other parts of the application, which may also be running at the same time.

JSON is fully operational with Python, PHP, and Java. It is this ability that allows the language to be fully used in producing the connectivity between different applications. Since it is able to retrieve data in almost any programming situation, it offers the support that every application needs to either import or export data, which is essential for the operations of the program.

Summary

The JSON generation is based on the methods identified in the Java object modeling structure. It is able to create a dedicated set of data elements that are related to each other in a non-linear manner. There are two main JSON elements. One is the parsing and the second is the array generation. The JSON generation provides a way of communicating between different programming languages. It has a unique standardization, which allows programmers to really use it in the Java 9 platform and prepare programs that have the best cross-functionality and are ideal for use on mobile platforms.

In the next chapter we will learn about JShell and the **Ahead-of-Time** (**AOT**) compiler. We will learn about **Read-Eval-Print Loop** (**REPL**) tool, which is quite similar to other languages such as Scala, Ruby and Python.

8
Tools for Higher Productivity and Faster Application

Since the dawn of programming as a profession, the standing goals of every aspiring coder were to quickly produce applications that perform the assigned tasks with lightning speed. Otherwise, why bother? We could slowly do whatever we were doing for thousands of years. In the course of the last century, we made substantial progress in both aspects, and now, Java 9 makes another step in each of these directions.

Two new tools were introduced in Java 9, JShell and the **Ahead-of-Time (AOT)** compiler-- both were expected for a long time. JShell is a **Read–Eval–Print Loop (REPL)** tool that is well-known for those who program in Scala, Ruby, or Python, for example. It takes a user input, evaluates it, and returns the result immediately. The AOT compiler takes Java bytecode and generates a native (system-dependent) machine code so that the resulting binary file can execute natively.

These tools will be the focus of this chapter.

The JShell tool usage

JShell helps a programmer to test fragments (snippets) of code as they are written. It shortens the time for development by avoiding the build-deploy-test part of the development cycle. Programmers can easily copy an expression or even several methods into the JShell session and run-test-modify them multiple times immediately. Such a quick turn around also helps to understand the library API better before using it and to tune the code to express exactly its purpose, thus facilitating better quality software.

How often have we guessed what the JavaDoc for a particular API meant and wasted build-deploy-test cycles for figuring it out? Or we want to recall, how exactly the string will be split by `substring(3)`? Sometimes, we create a small test application where we run the code we are not sure about, using again the same build-deploy-test cycle. With JShell, we can copy, paste, and run. In this section, we will describe and show how to do it.

JShell is built on the top of JVM, so it processes the code snippets exactly as JVM does. Only a few constructs that do not make sense for REPL are omitted. For example, you cannot use `package` declaration, `static`, or `final` in JShell (these keywords are going to be ignored). Also, the semicolon `;` is allowed but not required at the end of a statement.

JShell comes with API included in the module `jdk.jshell` which can be used for the integration of JShell into other tools (IDE, for example), but it is outside of the scope of this book.

Creating a JShell session and setting context

JShell comes with the JDK installation. You can find it in the `bin` directory as `$JAVA_HOME/bin/jshell`. Execute it to start the JShell session. Before you get familiar with JShell, we recommend starting the session with the option `-v`, which stands for *verbose*. This way, the shell will add more details to each of your actions, explaining what has been accomplished with each of them. After launching `jshell` in a terminal window, you will see the following output:

```
|  Welcome to JShell -- Version 9
|  For an introduction type: /help intro

jshell> []
```

This means that a JShell session is created and can be used for Java code running. Enter the recommended command `/help intro` and read the following JShell introduction:

```
jshell> /help intro
|
|  intro
|
|  The jshell tool allows you to execute Java code, getting immediate results.
|  You can enter a Java definition (variable, method, class, etc), like:  int x = 8
|  or a Java expression, like:  x + x
|  or a Java statement or import.
|  These little chunks of Java code are called 'snippets'.
|
|  There are also jshell commands that allow you to understand and
|  control what you are doing, like:  /list
|
|  For a list of commands: /help
```

The introduction tells us the very minimum we need to know in order to get going. So, let's follow the guide. If we enter `/help`, we get the list of possible JShell commands with a short description (we will go over every command in more detail later) and the following information:

```
|  /? [<command>|<subject>]
|        get information about jshell
|  /!
|        re-run last snippet
|  /<id>
|        re-run snippet by id
|  /-<n>
|        re-run n-th previous snippet
|
|  For more information type '/help' followed by the name of a
|  command or a subject.
|  For example '/help /list' or '/help intro'.
|
|  Subjects:
|
|  intro
|        an introduction to the jshell tool
|  shortcuts
|        a description of keystrokes for snippet and command completion,
|        information access, and automatic code generation
|  context
|        the evaluation context options for /env /reload and /reset
```

Those are important tips to remember. Notice that the /? and /help commands produce the same result, so from now on, we will use /? only. The commands /i, /<id> (id is assigned to each snippet automatically and shown to the left of the snippet when listed by the command /list), and /-<n> allow re-running of the snippets that have been run previously.

Subject intro we saw already. Subject shortcuts can be viewed by entering the command /? shortcuts:

```
<tab>
            After entering the first few letters of a Java identifier,
            a jshell command, or, in some cases, a jshell command argument,
            press the <tab> key to complete the input.
            If there is more than one completion, then possible completions will be shown.
            Will show documentation if available and appropriate.

Shift-<tab> v
            After a complete expression, hold down <shift> while pressing <tab>,
            then release and press "v", the expression will be converted to
            a variable declaration whose type is based on the type of the expression.

Shift-<tab> i
            After an unresolvable identifier, hold down <shift> while pressing <tab>,
            then release and press "i", and jshell will propose possible imports
            which will resolve the identifier based on the content of the specified classpath.
```

As you can see, the *Tab* key can be used to complete the current entry, while double *Tab* brings up possible completion options or JavaDoc, if available. Do not hesitate to press *Tab* several times after each command. It will help you to find more ways to utilize JShell features to your advantage.

Press *Shift* + *Tab* and then press *V* to create a variable based on the just completed expression. Here is an example:

1. Type 2*2 on the console and press *Enter*.
2. Press *Shift* + *Tab* together.
3. Release the keys and press *V*.
4. The shell will show int x = 2*2 and position the cursor just in front of =.

5. Enter the variable (x, for example, and press *Enter*). The resulting screen will show the following output:

```
jshell> 2 * 2
jshell> int x = 2 * 2
x ==> 4
|  created variable x : int
```

Press *Shift + Tab* and then press *I* after an unresolved identifier requests JShell to provide possible imports based on the content of the classpath. Here is an example:

6. Type `new Pair` and press *Enter.*
7. Press *Shift + Tab* together.
8. Release the keys and press *I*. The shell will show the following output:

```
jshell> new Pair
0: Do nothing
1: import: javafx.util.Pair
Choice:
```

9. You will get two options with the values 0 and 1, respectively.
10. In the shell, you will get a statement called `Choice`; type *1* and press *Enter*.
11. Now, the `javafx.util.Pair` class is imported.
12. You can continue entering the code snippet.

JShell was able to provide the suggestion because the JAR file with the compiled `Pair` class was on the classpath (set there by default as part of JDK libraries). You can also add to the classpath any other JAR file with the compiled classes you need for your coding. You can do it by setting it at JShell startup by the option `--class-path` (can be also used with one dash `-class-path`):

```
jshell --class-path ~/mylibrary/myclasses.jar
```

In the earlier example, the JAR file `myclasses.jar` is loaded from the folder `mylibrary` in the user's home directory. To set several JAR files, you can separate them by a colon : (for Linux and MacOS) or by a semicolon ; (for Windows).

The classpath can also be set by the command /env any time during the JShell session:

```
jshell> /env --class-path ~/mylibrary/myclasses.jar
|  Setting new options and restoring state.
```

Notice that every time the classpath is set, all the snippets of the current session are reloaded with the new classpath.

The commands /reset and /reload can be used instead of the /env command to set the classpath too. We will describe the difference between these commands in the next section.

If you do not want to collect your compiled classes in a JAR file, the option --class-path (or -class-path) could point to the directory where the compiled classes are located. Once the classpath is set, the classes associated with it can be imported during a snippet writing using keys *Shift + Tab* and then *I* as described earlier.

Other context options are related to the usage of modules and can be seen after entering the command /? context:

```
|     --module-path <module path>...
|             A list of directories, each directory
|             is a directory of modules.
|             The list is separated with the path separator
|             (a : on unix/linux/mac, and ; on windows).
|     --add-modules <modulename>[,<modulename>...]
|             root modules to resolve in addition to the initial module.
|             <modulename> can also be ALL-DEFAULT, ALL-SYSTEM,
|             ALL-MODULE-PATH.
|     --add-exports <module>/<package>=<target-module>(,<target-module>)*
|             updates <module> to export <package> to <target-module>,
|             regardless of module declaration.
|             <target-module> can be ALL-UNNAMED to export to all
|             unnamed modules. In jshell, if the <target-module> is not
|             specified (no =) then ALL-UNNAMED is used.
|
|  On the command-line these options must have two dashes, e.g.: --module-path
|  On jshell commands they can have one or two dashes, e.g.: -module-path
```

There are several more advanced options of running the jshell tool. To learn about them, refer to the Oracle documentation (for example, https://docs.oracle.com/javase/9/tools/jshell.htm).

The last important command we would like to mention in this section is /exit. It allows exiting the command mode and closing the JShell session.

JShell commands

As we mentioned in the previous section, the full list of JShell commands can be obtained by typing the /? command. Each command comes with a one-line description. There is another way to get the same list but without description, that is by typing / followed by *Tab*. The screen would show the following content:

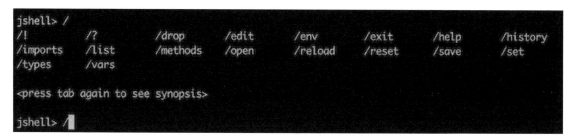

Pressing *Tab* the second time would bring the same list of the commands with a synopsis (one-line description) for each. To make it easier for a user, while typing, a command, subcommand, command argument, or command option can be abbreviated, as long as it remains unique so that the tool can recognize it unambiguously. For example, instead of the previous list of full-name commands, you can use the corresponding list of their abbreviated versions: /!, /?, /d, /ed, /en, /ex, /he, /hi, /i, /l, /m, /o, /rel, /res, /sa, /se, /t, /v. The preceding dash / is necessary for distinguishing commands from snippets.

Now, let's review each of these commands. While doing it, we will create a few snippets, variables, and types so that we can demonstrate each command more clearly using specific examples.

You can start a new JShell session by running jshell (with option -v) and enter the following commands:

- /en: To view or change the evaluation context
- /h: To view history of what you have typed
- /l [<name or id>|-all|-start]: To list the source you have typed
- /m [<name or id>|-all|-start]L: To list the declared methods and their signatures
- /t [<name or id>|-all|-start]: To list the declared types

- `/v [<name or id>|-all|-start]`: To list the declared variables and their values

The result would be like this:

```
|  Welcome to JShell -- Version 9
|  For an introduction type: /help intro

jshell> /en

jshell> /hi

/en
/hi

jshell> /l

jshell> /m

jshell> /t

jshell> /v
```

As you might be expecting, most of these commands yielded no results (except a short history of your typing until that moment) because we have not entered any code snippet yet. The last four commands have the same options:

- `<name or id>`: This is the name or ID of a specific snippet or method or type or variable (we will see examples later)
- `-start`: This shows snippets or methods or types or variables loaded at the JShell start (we will see later how to do it)
- `-all`: This shows snippets or methods or types or variables loaded at the JShell start and entered later during the session

By default, at the startup, several common packages are imported. You can see them by typing the `/l -start` or `/l -all` command:

```
jshell> /l -start

  s1 : import java.io.*;
  s2 : import java.math.*;
  s3 : import java.net.*;
  s4 : import java.nio.file.*;
  s5 : import java.util.*;
  s6 : import java.util.concurrent.*;
  s7 : import java.util.function.*;
  s8 : import java.util.prefs.*;
  s9 : import java.util.regex.*;
 s10 : import java.util.stream.*;
```

There is no `java.lang` package in this list, but it is always imported by default and not listed among the imports.

In the left column of the previously mentioned list, you can see the ID of each snippet. If you type the `/l s5` command, for example, it will retrieve the snippet with ID `s5`:

```
jshell> /l s5

  s5 : import java.util.*;
```

To customize the startup entries, you can use the command `/sa <file>` to save in the specified file all the settings and snippets you have entered in the current session. The next time you would like to continue with the same context, you can start the JShell session with this file `jshell <file>`.

Let's demonstrate this procedure with an example:

```
demo> jshell
|  Welcome to JShell -- Version 9
|  For an introduction type: /help intro

jshell> Pair
0: Do nothing
1: import: javafx.util.Pair
Choice:
Imported: javafx.util.Pair

jshell> Pair<Integer, String> pair = new Pair<>(1, "one")
pair ==> 1=one

jshell> /save ~/mysession.jsh

jshell> /ex
|  Goodbye
```

In the previous screenshot, you can see that we have started a JShell session and entered the name of the class Pair (not imported yet), then pressed *Shift + Tab* and *I* and selected option 1 (to import the class Pair). After that, we have finished typing the snippet (created a variable pair), saved the session entries in the file mysession.jsh (in the home directory), and closed the session. Let's look in the file mysession.jsh now:

```
demo> cat ~/mysession.jsh
import javafx.util.Pair;
Pair<Integer, String> pair = new Pair<>(1, "one");
demo>
```

As you can see, the file contains only the new entries from the saved session. If we would like to load them into the next session, we will use the command jshell ~/mysession.jsh and continue working in the same context:

```
demo> jshell ~/mysession.jsh
|  Welcome to JShell -- Version 9
|  For an introduction type: /help intro

jshell> /l

   1 : import javafx.util.Pair;
   2 : Pair<Integer, String> pair = new Pair<>(1, "one");

jshell> pair.getKey()
$3 ==> 1
```

In the previous screenshot, we started a new session, listed all the new entries (reloaded from the previous session), and got a key from the object `pair`. This has created variable `$3` automatically.

We can also create a variable explicitly. Type `pair.getValue()` and press *Shift + Tab* and then press *V*, which will prompt you to enter the variable name just in front of the sign `String = pair.getValue()`. Enter `value` and see the result:

```
jshell> pair.getValue()
jshell> String value = pair.getValue()
value ==> "one"
```

To see all the variables of the current session, type the command `/v`:

```
jshell> /v
|    Pair<Integer, String> pair = 1=one
|    Integer $3 = 1
|    String value = "one"
```

Let's now create a method `to2()` that multiplies any integer by 2:

```
jshell> int to2(int x){
   ...> return x*2;
   ...> }
|  created method to2(int)

jshell> /m
|    int to2(int)
```

To complete the demonstration of the commands `/l`, `/m`, `/t`, and `/v`, let's create a new type:

```
jshell> public class DemoClass {
   ...> private int x;
   ...> public DemoClass(int x) {
   ...> this.x = to2(x);
   ...> }
   ...> public int getX(){return this.x;}
   ...> }
|  created class DemoClass

jshell> /t
|    class DemoClass
```

Notice that the method `to2()` is visible inside a new class, which means that all standalone variables, standalone methods, and code inside classes are executed in the same context. This way, testing of a code fragment becomes easier but may introduce subtle errors and even unexpected behavior if the code's author relies on the encapsulation and behavior isolation in different parts of a more complex system than just a flat code fragment.

Now, by using the `/l` command, we can see everything we have typed:

```
jshell> /l

   1 : import javafx.util.Pair;
   2 : Pair<Integer, String> pair = new Pair<>(1, "one");
   3 : pair.getKey()
   4 : String value = pair.getValue();
   5 : int to2(int x){
       return x*2;
       }
   7 : public class DemoClass {
       private int x;
       public DemoClass(int x) {
       this.x = to2(x);
       }
       public int getX(){return this.x;}
       }
```

All these snippets are available for execution. Here is one example of using them:

```
jshell> new DemoClass(
DemoClass(

jshell> new DemoClass(2
Signatures:
DemoClass(int x)

<press tab again to see all possible completions>

jshell> new DemoClass(2
<press tab again to see documentation>

jshell> new DemoClass(2
DemoClass(int x)
<no documentation found>

jshell> new DemoClass(2)
$7 ==> DemoClass@e45f292
```

In the previous screenshot, we typed `new Demo` and pressed *Tab*. Then, we entered 2 and pressed *Tab* again. We saw the suggestion about pressing *Tab* to see documentation and did it. Well, there was no documentation found (we did not type any JavaDoc while creating the class `DemoClass`), so we just added `)` and pressed *Enter*. As a result, a new variable `$7` was created that held references to the object of the class `DemoClass`. We can use this variable now like this, for example:

```
jshell> int y = $7.
getX()        hashCode()

<press tab again to see all possible completions>

jshell> int y = $7.
equals(         getClass()   getX()        hashCode()   notify()   notifyAll()
toString()      wait(

jshell> int y = $7.getX()
getX()

jshell> int y = $7.getX()
y ==> 4
```

In the previous screenshot, we entered `int y = $7.` and pressed *Tab*, then pressed *Tab* the second time to see other options. We did it just for demo purposes. Then, we made our selection by typing `getX` after `.` and pressing `Tab`. JShell completed the statement with `()` for us and we pressed *Enter*, thus creating a new variable `y` (with the current evaluated value of 4).

Finally, let's try and test the function `substring()` to make sure it returns us the substring we need:

```
jshell> "012345".substring(3)
$13 ==> "345"

jshell> "012345".substring(1, 3)
$14 ==> "12"
```

We hope you now have a feel of how you can create and execute snippets.

Let's review other JShell commands. The command /i lists the imported packages and classes. In our case, if we use this command we will get the following output:

```
jshell> /i
|    import java.io.*
|    import java.math.*
|    import java.net.*
|    import java.nio.file.*
|    import java.util.*
|    import java.util.concurrent.*
|    import java.util.function.*
|    import java.util.prefs.*
|    import java.util.regex.*
|    import java.util.stream.*
|    import javafx.util.Pair
```

You can see that the class Pair is listed as imported, although we have done it in the previous JShell session and brought it in the new session by using the file ~/mysession.jsh.

The command /ed <name or id> allows you to edit any of the entries listed by the command /l. Let's do it:

```
jshell> /l

    1 : import javafx.util.Pair;
    2 : Pair<Integer, String> pair = new Pair<>(1, "one");
    3 : pair.getKey()
    4 : String value = pair.getValue();
    5 : int to2(int x){
        return x*2;
        }
    6 : public class DemoClass {
        private int x;
        public DemoClass(int x) {
        this.x = to2(x);
        }
        public int getX(){return this.x;}
        }
    7 : new DemoClass(2)
    8 : int y = $7.getX();

jshell> /e 7
| Command: '/e' is ambiguous: /edit, /exit, /env
| Type /help for help.

jshell> /ed 7
$9 ==> DemoClass@3f49dace
```

In the previous screenshot, we listed all the snippets and entered /e 7 to edit snippets with ID 7. It turned out that there are several commands starting with e, so we added d and got the following editor window:

In the previous window, we changed 2 to 3 and clicked the **Accept** button. As a result, a new variable $9 was created that holds the reference to the new DemoClass object. We can now use this new variable too:

```
jshell> $9.getX()
getX()

jshell> $9.getX()
$10 ==> 6
```

In the previous screenshot, we entered $9.getX and pressed *Tab*. The JShell completed the statement by adding (). We press *Enter*, and the new variable $10 (with the current evaluated value 6) was created.

The command /d <name or id> drops a snippet referenced by name or ID. Let's use it to delete a snippet with ID 7:

```
jshell> /drop 7
|  dropped variable $7

jshell> /l

   1 : import javafx.util.Pair;
   2 : Pair<Integer, String> pair = new Pair<>(1, "one");
   3 : pair.getKey()
   4 : String value = pair.getValue();
   5 : int to2(int x){
       return x*2;
       }
   6 : public class DemoClass {
       private int x;
       public DemoClass(int x) {
       this.x = to2(x);
       }
       public int getX(){return this.x;}
       }
   8 : int y = $7.getX();
   9 : new DemoClass(3);
  10 : $9.getX()
```

As you could guess, the expression that assigns a value to the variable 8 now cannot be evaluated:

```
jshell> $10
$10 ==> 6

jshell> $8
|  Error:
|  cannot find symbol
|    symbol:   variable $8
|  $8
|  ^^

jshell> /drop y
|  dropped variable y
```

In the earlier screenshot, we first requested to evaluate the expression that generates a value for variable 10 (for demonstration purposes), and it was correctly calculated as 6. Then, we attempted to do the same for variable 8 and received an error because its expression was broken after deleting the variable 7. So, we have deleted it now, too (this time by name, to demonstrate how a name can be used).

The command /sa [-all|-history|-start] <file> saves a snippet to a file. It is complemented by the command /o <file> that opens the file as the source input.

The commands /en, /res, and /rel have an overlapping functionality:

- /en [options]: This allows to view or change the evaluation context
- /res [options]: This discards all entered snippets and restarts the session
- /rel[options]: This reloads the session the same way the command /en does

See the official Oracle documentation (http://docs.oracle.com/javase/9/tools/jshell.htm) for more details and possible options.

The command [/se [setting] sets configuration information, including the external editor, startup settings, and feedback mode. This command is also used to create a custom feedback mode with customized prompt, format, and truncation values. If no setting is entered, then the current setting for the editor, startup settings, and feedback mode are displayed. The documentation referred to earlier describes all possible settings in all details.

The JShell is going to be even more helpful when integrated inside of the IDE so that a programmer can evaluate expressions on the fly or, even better, they can be evaluated automatically the same way the compiler today evaluates the syntax.

Ahead-of-Time (AOT)

The big claim of Java was write-once-run-anywhere. It was achieved by creating an implementation of **Java Runtime Environment (JRE)** for practically all platforms, so the bytecode generated once from the source by Java compiler (`javac` tool) could be executed everywhere where JRE was installed, provided the version of the compiler `javac` was compatible with the version of JRE.

The first releases of JRE were primarily the interpreters of the bytecode and yielded slower performance than some other languages and their compilers, such as C and C++. However, over time, JRE was improved substantially and now produces quite decent results, on a par with many other popular systems. In big part, it is due to the JIT dynamic compiler that converts the bytecodes of the most frequently used methods to the native code. Once generated, the compiled methods (the platform-specific machine code) is executed as needed without any interpretation, thus decreasing the execution time.

To utilize this approach, JRE needs some time for figuring out which methods of the application are used most often . The people working in this area of programming call them hot methods. This period of discovery, until the peak performance is reached, is often called a JVM's warm-up time. It is bigger for the larger and more complex Java applications and can be just a few seconds for smaller ones. However, even after the peak performance is reached, the application might, because of the particular input, start utilizing an execution path never used before and calling the methods that were not compiled yet, thus suddenly degrading the performance. It can be especially consequential when the code not compiled yet belongs to the complex procedures invoked in some rare critical situations, exactly when the best possible performance is needed.

The natural solution was to allow the programmer to decide which components of the application have to be precompiled into the native machine code--those that are more often used (thus decreasing the application's warm-up time), and those that are used not often but have to be executed as quickly as possible (in support of the critical situations and stable performance overall). That was the motivation of the *Java Enhancement Proposal JEP 295: Ahead-of-Time Compilation*:

> *JIT compilers are fast, but Java programs can become so large that it takes a long time for the JIT to warm up completely. Infrequently used Java methods might never be compiled at all, potentially incurring a performance penalty due to repeated interpreted invocations.*

It is worth noticing though that already in JIT compiler, it is possible to decrease the warm-up time by setting the compilation threshold--how many times a method has to be called before it gets compiled into the native code. By default, the number is 1,500. So, if we set it to less than that, the warm-up time will be shorter. It can be done using the option -XX:CompileThreshold with the java tool. For example, we can set the threshold to 500 as follows (where Test is the compiled Java class with the main() method in it):

```
java -XX:CompileThreshold=500 -XX:-TieredCompilation Test
```

The option -XX:-TieredCompilation was added to disable the tiered compilation because it is enabled by default and does not honor the compilation threshold. The possible drawback is that the 500 threshold might be too low and too many methods will be compiled, thus slowing down the performance and increasing the warm-up time. The best value for this option will vary from application to an application and may even depend on the particular data input with the same application.

Static versus dynamic compilation

Many higher level programming languages such as C or C++ used AOT compilation from the very beginning. They are also called *statically compiled* languages. Since AOT (or static) compilers are not constrained by performance requirements (at least not as much as the interpreters at runtime, also called *dynamic compilers*), they can afford to spend the time producing complex code optimizations. On the other hand, the static compilers do not have the runtime (profiling) data, which is especially limiting in the case of dynamically typed languages, Java being one of them. Since the ability of dynamic typing in Java--downcasting to the subtype, querying an object for its type, and other type operations--is one of the pillars of object-oriented programming (principle of polymorphism), AOT compilation for Java becomes even more limited. Lambda expressions pause another challenge for static compilation and are currently not supported yet.

Another advantage of a dynamic compiler is that it can make assumptions and optimize the code accordingly. If the assumption turned out to be wrong, the compiler can try another assumption until the performance goal is achieved. Such a procedure may slow down the application and/or increase the warm-up time, but it may result in a much better performance in the long run. The profile-guided optimization can help a static compiler to move along this path too, but it will always remain limited in its opportunity to optimize by comparison with a dynamic one.

That said, we should not be surprised that the current AOT implementation in JDK 9 is experimental and limited, so far, to 64-bit Linux-based systems only, with either Parallel or G1 garbage collection and the only supported module being `java.base`. Further, AOT compilation should be executed on the same system or a system with the same configuration on which the resulting machine code will be executed. Yet, despite all that, the JEP 295 states:

> *Performance testing shows that some applications benefit from AOT-compiled code, while others clearly show regressions.*

It is worth noting that AOT compilation has been long supported in **Java Micro Edition** (**ME**), but more use cases for AOT in **Java Standard Edition** (**SE**) are yet to be identified, which was one of the reasons the experimental AOT implementation was released with JDK 9-- in order to facilitate the community to try and tell about the practical needs.

The AOT commands and procedures

The underlying AOT compilation in JDK 9 is based on the Oracle project *Graal*--an open source compiler introduced with JDK 8 with a goal of improving the performance of the Java dynamic compiler. The AOT group had to modify it, mostly around constants processing and optimization. They have also added probabilistic profiling and a special inlining policy, thus making Grall more suitable for static compilation.

In addition to the existing compiling tool `javac`, a new `jaotc` tool is included in the JDK 9 installation. The resulting AOT shared libraries `.so` are generated using the `libelf` library--the dependency that is going to be removed in the future releases.

To start AOT compilation, a user has to launch `jaotc` and specify classes, JAR files, or modules that have to be compiled. The name of the output library (that holds the generated machine code) can also be passed as the `jaotc` parameter. If not specified, the default name of the output will be `unnamed.so`. As an example, let's look at how the AOT compiler can work with the class `HelloWorld`:

```
public class HelloWorld {
    public static void main(String... args) {
        System.out.println("Hello, World!");
    }
}
```

First, we will generate the bytecode and produce `HelloWorld.class` using `javac`:

```
javac HelloWorld.java
```

Then, we will use the bytecode from the file `HelloWorld.class` to generate machine code into the library `libHelloWorld.so`:

```
jaotc --output libHelloWorld.so HelloWorld.class
```

Now, we can execute the generated library (on the platform with the same specification as the one where `jaotc` was executed) using the `java` tool with an option `-XX:AOTLibrary`:

```
java -XX:AOTLibrary=./libHelloWorld.so HelloWorld
```

The option `-XX:AOTLibrary` allows us to list several AOT libraries separated by commas.

Notice that the `java` tool requires bytecode of all the applications in addition to the native code of some of its components. This fact diminishes the alleged advantage of static compilation, which some AOT enthusiasts claim, that it protects code better from being decompiled. It might be so in the future when bytecode will not be required at runtime if the same class or method is in the AOT library already. However, as of today, it is not the case.

To see if AOT-compiled methods were used, you can add an option `-XX:+PrintAOT`:

```
java -XX:AOTLibrary=./libHelloWorld.so -XX:+PrintAOT HelloWorld
```

It will allow you to see the line loaded `./libHelloWorld.so` AOT library in the output.

If the source code of a class was changed but not pushed (through the `jaotc` tool) into the AOT library, JVM will notice it at runtime because the fingerprint of each compiled class is stored with its native code in the AOT library. JIT will then ignore the code in the AOT library and use the bytecode instead.

The `java` tool in JDK 9 supports a few other flags and options related to AOT:

- `-XX:+/-UseAOT` tells the JVM to use or to ignore AOT-compiled files (by default, it is set to use AOT)
- `-XX:+/-UseAOTStrictLoading` turns on/off the AOT strict loading; if on, it directs JVM to exit if any of the AOT libraries were generated on a platform with a configuration different from the current runtime configuration

The JEP 295 describes the `jaotc` tool's command format as follows:

```
jaotc <options> <name or list>
```

The `name` is a class name or JAR file. The `list` is a colon : separated list of class names, modules, JAR files, or directories that contain class files. The `options` is one or many flags from the following list:

- `--output <file>`: This is the output file name (by default, `unnamed.so`)
- `--class-name <class names>`: This is the list of Java classes to compile
- `--jar <jar files>`: This is the list of JAR files to compile
- `--module <modules>`: This is the list of Java modules to compile
- `--directory <dirs>`: This is the list of directories where you can search for files to compile
- `--search-path <dirs>`: This is the list of directories where to search for specified files
- `--compile-commands <file>`: This is the name of the file with compile commands; here is an example:

```
exclude
sun.util.resources..*.TimeZoneNames_.*.getContents\(\)\[\[Ljava
/lang/Object;
 exclude sun.security.ssl.*
 compileOnly java.lang.String.*
```

AOT recognizes two compile commands currently:

- `exclude`: This excludes the compilation of specified methods
- `compileOnly`: This compiles only specified methods

Regular expressions are used to specify classes and methods, which are mentioned here:

- `--compile-for-tiered`: This generates profiling code for tiered compilation (by default, profiling code is not generated)
- `--compile-with-assertions`: This generates code with Java assertions (by default, assertions code is not generated)
- `--compile-threads <number>`: This is the number of compilation threads to be used (by default, the smaller value of 16 and number of available CPUs)
- `--ignore-errors`: This ignores all exceptions thrown during class loading (by default, exits on compilation if class loading throws an exception)
- `--exit-on-error`: This exits on compilation errors (by default, failed compilation is skipped, while the compilation of other methods continues)
- `--info`: This prints information about compilation phases
- `--verbose`: This prints more details about compilation phases

- `--debug`: This prints even more details
- `--help`: This prints help information
- `--version`: This prints version information
- `-J<flag>`: This passes a flag directly to the JVM runtime system

As we mentioned already, some applications can improve performance using AOT, while others may become slower. Only testing will provide a definite answer to the question about the usefulness of AOT for each application. In any case, one of the ways to improve performance is to compile and use the AOT library of the `java.base` module:

```
jaotc --output libjava.base.so --module java.base
```

At runtime, the AOT initialization code looks for shared libraries in the `$JAVA_HOME/lib` directory or among the libraries listed by the `-XX:AOTLibrary` option. If shared libraries are found, they are picked up and used. If no shared libraries can be found, AOT will be turned off.

Summary

In this chapter, we described two new tools that can help a developer be more productive (JShell tool) and help improve Java application performance (`jaotc` tool). The examples and steps to use them will help you understand the benefits of their usage and get you started in case you decide to try them.

In the next chapter, we will discuss how to monitor Java applications programmatically using command-line tools. We will also explore how to improve the application performance via multithreading and how to tune the JVM itself after learning about the bottlenecks through monitoring.

9
Multithreading and Reactive Programming

In the previous chapter, we have described the Ahead-of-Time compiler of JDK 9 as one of the tools that can help to improve the performance of a Java application. In this chapter, we will look at another approach to support a high performance of an application by programmatically splitting the task between several workers. That was how the pyramids were built 4,500 years ago, and this method has not failed to deliver since then. But there is a limitation on how many laborers can be brought to work on the same project. The shared resources provide a ceiling to how much the workforce can be increased, whether the resources are counted in square feet and gallons (as the living quarters and water in the time of the pyramids) or in gigabytes and gigahertz (as the memory and processing power of a computer).

Allocation, usage, and limitations of a living space and computer memory are very similar. However, we perceive the processing power of the human workforce and CPU quite differently. Historians tell us that thousands of ancient Egyptians worked on cutting and moving massive stone blocks at the same time. We do not have any problem understanding what they mean even if we know that these workers rotated all the time, some of them resting or attending to other matters temporarily and then coming back to replace the ones who have finished their annual assignment, others died or got injured and were replaced by the new recruits.

But in case of computer data processing, when we hear about working threads executing at the same time, we automatically assume that they literally do what they are programmed to do in parallel. Only after we look under the hood of such a system we realize that such parallel processing is possible only when the threads are executed each by a different CPU. Otherwise, they time share the same processing power, and we perceive them working at the same time only because the time slots they use are very short--a fraction of the time units we have used in our everyday life. When the threads share the same resource, in computer science we say they do it *concurrently*.

In this chapter, we will discuss the ways to increase Java application performance by using the workers (threads) that process data concurrently. We will show how to use threads effectively by pooling them, how to synchronize the concurrently accessed data, how to monitor and tune worker threads at runtime, and how to take advantage of the reactive programming concept.

But before doing that, let's revisit the basics of creating and running multiple threads in the same Java process.

Prerequisites

There are principally two ways to create worker threads--by extending the `java.lang.Thread` class and by implementing the `java.lang.Runnable` interface. While extending the `java.lang.Thread` class, we are not required to implement anything:

```
class MyThread extends Thread {
}
```

Our `MyThread` class inherits the `name` property with an automatically generated value and the `start()` method. We can run this method and check the `name`:

```
System.out.print("demo_thread_01(): ");
MyThread t1 = new MyThread();
t1.start();
System.out.println("Thread name=" + t1.getName());
```

If we run this code, the result will be as follows:

```
demo_thread_01(): Thread name=Thread-0
```

As you can see, the generated name is Thread-0. If we created another thread in the same Java process, the name would be Thread-1 and so on. The start() method does nothing. The source code shows that it calls the run() method if such a method is implemented.

We can add any other method to the MyThread class as follows:

```
class MyThread extends Thread {
    private double result;
    public MyThread(String name){ super(name); }
    public void calculateAverageSqrt(){
        result =  IntStream.rangeClosed(1, 99999)
                            .asDoubleStream()
                            .map(Math::sqrt)
                            .average()
                            .getAsDouble();
    }
    public double getResult(){ return this.result; }
}
```

The calculateAverageSqrt() method calculates the average square root of the first 99,999 integers and assigns the result to a property that can be accessed anytime. The following code demonstrates how we can use it:

```
System.out.print("demo_thread_02(): ");
MyThread t1 = new MyThread("Thread01");
t1.calculateAverageSqrt();
System.out.println(t1.getName() + ": result=" + t1.getResult());
```

Running this brings up the following result:

```
demo_thread_02(): Thread01: result=210.81798155929968
```

As you would expect, the calculateAverageSqrt() method blocks until the calculations are completed. It was executed in the main thread without it taking advantage of multithreading. To do this, we move the functionality in the run() method:

```
class MyThread01 extends Thread {
    private double result;
    public MyThread01(String name){ super(name); }
    public void run(){
        result =  IntStream.rangeClosed(1, 99999)
                            .asDoubleStream()
                            .map(Math::sqrt)
                            .average()
                            .getAsDouble();
```

```
    }
    public double getResult(){ return this.result; }
}
```

Now we call the `start()` method again, as in the first example and expect the result to be calculated:

```
System.out.print("demo_thread_03(): ");
MyThread01 t1 = new MyThread01("Thread01");
t1.start();
System.out.println(t1.getName() + ": result=" + t1.getResult());
```

However, the output of this code may surprise you:

```
demo_thread_03(): Thread01: result=0.0
```

This means that the main thread accessed (and printed) the `t1.getResult()` function before the new `t1` thread finished its calculations. We can experiment and change the implementation of the `run()` method to see if the `t1.getResult()` function can get a partial result:

```
public void run() {
    for (int i = 1; i < 100000; i++) {
        double s = Math.sqrt(1. * i);
        result = result + s;
    }
    result = result / 99999;
}
```

However, if we run the `demo_thread_03()` method again, the result remains the same:

```
demo_thread_03(): Thread01: result=0.0
```

It takes time to create a new thread and get it going. Meanwhile, the `main` thread calls the `t1.getResult()` function immediately, thus getting no results yet.

To give the new (child) thread time to complete the calculations, we add the following code:

```
try {
    t1.join();
} catch (InterruptedException e) {
    e.printStackTrace();
}
```

The `join()` method tells the current thread to wait until the `t1` thread is finished executing. Let's run the following snippet of code:

```
System.out.print("demo_thread_04(): ");
MyThread01 t1 = new MyThread01("Thread01");
t1.start();
try {
    t1.join();
} catch (InterruptedException e) {
    e.printStackTrace();
}
System.out.println(t1.getName()
            + ": result=" + t1.getResult());
System.out.println("Thread name="
        + Thread.currentThread().getName());
```

You have noticed that we have paused the main thread by 100 ms and added printing of the current thread name, to illustrate what we mean by `main` thread, the name that is assigned automatically to the thread that executes the `main()` method. The output of the previous code is as follows:

```
demo_thread_04(): Thread01: result=210.81903565187375
Thread name=main
```

The delay of 100 ms was enough for the `t1` thread to finish the calculations. That was the first of two ways of creating threads for multithreaded calculation. The second way is to implement the `Runnable` interface. It may be the only way possible if the class that does calculations already extends some other class and you cannot or don't want to use composition for some reasons. The `Runnable` interface is a functional interface (has only one abstract method) with the `run()` method that has to be implemented:

```
@FunctionalInterface
public interface Runnable {
    /**
     * When an object implementing interface <code>Runnable</code> is used
     * to create a thread, starting the thread causes the object's
     * <code>run</code> method to be called in that separately executing
```

```
    * thread.
    */
    public abstract void run();
```

We implement this interface in the MyRunnable class:

```
class MyRunnable01 implements Runnable {
    private String id;
    private double result;
    public MyRunnable01(int id) {
        this.id = String.valueOf(id);
    }
    public String getId() { return this.id; }
    public double getResult() { return this.result; }
    public void run() {
        result = IntStream.rangeClosed(1, 99999)
                        .asDoubleStream()
                        .map(Math::sqrt)
                        .average()
                        .getAsDouble();

    }
}
```

It has the same functionality as the Thread01 class earlier plus we have added id that allows identifying the thread if necessary since the Runnable interface does not have the built-in getName() method like the Thread class has.

Similarly, if we execute this class without pausing the main thread, like this:

```
System.out.print("demo_runnable_01(): ");
MyRunnable01 myRunnable = new MyRunnable01(1);
Thread t1 = new Thread(myRunnable);
t1.start();
System.out.println("Worker " + myRunnable.getId()
            + ": result=" + myRunnable.getResult());
```

The output will be as follows:

```
demo_runnable_01(): Worker 1: result=0.0
```

We will now add the pause as follows:

```
System.out.print("demo_runnable_02(): ");
MyRunnable01 myRunnable = new MyRunnable01(1);
Thread t1 = new Thread(myRunnable);
t1.start();
try {
    t1.join();
} catch (InterruptedException e) {
    e.printStackTrace();
}
System.out.println("Worker " + myRunnable.getId()
            + ": result=" + myRunnable.getResult());
```

The result is exactly the same as the one produced by the `Thread01` class:

```
demo_runnable_02(): Worker 1: result=210.81903565187375
```

All the previous examples stored the generated result in the class property. But it is not always the case. Typically, the worker thread either passes its value to another thread or stores it in a database or somewhere else externally. In such a case, one can take advantage of the `Runnable` interface being a functional interface and pass the necessary processing function into a new thread as a lambda expression:

```
System.out.print("demo_lambda_01(): ");
String id = "1";
Thread t1 =
    new Thread(() -> IntStream.rangeClosed(1, 99999)
            .asDoubleStream().map(Math::sqrt).average()
            .ifPresent(d -> System.out.println("Worker "
                        + id + ": result=" + d)));
t1.start();
try {
    t1.join();
} catch (InterruptedException e) {
    e.printStackTrace();
}
```

The result is going to be exactly the same, as shown here:

```
demo_lambda_01(): Worker 1: result=210.81903565187375
```

Depending on the preferred style, you can re-arrange the code and isolate the lambda expression in a variable, as follows:

```
Runnable r = () -> IntStream.rangeClosed(1, 99999)
        .asDoubleStream().map(Math::sqrt).average()
    .ifPresent(d -> System.out.println("Worker "
                        + id + ": result=" + d));
Thread t1 = new Thread(r);
```

Alternatively, you can put the lambda expression in a separate method:

```
void calculateAverage(String id) {
    IntStream.rangeClosed(1, 99999)
        .asDoubleStream().map(Math::sqrt).average()
    .ifPresent(d -> System.out.println("Worker "
                        + id + ": result=" + d));
}
void demo_lambda_03() {
    System.out.print("demo_lambda_03(): ");
    Thread t1 = new Thread(() -> calculateAverage("1"));
    ...
}
```

The result is going to be the same, as shown here:

```
demo_lambda_03(): Worker 1: result=210.81903565187375
```

With the basic understanding of threads creation in place, we can now return to the discussion about using the multithreading for building a high-performance application. In other words, after we understand the abilities and resources needed for each worker, we can now talk about logistics of bringing in many of them for such a big-scale project as the Great Pyramid of Giza.

To write code that manages the life cycle of worker threads and their access to the shared resources is possible, but it is quite the same from one application to another. That's why, after several releases of Java, the thread management plumbing became part of the standard JDK library as the `java.util.concurrent` package. This package has a wealth of interfaces and classes that support multithreading and concurrency. We will discuss how to use most of this functionality in the subsequent sections, while talking about thread pools, threads monitoring, thread synchronization, and the related subjects.

Thread pools

In this section, we will look into the `Executor` interfaces and their implementations provided in the `java.util.concurrent` package. They encapsulate thread management and minimize the time an application developer spends on the writing code related to threads' life cycles.

There are three `Executor` interfaces defined in the `java.util.concurrent` package:

- The base `Executor` interface has only one `void execute(Runnable r)` method in it. It basically replaces the following:

      ```
      Runnable r = ...;
      (new Thread(r)).start()
      ```

  However, we can also avoid a new thread creation by getting it from a pool.

- The `ExecutorService` interface extends `Executor` and adds four groups of methods that manage the life cycle of the worker threads and of the executor itself:
- Methods `submit()`: Place in the queue for the execution of an object of the interface `Runnable` or interface `Callable` (allows the worker thread to return a value); return object of `Future` interface, which can be used to access the value returned by the `Callable` and to manage the status of the worker thread
- Methods `invokeAll()`: Place in the queue for the execution of a collection of interface `Callable` objects return, list of `Future` objects when all the worker threads are complete (there is also an overloaded `invokeAll()` method with timeout)
- Methods `invokeAny()`: Place in the queue for the execution of a collection of interface `Callable` objects; return one `Future` object of any of the worker threads, which has completed (there is also an overloaded `invokeAny()` method with timeout);
- Methods that manage the worker threads status and the service itself:
    - `shutdown()`: This prevents new worker threads from being submitted to the service
    - `isShutdown()`: This checks whether the shutdown of the executor was initiated

- `awaitTermination(long timeout, TimeUnit timeUnit)`: This waits until all worker threads have completed execution after a shutdown request, or the timeout occurs, or the current thread is interrupted, whichever happens first
- `isTerminated()`: This checks whether all the worker threads have completed after the shutdown was initiated; it never returns `true` unless either `shutdown()` or `shutdownNow()` was called first
- `shutdownNow()`: This interrupts each worker thread that is not completed; a worker thread should be written so that it checks its own status (using `Thread.currentThread().isInterrupted()`, for example) periodically and gracefully shuts down on its own; otherwise, it will continue running even after `shutdownNow()` was called.

- The `ScheduledExecutorService` interface extends `ExecutorService` and adds methods that allow scheduling of the execution (one-time and periodic one) of the worker threads.

A pool-based implementation of `ExecutorService` can be created using the `java.util.concurrent.ThreadPoolExecutor` or `java.util.concurrent.ScheduledThreadPoolExecutor` class. There is also a `java.util.concurrent.Executors` factory class that covers most of the practical cases. So, before writing a custom code for worker threads pool creation, we highly recommend looking into using the following factory methods of the `java.util.concurrent.Executors` class:

- `newSingleThreadExecutor()`: This creates an `ExecutorService` (pool) instance that executes worker threads sequentially
- `newFixedThreadPool()`: This creates a thread pool that reuses a fixed number of worker threads; if a new task is submitted when all the worker threads are still executing, it will be set into the queue until a worker thread is available
- `newCachedThreadPool()`: This creates a thread pool that adds a new thread as needed, unless there is an idle thread created before; threads that have been idle for sixty seconds are removed from the cache
- `newScheduledThreadPool()`: This creates a thread pool of a fixed size that can schedule commands to run after a given delay, or to execute periodically
- `newSingleThreadScheduledExecutor()`: This creates a single-threaded executor that can schedule commands to run after a given delay, or to execute periodically

- `newWorkStealingThreadPool()`: This creates a thread pool that uses the same work-stealing mechanism used by `ForkJoinPool`, which is particularly useful in case the worker threads generate other threads, such as in recursive algorithms

Each of these methods has an overloaded version that allows passing in a `ThreadFactory` that is used to create a new thread when needed. Let's see how it all works in a code sample.

First, we create a `MyRunnable02` class that implements `Runnable`--our future worker threads:

```
class MyRunnable02 implements Runnable {
    private String id;
    public MyRunnable02(int id) {
        this.id = String.valueOf(id);
    }
    public String getId(){ return this.id; }
    public void run() {
        double result = IntStream.rangeClosed(1, 100)
            .flatMap(i -> IntStream.rangeClosed(1, 99999))
            .takeWhile(i ->
                !Thread.currentThread().isInterrupted())
            .asDoubleStream()
            .map(Math::sqrt)
            .average()
            .getAsDouble();
        if(Thread.currentThread().isInterrupted()){
            System.out.println(" Worker " + getId()
                        + ": result=ignored: " + result);
        } else {
            System.out.println(" Worker " + getId()
                            + ": result=" + result);
        }
    }
}
```

Notice the important difference of this implementation from the previous examples--the `takeWhile(i -> !Thread.currentThread().isInterrupted())` operation allows the stream flowing as long as the thread worker status is not set to interrupted, which happens when the `shutdownNow()` method is called. As soon as the predicate of the `takeWhile()` returns `false` (the worker thread is interrupted), the thread stops producing the result (just ignores the current `result` value). In a real system, it would equate to skipping storing `result` value in the database, for example.

It is worth noting here that using the `interrupted()` status method for checking the thread status in the preceding code may lead to inconsistent results. Since the `interrupted()` method returns the correct state value and then clears the thread state, the second call to this method (or the call to the method `isInterrupted()` after the call to the method `interrupted()`) always returns `false`.

Although it is not the case in this code, we would like to mention here a mistake some developers make while implementing `try`/`catch` block in a worker thread. For example, if the worker needs to pause and wait for an interrupt signal, the code often looks like this:

```
try {
    Thread.currentThread().wait();
} catch (InterruptedException e) {}
// Do what has to be done
```

The problem with the preceding snippet is that the thread status never becomes interrupted, while the higher level code might be monitoring the worker thread and changes behavior depending on whether the worker has been interrupted or not.

The better implementation is as follows:

```
try {
    Thread.currentThread().wait();
} catch (InterruptedException e) {
    Thread.currentThread().interrupt();
}
// Do what has to be done
```

This way the status *interrupted* is set on the thread and can be checked later by the `isInterrupted()` method. To be fair, in many applications, once the thread is interrupted, its code is not checked again. But setting the correct state is a good practice, especially in the cases when you are not the author of the client code.

In the snippet of code with the `join()` method, we did not need to do that because that was the main code (the highest level code) that had to be paused.

Now we can show how to execute the earlier `MyRunnable02` class with a cached pool implementation of the `ExecutiveService` pool (other types of thread pool are used similarly). First, we create the pool, submit three instances of the `MyRunnable02` class for execution and shut down the pool:

```
ExecutorService pool = Executors.newCachedThreadPool();
IntStream.rangeClosed(1, 3).
        forEach(i -> pool.execute(new MyRunnable02(i)));
System.out.println("Before shutdown: isShutdown()="
```

```
            + pool.isShutdown() + ", isTerminated()="
                            + pool.isTerminated());
pool.shutdown(); // New threads cannot be submitted
System.out.println("After  shutdown: isShutdown()="
        + pool.isShutdown() + ", isTerminated()="
                            + pool.isTerminated());
```

If we run these lines, we will see the following output:

```
Before shutdown: isShutdown()=false, isTerminated()=false
After   shutdown: isShutdown()=true, isTerminated()=false
```

No surprises here! The isShutdown() method returns a false value before the
shutdown() method is called and a true value afterward. The isTerminated() method
returns a false value, because none of the worker threads has completed yet.

Let's test the shutdown() method by adding the following code after it:

```
try {
    pool.execute(new MyRunnable02(100));
} catch(RejectedExecutionException ex){
    System.err.println("Cannot add another worker-thread to the service
queue:\n" + ex.getMessage());
}
```

The output will now have the following message (the screenshot would be either too big for
this page or not readable when fitting):

```
Cannot add another worker-thread to the service queue:
Task com.packt.java9hp.ch09_threads.MyRunnable02@6f7fd0e6
    rejected from java.util.concurrent.ThreadPoolExecutor
    [Shutting down, pool size = 3, active threads = 3,
    queued tasks = 0, completed tasks = 0]
```

As expected, after the shutdown() method is called, no more worker threads can be added
to the pool.

Now, let's see what can we do after the shutdown was initiated:

```
long timeout = 100;
TimeUnit timeUnit = TimeUnit.MILLISECONDS;
System.out.println("Waiting for all threads completion "
                + timeout + " " + timeUnit + "...");
// Blocks until timeout or all threads complete execution
boolean isTerminated =
                pool.awaitTermination(timeout, timeUnit);
```

```
System.out.println("isTerminated()=" + isTerminated);
if (!isTerminated) {
    System.out.println("Calling shutdownNow()...");
    List<Runnable> list = pool.shutdownNow();
    printRunningThreadIds(list);
    System.out.println("Waiting for threads completion "
                    + timeout + " " + timeUnit + "...");
    isTerminated =
                pool.awaitTermination(timeout, timeUnit);
    if (!isTerminated){
        System.out.println("Some threads are running...");
    }
    System.out.println("Exiting.");
}
```

The `printRunningThreadIds()` method looks like this:

```
void printRunningThreadIds(List<Runnable> l){
    String list = l.stream()
            .map(r -> (MyRunnable02)r)
            .map(mr -> mr.getId())
            .collect(Collectors.joining(","));
    System.out.println(l.size() + " thread"
        + (l.size() == 1 ? " is" : "s are") + " running"
            + (l.size() > 0 ? ": " + list : "") + ".");
}
```

The output of the preceding code will be as follows:

```
Waiting for all threads completion 100 MILLISECONDS...
    Worker 1: result=210.81903565187375
    Worker 2: result=210.81903565187375
    Worker 3: result=210.81903565187375
isTerminated()=true
```

This means that 100 ms was enough for each worker thread to complete the calculations. (Notice, if you try to reproduce this data on your computer, the results might be slightly different because of the difference in performance, so you would need to adjust the timeout.)

When we have decreased the wait time to 75 ms, the output became as follows:

```
Waiting for all threads completion 75 MILLISECONDS...
isTerminated()=false
Calling shutdownNow()...
    Worker 1: result=ignored: 210.50563195472404
    Worker 3: result=ignored: 210.48567155912065
    Worker 2: result=ignored: 210.52551215481083
0 threads are running.
Waiting for threads completion 75 MILLISECONDS...
Exiting.
```

The 75 ms on our computer was not enough to let all the threads complete, so they were interrupted by `shutdownNow()` and their partial results were ignored.

Let's now remove the check of the interrupted status in the `MyRunnable01` class:

```java
class MyRunnable02 implements Runnable {
    private String id;
    public MyRunnable02(int id) {
        this.id = String.valueOf(id);
    }
    public String getId(){ return this.id; }
    public void run() {
        double result = IntStream.rangeClosed(1, 100)
            .flatMap(i -> IntStream.rangeClosed(1, 99999))
            .asDoubleStream()
            .map(Math::sqrt)
            .average()
            .getAsDouble();
        System.out.println(" Worker " + getId()
                                + ": result=" + result);
    }
}
```

Without the check, even if we decrease the timeout to 1 ms, the result will be as follows:

```
Waiting for all threads completion 1 MILLISECONDS...
isTerminated()=false
Calling shutdownNow()...
0 threads are running.
Waiting for threads completion 1 MILLISECONDS...
Some threads running...
Exiting.

    Worker 2: result=210.81903565187375
    Worker 3: result=210.81903565187375
    Worker 1: result=210.81903565187375
```

That is because the worker threads have never noticed that somebody tried to interrupt them and completed their assigned calculations. This last test demonstrates the importance of watching for the interrupted state in a work thread in order to avoid many possible problems, namely, data corruption and memory leak.

The demonstrated cached pool works fine and poses no problem if the worker threads perform short tasks and their number cannot grow excessively large. If you need to have more control over the max number of worker threads running at any time, use the fixed size thread pool. We will discuss how to choose the pool size in one of the following sections of this chapter.

The single-thread pool is a good fit for executing tasks in a certain order or in the case when each of them requires so many resources that cannot be executed in parallel with another. Yet another case for using a single-thread execution would be for workers that modify the same data, but the data cannot be protected from the parallel access another way. The thread synchronization will be discussed in more detail in one of the following sections of this chapter, too.

In our sample code, so far we have only included the `execute()` method of the `Executor` interface. We will demonstrate the other methods of the `ExecutorService` pool in the following section while discussing threads monitoring.

And the last remark in this section. The worker threads are not required to be objects of the same class. They may represent completely different functionality and still be managed by one pool.

Monitoring threads

There are two ways to monitor threads, programmatically and using the external tools. We have already seen how the result of a worker calculation could be checked. Let's revisit that code. We will also slightly modify our worker implementation:

```java
class MyRunnable03 implements Runnable {
  private String name;
  private double result;
  public String getName(){ return this.name; }
  public double getResult() { return this.result; }
  public void run() {
    this.name = Thread.currentThread().getName();
    double result = IntStream.rangeClosed(1, 100)
      .flatMap(i -> IntStream.rangeClosed(1, 99999))
      .takeWhile(i -> !Thread.currentThread().isInterrupted())
      .asDoubleStream().map(Math::sqrt).average().getAsDouble();
```

```
        if(!Thread.currentThread().isInterrupted()){
          this.result = result;
        }
      }
    }
  }
```

For the worker thread identification, instead of custom ID, we now use the thread name assigned automatically at the time of the execution (that is why we assign the `name` property in the `run()` method that is called in the context of the execution when the thread acquires its name). The new class `MyRunnable03` can be used like this:

```
void demo_CheckResults() {
    ExecutorService pool = Executors.newCachedThreadPool();
    MyRunnable03 r1 = new MyRunnable03();
    MyRunnable03 r2 = new MyRunnable03();
    pool.execute(r1);
    pool.execute(r2);
    try {
        t1.join();
    } catch (InterruptedException e) {
        e.printStackTrace();
    }
    System.out.println("Worker " + r1.getName() + ": result=" +
r1.getResult());
    System.out.println("Worker " + r2.getName() + ": result=" +
r2.getResult());
    shutdown(pool);
}
```

The `shutdown()` method contains the following code:

```
void shutdown(ExecutorService pool) {
    pool.shutdown();
    try {
        if(!pool.awaitTermination(1, TimeUnit.SECONDS)){
            pool.shutdownNow();
        }
    } catch (InterruptedException ie) {}
}
```

If we run the preceding code, the output will be as follows:

```
Worker pool-1-thread-1: result=210.81903565187375
Worker pool-1-thread-2: result=210.81903565187375
```

If the result on your computer is different, try to increase the input value to the `sleepMs()` method.

Another way to get information about the application worker threads is by using the `Future` interface. We can access this interface using the `submit()` method of the `ExecutorService` pool, instead of the `execute()`, `invokeAll()`, or `invokeAny()` methods. This code shows how to use the `submit()` method:

```
ExecutorService pool = Executors.newCachedThreadPool();
Future f1 = pool.submit(new MyRunnable03());
Future f2 = pool.submit(new MyRunnable03());
printFuture(f1, 1);
printFuture(f2, 2);
shutdown(pool);
```

The `printFuture()` method has the following implementation:

```
void printFuture(Future future, int id) {
    System.out.println("printFuture():");
    while (!future.isCancelled() && !future.isDone()){
        System.out.println("    Waiting for worker "
                                    + id + " to complete...");
        sleepMs(10);
    }
    System.out.println("    Done...");
}
```

The `sleepMs()` method contains the following code:

```
void sleepMs(int sleepMs) {
    try {
        TimeUnit.MILLISECONDS.sleep(sleepMs);
    } catch (InterruptedException e) {}
}
```

We prefer this implementation instead of the traditional `Thread.sleep()` because it is explicit about the time units used.

If we execute the previous code, the result will be similar to the following:

```
printFuture():
    Waiting for worker 1 to complete...
    Waiting for worker 1 to complete...
    Waiting for worker 1 to complete...
    Waiting for worker 1 to complete...
    Waiting for worker 1 to complete...
    Waiting for worker 1 to complete...
    Waiting for worker 1 to complete...
    Waiting for worker 1 to complete...
    Waiting for worker 1 to complete...
    Waiting for worker 1 to complete...
    Done...
printFuture():
    Done...
```

The `printFuture()` method has blocked the main thread execution until the first thread has completed. Meanwhile, the second thread has completed too. If we call the `printFuture()` method after the `shutdown()` method, both the threads would complete by that time already because we have set a wait time of 1 second (see the `pool.awaitTermination()` method), which is enough for them to finish their job:

```
printFuture():
    Done...
printFuture():
    Done...
```

If you think it is not much information from a threads monitoring point of view, the `java.util.concurrent` package provides more capabilities via the `Callable` interface. It is a functional interface that allows returning any object (containing results of the worker thread calculations) via the `Future` object using `ExecutiveService` methods--`submit()`, `invokeAll()`, and `invokeAny()`. For example, we can create a class that contains the result of a worker thread:

```
class Result {
    private double result;
    private String workerName;
    public Result(String workerName, double result) {
        this.result = result;
        this.workerName = workerName;
    }
    public String getWorkerName() { return workerName; }
    public double getResult() { return result; }
}
```

We have included the name of the worker thread too for monitoring which thread generated the result that is presented. The class that implements the `Callable` interface may look like this:

```
class MyCallable01<T> implements Callable {
  public Result call() {
    double result = IntStream.rangeClosed(1, 100)
      .flatMap(i -> IntStream.rangeClosed(1, 99999))
      .takeWhile(i -> !Thread.currentThread().isInterrupted())
      .asDoubleStream().map(Math::sqrt).average().getAsDouble();
    String workerName = Thread.currentThread().getName();
    if(Thread.currentThread().isInterrupted()){
      return new Result(workerName, 0);
    } else {
      return new Result(workerName, result);
    }
  }
}
```

And here is the code that uses the `MyCallable01` class:

```
ExecutorService pool = Executors.newCachedThreadPool();
Future f1 = pool.submit(new MyCallable01<Result>());
Future f2 = pool.submit(new MyCallable01<Result>());
printResult(f1, 1);
printResult(f2, 2);
shutdown(pool);
```

The `printResult()` method contains the following code:

```
void printResult(Future<Result> future, int id) {
    System.out.println("printResult():");
    while (!future.isCancelled() && !future.isDone()){
        System.out.println("   Waiting for worker "
                            + id + " to complete...");
        sleepMs(10);
    }
    try {
        Result result = future.get(1, TimeUnit.SECONDS);
        System.out.println("   Worker "
                + result.getWorkerName() + ": result = "
                            + result.getResult());
    } catch (Exception ex) {
        ex.printStackTrace();
    }
}
```

The output of this code may look like this:

```
printResult():
    Waiting for worker 1 to complete...
    Waiting for worker 1 to complete...
    Waiting for worker 1 to complete...
    Waiting for worker 1 to complete...
    Waiting for worker 1 to complete...
    Waiting for worker 1 to complete...
    Waiting for worker 1 to complete...
    Waiting for worker 1 to complete...
    Waiting for worker 1 to complete...
    Waiting for worker 1 to complete...
    Waiting for worker 1 to complete...
    Worker pool-1-thread-1: result = 210.81903565187375
printResult():
    Worker pool-1-thread-2: result = 210.81903565187375
```

The earlier output shows, as in the previous examples, that the printResult() method waits until the first of the worker threads finishes, so the second thread manages to finish its job at the same time. The advantage of using Callable, as you can see, is that we can retrieve the actual result from a Future object, if we need it.

The usage of the invokeAll() and invokeAny() methods looks similar:

```
ExecutorService pool = Executors.newCachedThreadPool();
try {
    List<Callable<Result>> callables =
            List.of(new MyCallable01<Result>(),
                        new MyCallable01<Result>());
    List<Future<Result>> futures =
                        pool.invokeAll(callables);
    printResults(futures);
} catch (InterruptedException e) {
    e.printStackTrace();
}
shutdown(pool);
```

The `printResults()` method is using the `printResult()` method, which you already know:

```
void printResults(List<Future<Result>> futures) {
    System.out.println("printResults():");
    int i = 1;
    for (Future<Result> future : futures) {
        printResult(future, i++);
    }
}
```

If we run the preceding code, the output will be as follows:

```
printResults():
printResult():
    Worker pool-1-thread-1: result = 210.81903565187375
printResult():
    Worker pool-1-thread-2: result = 210.81903565187375
```

As you can see, there is no more waiting for the worker thread completing the job. That is so because the `invokeAll()` method returns the collection of the `Future` object after all the jobs have completed.

The `invokeAny()` method behaves similarly. If we run the following code:

```
System.out.println("demo_InvokeAny():");
ExecutorService pool = Executors.newCachedThreadPool();
try {
    List<Callable<Result>> callables =
                    List.of(new MyCallable01<Result>(),
                            new MyCallable01<Result>());
    Result result = pool.invokeAny(callables);
    System.out.println("    Worker "
                    + result.getWorkerName()
                + ": result = " + result.getResult());
} catch (InterruptedException | ExecutionException e) {
    e.printStackTrace();
}
shutdown(pool);
```

The following will be the output:

```
demo_InvokeAny():
    Worker pool-1-thread-2: result = 210.81903565187375
```

These are the basic techniques for monitoring the threads programmatically, but one can easily extend our examples to cover more complicated cases tailored to the needs of a specific application. In Chapter 11, *Making Use of New APIs to Improve Your Code*, we will also discuss another way to programmatically monitor worker threads using the `java.util.concurrent.CompletableFuture` class introduced in JDK 8 and extended in JDK 9.

If necessary, it is possible to get information not only about the application worker threads, but also about all other threads in the JVM process using the `java.lang.Thread` class:

```java
void printAllThreads() {
    System.out.println("printAllThreads():");
    Map<Thread, StackTraceElement[]> map = Thread.getAllStackTraces();
    for(Thread t: map.keySet()){
        System.out.println("    " + t);
    }
}
```

Now, let's call this method as follows:

```java
void demo_CheckResults() {
    ExecutorService pool = Executors.newCachedThreadPool();
    MyRunnable03 r1 = new MyRunnable03();
    MyRunnable03 r2 = new MyRunnable03();
    pool.execute(r1);
    pool.execute(r2);
    sleepMs(1000);
    printAllThreads();
    shutdown(pool);
}
```

The result looks like this:

```
printAllThreads():
    Thread[Signal Dispatcher,9,system]
    Thread[pool-1-thread-2,5,main]
    Thread[Monitor Ctrl-Break,5,main]
    Thread[Common-Cleaner,8,InnocuousThreadGroup]
    Thread[main,5,main]
    Thread[pool-1-thread-1,5,main]
    Thread[Finalizer,8,system]
    Thread[Reference Handler,10,system]
```

We took advantage of the `toString()` method of the `Thread` class that prints only the thread name, priority, and the thread group it belongs to. And we see the two application threads we have created explicitly (in addition to the `main` thread) in the list under the names `pool-1-thread-1` and `pool-1-thread-2`. But if we call the `printAllThreads()` method after calling the `shutdown()` method, the output will be as follows:

```
printAllThreads():
    Thread[Monitor Ctrl-Break,5,main]
    Thread[Reference Handler,10,system]
    Thread[Finalizer,8,system]
    Thread[Common-Cleaner,8,InnocuousThreadGroup]
    Thread[Signal Dispatcher,9,system]
    Thread[main,5,main]
```

We do not see the `pool-1-thread-1` and `pool-1-thread-2` threads in the list anymore because the `ExecutorService` pool has been shut down.

We could easily add the stack trace information pulled from the same map:

```java
void printAllThreads() {
    System.out.println("printAllThreads():");
    Map<Thread, StackTraceElement[]> map
                        = Thread.getAllStackTraces();
    for(Thread t: map.keySet()){
        System.out.println("   " + t);
        for(StackTraceElement ste: map.get(t)){
            System.out.println("        " + ste);
        }
    }
}
```

However, that would take too much space on the book page. In Chapter 11, *Making Use of New APIs to Improve Your Code* while presenting new Java capabilities that came with JDK 9, we will also discuss a better way to access a stack trace via the `java.lang.StackWalker` class.

The `Thread` class object has several other methods that provide information about the thread, which are as follows:

- `dumpStack()`: This prints a stack trace to the standard error stream
- `enumerate(Thread[] arr)`: This copies active threads in the current thread's thread group and its subgroups into the specified array `arr`
- `getId()`: This provides the thread's ID

- getState(): This reads the state of the thread; the possible values from enum Thread.State can be one of the following:
    - NEW: This is the thread that has not yet started
    - RUNNABLE: This is the thread that is currently being executed
    - BLOCKED: This is the thread that is blocked waiting for a monitor lock to be released
    - WAITING: This is the thread that is waiting for an interrupt signal
    - TIMED_WAITING: This is the thread that is waiting for an interrupt signal up to a specified waiting time
    - TERMINATED: This is the thread that has exited
- holdsLock(Object obj): This indicates whether the thread holds the monitor lock on the specified object
- interrupted() or isInterrupted(): This indicates whether the thread has been interrupted (received an interrupt signal, meaning that the flag interrupted was set to true)
- isAlive(): This indicates whether the thread is alive
- isDaemon(): This indicates whether the thread is a daemon thread.

The java.lang.management package provides similar capabilities for monitoring threads. Let's run this code snippet, for example:

```
void printThreadsInfo() {
    System.out.println("printThreadsInfo():");
    ThreadMXBean threadBean =
                    ManagementFactory.getThreadMXBean();
    long ids[] = threadBean.getAllThreadIds();
    Arrays.sort(ids);
    ThreadInfo[] tis = threadBean.getThreadInfo(ids, 0);
    for (ThreadInfo ti : tis) {
        if (ti == null) continue;
        System.out.println("    Id=" + ti.getThreadId()
                    + ", state=" + ti.getThreadState()
                        + ", name=" + ti.getThreadName());
    }
}
```

For better presentation, we took advantage of having thread IDs listed and, as you could see previously, have sorted the output by ID. If we call the `printThreadsInfo()` method before the `shutdown()` method the output will be as follows:

```
printThreadsInfo():
    Id=1, state=RUNNABLE, name=main
    Id=2, state=RUNNABLE, name=Reference Handler
    Id=3, state=WAITING, name=Finalizer
    Id=4, state=RUNNABLE, name=Signal Dispatcher
    Id=10, state=TIMED_WAITING, name=Common-Cleaner
    Id=11, state=RUNNABLE, name=Monitor Ctrl-Break
    Id=13, state=TIMED_WAITING, name=pool-1-thread-1
    Id=14, state=TIMED_WAITING, name=pool-1-thread-2
```

However, if we call the `printThreadsInfo()` method after the `shutdown()` method, the output will not include our worker threads anymore, exactly as in the case of using the `Thread` class API:

```
printThreadsInfo():
    Id=1, state=RUNNABLE, name=main
    Id=2, state=RUNNABLE, name=Reference Handler
    Id=3, state=WAITING, name=Finalizer
    Id=4, state=RUNNABLE, name=Signal Dispatcher
    Id=10, state=TIMED_WAITING, name=Common-Cleaner
    Id=11, state=RUNNABLE, name=Monitor Ctrl-Break
```

The `java.lang.management.ThreadMXBean` interface provides a lot of other useful data about threads. You can refer to the official API on the Oracle website about this interface for more information check this link: `https://docs.oracle.com/javase/8/docs/api/index.html?java/lang/management/ThreadMXBean.html`).

In the list of threads mentioned earlier, you may have noticed the `Monitor Ctrl-Break` thread. This thread provides another way to monitor the threads in the JVM process. Pressing the *Ctrl* and *Break* keys on Windows causes the JVM to print a thread dump to the application's standard output. On Oracle Solaris or Linux operating systems, the same effect has the combination of the *Ctrl* key and the backslash \. This brings us to the external tools for thread monitoring.

In case you don't have access to the source code or prefer to use the external tools for the threads monitoring, there are several diagnostic utilities available with the JDK installation. In the following list, we mention only the tools that allow for thread monitoring and describe only this capability of the listed tools (although they have other extensive functionality too):

- The `jcmd` utility sends diagnostic command requests to the JVM on the same machine using the JVM process ID or the name of the main class: `jcmd <process id/main class> <command> [options]`, where the `Thread.print` option prints the stack traces of all the threads in the process.

- The JConsole monitoring tool uses the built-in JMX instrumentation in the JVM to provide information about the performance and resource consumption of running applications. It has a thread tab pane that shows thread usage over time, the current number of live threads, the highest number of live threads since the JVM started. It is possible to select the thread and its name, state, and stack trace, as well as, for a blocked thread, the synchronizer that the thread is waiting to acquire, and the thread owning the lock. Use the **Deadlock Detection** button to identify the deadlock. The command to run the tool is `jconsole <process id>` or (for remote application) `jconsole <hostname>:<port>`, where `port` is the port number specified with the JVM start command that enabled the JMX agent.

- The `jdb` utility is an example command line debugger. It can be attached to the JVM process and allows you to examine threads.

- The `jstack` command line utility can be attached to the JVM process and print the stack traces of all threads, including JVM internal threads, and optionally native stack frames. It allows you to detect deadlocks too.

- **Java Flight Recorder** (**JFR**) provides information about the Java process, including threads waiting for locks, garbage collections, and so on. It also allows getting thread dumps, which are similar to the one generated by the `Thread.print` diagnostic command or by using the jstack tool. It is possible to set up **Java Mission Control** (**JMC**) to dump a flight recording if a condition is met. JMC UI contains information about threads, lock contention, and other latencies. Although JFR is a commercial feature, it is free for developer desktops/laptops, and for evaluation purposes in test, development, and production environments.

You can find more details about these and other diagnostic tools in the official Oracle documentation at `https://docs.oracle.com/javase/9/troubleshoot/diagnostic-tools.htm`.

Sizing thread pool executors

In our examples, we have used a cached thread pool that creates a new thread as needed or, if available, reuses the thread already used, but which completed its job and returned to the pool for a new assignment. We did not worry about too many threads created because our demo application had two worker threads at the most and they were quite short lived.

But in the case where an application does not have a fixed limit of the worker threads it might need or there is no good way to predict how much memory a thread may take or how long it can execute, setting a ceiling on the worker thread count prevents an unexpected degradation of the application performance, running out of memory or depletion of any other resources the worker threads use. If the thread behavior is extremely unpredictable, a single thread pool might be the only solution, with an option of using a custom thread pool executor (more about this last option is explained later). But in most of the cases, a fixed-size thread pool executor is a good practical compromise between the application needs and the code complexity. Depending on the specific requirements, such an executor might be one of these three flavors:

- A straightforward, fixed-sized `ExecutorService.newFixedThreadPool(int nThreads)` pool that does not grow beyond the specified size, but does not adopt either
- Several `ExecutorService.newScheduledThreadPool(int nThreads)` pools that allow scheduling different groups of threads with a different delay or cycle of execution
- `ExecutorService.newWorkStealingPool(int parallelism)` that adapts to the specified number of CPUs, which you may set higher or smaller than the actual CPUs count on your computer

Setting the fixed size in any of the preceding pools too low may deprive the application of the chance to utilize the available resources effectively. So, before selecting the pool size, it is advisable to spend some time on monitoring it and tuning JVM (see how to do it in one of the sections of this chapter) with the goal of the identification of the idiosyncrasy of the application behavior. In fact, the cycle deploy-monitor-tune-adjust has to be repeated throughout the application life cycle in order to accommodate and take advantage of the changes that happened in the code or the executing environment.

The first parameter you take into account is the number of CPUs in your system, so the thread pool size can be at least as big as the CPU's count. Then, you can monitor the application and see how much time each thread engages the CPU and how much of the time it uses other resources (such as I/O operations). If the time spent not using the CPU is comparable with the total executing time of the thread, then you can increase the pool size by *time not using CPU/total executing time*. But that is in the case that another resource (disk or database) is not a subject of contention between the threads. If the latter is the case, then you can use that resource instead of the CPU as the delineating factor.

Assuming the worker threads of your application are not too big or too long executing and belong to the mainstream population of the typical working threads that complete their job in a reasonably short period of time, you can increase the pool size by adding the (rounded up) ratio of the desired response time and the time a thread uses CPU or another most contentious resource. This means that, with the same desired response time, the less a thread uses CPU or another concurrently accessed resource, the bigger the pool size should be. If the contentious resource has its own ability to improve concurrent access (like a connection pool in the database), consider utilizing that feature first.

If the required number of threads running at the same time changes at runtime under the different circumstances, you can make the pool size dynamic and create a new pool with a new size (shutting down the old pool after all its threads have completed). The recalculation of the size of a new pool might be necessary also after you add to remove the available resources. You can use `Runtime.getRuntime().availableProcessors()` to programmatically adjust the pool size based on the current count of the available CPUs, for example.

If none of the ready-to-use thread pool executor implementations that come with the JDK suit the needs of a particular application, before writing the thread managing code from scratch, try to use the `java.util.concurrent.ThreadPoolExecutor` class first. It has several overloaded constructors. To give you an idea of its capabilities, here is the constructor with the biggest number of options:

```
ThreadPoolExecutor (int corePoolSize, int maximumPoolSize, long
keepAliveTime, TimeUnit unit, BlockingQueue<Runnable> workQueue,
ThreadFactory threadFactory, RejectedExecutionHandler handler)
```

The earlier mentioned parameters are (quoting from the JavaDoc):

- `corePoolSize`: This is the number of threads to keep in the pool, even if they are idle unless `allowCoreThreadTimeOut` is set
- `maximumPoolSize`: This is the maximum number of threads to allow in the pool
- `keepAliveTime`: When the number of threads is greater than the core, this is the maximum time that excess idle threads will wait for new tasks before terminating

- `unit`: This is the time unit for the `keepAliveTime` argument
- `workQueue`: This is the queue to use for holding tasks before they are executed, this queue will hold only the `Runnable` tasks submitted by the execute method
- `threadFactory`: This is the factory to use when the executor creates a new thread
- `handler`: This is the handler to use when the execution is blocked because the thread bounds and queue capacities are reached

Each of the previous constructor parameters except the `workQueue` parameter can also be set via the corresponding setter after the object of the `ThreadPoolExecutor` method has been created, thus allowing more flexibility in dynamic adjustment of the existing pool characteristics.

Thread synchronization

We have collected enough people and resources such as food, water, and tools for the pyramid building. We have divided people into teams and assigned each team a task. A number (a pool) of people are living in the nearby village on a standby mode, ready to replace the ones that got sick or injured on their assignment. We adjusted the workforce count so that there are only a few people who will remain idle in the village. We rotate the teams through the work-rest cycle to keep the project going at maximum speed. We monitored the process and have adjusted the number of teams and the flow of supplies they need so that there are no visible delays and there is steady measurable progress in the project as a whole. Yet, there are many moving parts overall and various small and big unexpected incidents and problems happen all the time.

To make sure that the workers and teams do not step on each other and that there is some kind of traffic regulation so that the next technological step does not start until the previous one is finished, the main architect sends his representatives to all the critical points of the construction site. These representatives make sure that the tasks are executed with the expected quality and in the prescribed order. They have the power to stop the next team from starting their job until the previous team has not finished yet. They act like traffic cops or the locks that can shut down the access to the workplace or allow it, if/when necessary.

The job these representatives are doing can be defined in the modern language as a coordination or synchronization of actions of the executing units. Without it, the results of the efforts of the thousands of workers would be unpredictable. The big picture from ten thousand feet would look smooth and harmonious, as the farmers' fields from the windows of an airplane. But without closer inspection and attention to the critical details, this perfect looking picture may bring a poor harvest, if any.

Similarly, in the quiet electronic space of the multithreaded execution environment, the working threads have to be synchronized if they share access to the same working place. For example, let's create the following class-worker for a thread:

```
class MyRunnable04 implements Runnable {
  private int id;
  public MyRunnable04(int id) { this.id = id; }
  public void run() {
    IntStream.rangeClosed(1, 5)
      .peek(i -> System.out.println("Thread "+id+": "+ i))
      .forEach(i -> Demo04Synchronization.result += i);
  }
}
```

As you can see, it sequentially adds 1, 2, 3, 4, 5 (so, that the resulting total is expected to be 15) to the static property of the Demo04Synchronization class:

```
public class Demo04Synchronization {
    public static int result;
    public static void main(String... args) {
        System.out.println();
        demo_ThreadInterference();
    }
    private static void demo_ThreadInterference(){
        System.out.println("demo_ThreadInterference: ");
        MyRunnable04 r1 = new MyRunnable04(1);
        Thread t1 = new Thread(r1);
        MyRunnable04 r2 = new MyRunnable04(2);
        Thread t2 = new Thread(r2);
        t1.start();
        sleepMs(100);
        t2.start();
        sleepMs(100);
        System.out.println("Result=" + result);
    }
    private static void sleepMs(int sleepMs) {
        try {
            TimeUnit.MILLISECONDS.sleep(sleepMs);
        } catch (InterruptedException e) {}
    }
}
```

In the earlier code, while the main thread pauses for 100 ms the first time, the thread t1 brings the value of the variable result to 15, then the thread t2 adds another 15 to get the total of 30. Here is the output:

```
demo_ThreadInterference:
Thread 1: 1
Thread 1: 2
Thread 1: 3
Thread 1: 4
Thread 1: 5
Thread 2: 1
Thread 2: 2
Thread 2: 3
Thread 2: 4
Thread 2: 5
Result=30
```

If we remove the first pause of 100 ms, the threads will work concurrently:

```
demo_ThreadInterference:
Thread 1: 1
Thread 2: 1
Thread 1: 2
Thread 2: 2
Thread 2: 3
Thread 2: 4
Thread 1: 3
Thread 1: 4
Thread 1: 5
Thread 2: 5
Result=30
```

The final result is still 30. We feel good about this code and deploy it to production as a well-tested code. However, if we increase the number of additions from 5 to 250, for example, the result becomes unstable and changes from run to run. Here is the first run (we commented out the printout in each thread in order to save space):

```
demo_ThreadInterference:
Result=55946
```

And here is the output of another run:

```
demo_ThreadInterference:
Result=62210
```

It demonstrates the fact that the `Demo04Synchronization.result += i` operation is not atomic. This means it consists of several steps, reading the value from the `result` property, adding a value to it, assigning the resulting sum back to the `result` property. This allows the following scenario, for example:

- Both the threads have read the current value of `result` (so each of the threads has a copy of the same original `result` value)
- Each thread adds another integer to the same original one
- The first thread assigns the sum to the `result` property
- The second thread assigns its sum to the `result` property

As you can see, the second thread did not know about the addition the first thread made and has overwritten the value assigned to the `result` property by the first thread. But such thread interleaving does not happen every time. It is just a game of chance. That's why we did not see such an effect with five numbers only. But the probability of this happening increases with the growth of the number of concurrent actions.

A similar thing could happen during the pyramid building too. The second team could start doing something before the first team has finished their task. We definitely need a *synchronizer* and it comes with a `synchronized` keyword. Using it, we can create a method (an architect representative) in the `Demo04Synchronization` class that will control access to the `result` property and add to it this keyword:

```
private static int result;
public static synchronized void incrementResult(int i){
    result += i;
}
```

Now we have to modify the `run()` method in the worker thread too:

```
public void run() {
    IntStream.rangeClosed(1, 250)
        .forEach(Demo04Synchronization::incrementResult);
}
```

The output now shows the same final number for every run:

```
demo_ThreadInterference:
Result=62750
```

The synchronized keyword tells JVM that only one thread at a time is allowed to enter this method. All the other threads will wait until the current visitor of the method exits from it.

The same effect could be achieved by adding the synchronized keyword to a block of code:

```
public static void incrementResult(int i){
    synchronized (Demo04Synchronization.class){
        result += i;
    }
}
```

The difference is that the block synchronization requires an object--a class object in the case of static property synchronization (as in our case) or any other object in the case of an instance property synchronization. Each object has an intrinsic lock or monitor lock, often referred to simply as a monitor. Once a thread acquires a lock on an object, no other thread can acquire it on the same object until the first thread releases the lock after normal exit from the locked code or if the code throws an exception.

In fact, in the case of a synchronized method, an object (the one to which the method belongs) is used for locking, too. It just happens behind the scene automatically and does not require the programmer to use an object's lock explicitly.

In case you do not have access to the main class code (as in the example earlier) you can keep the result property public and add a synchronized method to the worker thread (instead of the class as we have done):

```
class MyRunnable05 implements Runnable {
    public synchronized void incrementResult(int i){
        Demo04Synchronization.result += i;
    }
    public void run() {
        IntStream.rangeClosed(1, 250)
                .forEach(this::incrementResult);
    }
}
```

In this case, the object of the MyRunnable05 worker class provides its intrinsic lock by default. This means, you need to use the same object of the MyRunnable05 class for all the threads:

```
void demo_Synchronized(){
    System.out.println("demo_Synchronized: ");
    MyRunnable05 r1 = new MyRunnable05();
    Thread t1 = new Thread(r1);
    Thread t2 = new Thread(r1);
    t1.start();
    t2.start();
    sleepMs(100);
    System.out.println("Result=" + result);
}
```

The output of the preceding code is the same as before:

```
demo_Synchronized:
Result=62750
```

One can argue that this last implementation is preferable because it allocates the responsibility of the synchronization with the thread (and the author of its code) and not with the shared resource. This way the need for synchronization changes along with the thread implementation evolution, provided that the client code (that uses the same or different objects for the threads) can be changed as needed as well.

There is another possible concurrency issue that may happen in some operating systems. Depending on how the thread caching is implemented, a thread might preserve a local copy of the property result and not update it after another thread has changed its value. By adding the volatile keyword to the shared (between threads) property guarantees that its current value will be always read from the main memory, so each thread will see the updates done by the other threads. In our previous examples, we just set the Demo04Synchronization class property as private static volatile int result, add a synchronized incrementResult() method to the same class or to the thread and do not worry anymore about threads stepping on each other.

The described thread synchronization is usually sufficient for the mainstream application. But the higher performance and highly concurrent processing often require looking closer into the thread dump, which typically shows that method synchronization is more efficient than block synchronization. Naturally, it also depends on the size of the method and the block. Since all the other threads that try to access the synchronized method or block are going to stop execution until the current visitor of the method or block exits it, it is possible that despite the overhead a small synchronized block yields better performance than the big synchronized method.

For some applications, the behavior of the default intrinsic lock, which just blocks until the lock is released, maybe not well suited. If that is the case, consider using locks from the `java.util.concurrent.locks` package. The access control based on locks from that package has several differences if compared with using the default intrinsic lock. These differences may be advantageous for your application or provide the unnecessary complication, but it's important to know them, so you can make an informed decision:

- The synchronized fragment of code does not need to belong to one method; it can span several methods, delineated by the calls to the `lock()` and `unlock()` methods (invoked on the object that implements the `Lock` interface)
- While creating an object of the `Lock` interface called `ReentrantLock`, it is possible to pass into the constructor a `fair` flag that makes the lock able to grant an access to the longest-waiting thread first, which helps to avoid starvation (when the low priority thread never can get access to the lock)
- Allows a thread to test whether the lock is accessible before committing to be blocked
- Allows interrupting a thread waiting for the lock, so it does not remain blocked indefinitely
- You can implement the `Lock` interface yourself with whatever features you need for your application

A typical pattern of usage of the `Lock` interface looks like this:

```
Lock lock = ...;
...
    lock.lock();
    try {
        // the fragment that is synchronized
    } finally {
        lock.unlock();
    }
...
}
```

Notice the `finally` block. It is the way to guarantee that the `lock` is released eventually. Otherwise, the code inside the `try-catch` block can throw an exception and the lock is never released.

In addition to the `lock()` and `unlock()` methods, the `Lock` interface has the following methods:

- `lockInterruptibly()`: This acquires the lock unless the current thread is interrupted. Similar to the `lock()` method, this method blocks while waiting until the lock is acquired, in difference to the `lock()` method, if another thread interrupts the waiting thread, this method throws the `InterruptedException` exception
- `tryLock()`: This acquires the lock immediately if it is free at the time of invocation
- `tryLock(long time, TimeUnit unit)`: This acquires the lock if it is free within the given waiting time and the current thread has not been interrupted
- `newCondition()`: This returns a new `Condition` instance that is bound to this `Lock` instance, after acquiring the lock, the thread can release it (calling the `await()` method on the `Condition` object) until some other thread calls `signal()` or `signalAll()` on the same `Condition` object, it is also possible to specify the timeout period (by using an overloaded `await()` method), so the thread will resume after the timeout if there was no signal received, see the `Condition` API for more details

The scope of this book does not allow us to show all the possibilities for thread synchronization provided in the `java.util.concurrent.locks` package. It would take several chapters to describe all of them. But even from this short description, you can see that one would be hard pressed to find a synchronization problem that cannot be solved using the `java.util.concurrent.locks` package.

The synchronization of a method or block of code makes sense when several lines of code have to be isolated as an atomic (all or nothing) operation. But in the case of a simple assignment to a variable or increment/decrement of a number (as in our earlier examples), there is a much better way to synchronize this operation by using classes from the `java.util.concurrent.atomic` package that support lock-free thread-safe programming on a single variable. The variety of classes covers all the numbers and even arrays and reference types such as `AtomicBoolean`, `AtomicInteger`, `AtomicIntegerArray`, `AtomicReference`, and `AtomicReferenceArray`.

There are 16 classes in total. Depending on the value type, each of them allows a full imaginable range of operations, that is, `set()`, `get()`, `addAndGet()`, `compareAndSet()`, `incrementAndGet()`, `decrementAndGet()`, and many others. Each operation is implemented much more efficiently than the same operations implemented with the `synchronized` keyword. And there is no need for the `volatile` keyword because it uses it under the hood.

If the concurrently accessed resource is a collection, the `java.util.concurrent` package offers a variety of thread-safe implementations that perform better than synchronized `HashMap`, `Hashtable`, `HashSet`, `Vector`, and `ArrayList` (if we compare the corresponding `ConcurrentHashMap`, `CopyOnWriteArrayList`, and `CopyOnWriteHashSet`). The traditional synchronized collections lock the whole collection while concurrent collections use such advanced techniques such as lock stripping to achieve thread safety. The concurrent collections especially shine with more reading and fewer updates and they are much more scalable than synchronized collections. But if the size of your shared collection is small and writes dominate, the advantage of concurrent collections is not as obvious.

Tuning JVM

Each pyramid building, as any big project, goes through the same life cycle of design, planning, execution, and delivery. And throughout each of these phases, a continuous tuning is going on, a complex project is called so for a reason. A software system is not different in this respect. We design, plan and build it, then change and tune continuously. If we are lucky, then the new changes do not go too far back to the initial stages and do not require changing the design. To hedge against such drastic steps, we use prototypes (if the waterfall model is used) or iterative delivery (if the agile process is adopted) for early detection of possible problems. Like young parents, we are always on alert, monitoring the progress of our child, day and night.

As we mentioned already in one of the previous sections, there are several diagnostic tools that come with each JDK 9 installation or can be used in addition to them for monitoring your Java application. The full list of these tools (and the recommendations how to create a custom tool, if needed) can be found in official Java SE documentation on the Oracle site: `https://docs.oracle.com/javase/9/troubleshoot/diagnostic-tools.htm`.

Using these tools one identifies the bottleneck of the application and addresses it either programmatically or by tuning the JVM itself or both. The biggest gain usually comes with the good design decisions and from using certain programming techniques and frameworks, some of which we have described in other sections. In this section, we are going to look at the options available after all possible code changes are applied or when changing code is not an option, so all we can do is to tune JVM itself.

The goal of the effort depends on the results of the application profiling and the nonfunctional requirements for:

- Latency, or how responsive the application is to the input
- Throughput, or how much work the application is doing in a given unit of time
- Memory footprint, or how much memory the application requires

The improvements in one of them often are possible only at the expense of the one or both of the others. The decrease in the memory consumption may bring down the throughput and latency, while the decrease in latency typically can be achieved only via the increase in memory footprint unless you can bring in faster CPUs thus improving all three characteristics.

Application profiling may show that one particular operation keeps allocating a lot of memory in the loop. If you have an access to the code, you can try to optimize this section of the code and thus ease the pressure on JVM. Alternatively, it may show that there is an I/O or another interaction with a low device is involved, and there is nothing you can do in the code to improve it.

Defining the goal of the application and JVM tuning requires establishing metrics. For example, it is well known already that the traditional measure of latency as the average response time hides more than it reveals about the performance. The better latency metrics would be the maximum response time in conjunction with 99% best response time. For throughput, a good metrics would be the number of transactions per a unit of time. Often the inverse of this metrics (time per transaction) closely reflects latency. For the memory footprint, the maximum allocated memory (under the load) allows for the hardware planning and setting guards against the dreaded OutOfMemoryError exception. Avoiding full (stop-the-world) garbage collection cycle would be ideal. In practice, though, it would be good enough if *Full GC* happens not often, does not visibly affect the performance and ends up with approximately the same heap size after several cycles.

Unfortunately, such simplicity of the requirements does happen in practice. Real life brings more questions all the time as follows:

- Can the target latency (response time) be ever exceeded?
- If yes, how often and by how much?
- How long can the period of the poor response time last?
- Who/what measures the latency in production?
- Is the target performance the peak performance?
- What is the expected peak load?
- How long is the expected peak load going to last?

Only after all these and similar questions are answered and the metrics (that reflect the nonfunctional requirements) are established, we can start tweaking the code, running it and profiling again and again, then tweaking the code and repeating the cycle. This activity has to consume most of the efforts because tuning of the JVM itself can bring only the fraction of the performance improvements by comparison with the performance gained by the code changes.

Nevertheless, several passes of the JVM tuning must happen early in order to avoid wasting of the efforts and trying to force the code in the not well-configured environment. The JVM configuration has to be as generous as possible for the code to take advantage of all the available resources.

First of all, select garbage collector from the four that JVM 9 supports, which are as follows:

- **Serial collector**: This uses a single thread to perform all the garbage collection work
- **Parallel collector**: This uses multiple threads to speed up garbage collection
- **Concurrent Mark Sweep (CMS) collector**: This uses shorter garbage collection pauses at the expense of taking more of the processor time
- **Garbage-First (G1) collector**: This is intended for multiprocessor machines with a large memory, but meets garbage collection pause-time goals with high probability, while achieving high throughput.

The official Oracle documentation (https://docs.oracle.com/javase/9/gctuning/available-collectors.htm) provides the following initial guidelines for the garbage collection selection:

- If the application has a small dataset (up to approximately 100 MB), then select the serial collector with the -XX:+UseSerialGC option

- If the application will be run on a single processor and there are no pause-time requirements, then select the serial collector with the `-XX:+UseSerialGC` option
- If (a) peak application performance is the first priority and (b) there are no pause-time requirements or pauses of one second or longer are acceptable, then let the VM select the collector or select the parallel collector with `-XX:+UseParallelGC`
- If the response time is more important than the overall throughput and garbage collection pauses must be kept shorter than approximately one second, then select a concurrent collector with `-XX:+UseG1GC` or `-XX:+UseConcMarkSweepGC`

But if you do not have particular preferences yet, let the JVM select garbage collector until you learn more about your application's needs. In JDK 9, the G1 is selected by default on certain platforms, and it is a good start if the hardware you use has enough resources.

Oracle also recommends using G1 with its default settings, then later playing with a different pause-time goal using the `-XX:MaxGCPauseMillis` option and maximum Java heap size using the `-Xmx` option. Increasing either the pause-time goal or the heap size typically leads to a higher throughput. The latency is affected by the change of the pause-time goal too.

While tuning the GC, it is beneficial to keep the `-Xlog:gc*=debug` logging option. It provides many useful details about garbage collection activity. The first goal of JVM tuning is to decrease the number of full heap GC cycles (Full GC) because they are very resource consuming and thus may slow down the application. It is caused by too high occupancy of the old generation area. In the log, it is identified by the words `Pause Full (Allocation Failure)`. The following are the possible steps to reduce chances of Full GC:

- Bring up the size of the heap using `-Xmx`. But make sure it does not exceed the physical size of RAM. Better yet, leave some RAM space for other applications.
- Increase the number of concurrent marking threads explicitly using `-XX:ConcGCThreads`.
- If the humongous objects take too much of the heap (watch for *gc+heap=info* logging that shows the number next to humongous regions) try to increase the region size using `-XX: G1HeapRegionSize`.
- Watch the GC log and modify the code so that almost all the objects created by your application are not moved beyond the young generation (dying young).
- Add or change one option at a time, so you can understand the causes of the change in the JVM's behavior clearly.

These few steps will help you go and create a trial-and-error cycle that will bring you a better understanding of the platform you are using, the needs of your application, and the sensitivity of the JVM and the selected GC to different options. Equipped with this knowledge, you will then be able to meet the nonfunctional performance requirements whether by changing the code, tuning the JVM, or reconfiguring the hardware.

Reactive programming

After several false starts and a few disastrous disruptions, followed by heroic recoveries, the process of pyramid building took shape and ancient builders were able to complete a few projects. The final shape sometimes did not look exactly as envisioned (the first pyramids have ended up bent), but, nevertheless, the pyramids still decorate the desert today. The experience was passed from generation to generation, and the design and the process were tuned well enough to produce something magnificent and pleasant to look at more than 4,000 years later.

The software practices also change over time, albeit we have had only some 70 years since Mr. Turing wrote the first modern program. In the beginning, when there were only a handful of programmers in the world, a computer program used to be a continuous list of instructions. Functional programming (pushing a function around like a first-class citizen) was introduced very early too but has not become a mainstream. Instead, the *GOTO* instruction allowed you to roll code in a spaghetti bowl. Structural programming followed, then object-oriented programming, with functional programming moving along and even thriving in certain areas. Asynchronous processing of the events generated by the pressed keys became routine for many programmers. JavaScript tried to use all of the best practices and gained a lot of power, even if at the expense of programmers' frustration during the debugging (fun) phase. Finally, with thread pools and lambda expressions being part of JDK SE, adding reactive streams API to JDK 9 made Java part of the family that allows reactive programming--programming with asynchronous data streams.

To be fair, we were able to process data asynchronously even without this new API--by spinning worker threads and using thread pools and callables (as we described in the previous sections) or by passing the callbacks (even if lost once in a while in the maze of the who-calls-whom). But, after writing such a code a few times, one notices that most of such code is just a plumbing that can be wrapped inside a framework that can significantly simplify asynchronous processing. That's how the Reactive Streams initiative (http://www.reactive-streams.org) came to be created and the scope of the effort is defined as follows:

> *The scope of Reactive Streams is to find a minimal set of interfaces, methods and protocols that will describe the necessary operations and entities to achieve the goal--asynchronous streams of data with non-blocking back pressure.*

The term *non-blocking back pressure* is an important one because it identifies one of the problems of the existed asynchronous processing--coordination of the speed rate of the incoming data with the ability of the system to process them without the need of stopping (blocking) the data input. The solution would still include some back pressure by informing the source that the consumer has difficulty in keeping up with the input, but the new framework should react to the change of the rate of the incoming data in a more flexible manner than just blocking the flow, thus the name *reactive*.

The Reactive Streams API consists of the five interfaces included in the class which are `java.util.concurrent.Flow`, `Publisher`, `Subscriber`, `Subscription`, and `Processor`:

```
@FunctionalInterface
public static interface Flow.Publisher<T> {
  public void subscribe(Flow.Subscriber<? super T> subscriber);
}

public static interface Flow.Subscriber<T> {
  public void onSubscribe(Flow.Subscription subscription);
  public void onNext(T item);
  public void onError(Throwable throwable);
  public void onComplete();
}

public static interface Flow.Subscription {
  public void request(long numberOfItems);
  public void cancel();
}

public static interface Flow.Processor<T,R>
          extends Flow.Subscriber<T>, Flow.Publisher<R> {
}
```

A `Flow.Subscriber` object becomes a subscriber of the data produced by the object of `Flow.Publisher` after the object of `Flow.Subscriber` is passed as a parameter into the `subscribe()` method. The publisher (object of `Flow.Publisher`) calls the subscriber's `onSubscribe()` method and passes as a parameter a `Flow.Subsctiption` object. Now, the subscriber can request `numberOffItems` of data from the publisher by calling the subscription's `request()` method. That is the way to implement the pull model when a subscriber decides when to request another item for processing. The subscriber can unsubscribe from the publisher services by calling the `cancel()` subscription method.

In return (or without any request, if the implementer has decided to do so, that would be a push model), the publisher can pass to the subscriber a new item by calling the subscriber's `onNext()` method. The publisher can also tell the subscriber that the item production has encountered a problem (by calling the subscriber's `onError()` method) or that no more data will be coming (by calling the subscriber's `onComplete()` method).

The `Flow.Processor` interface describes an entity that can act as both a subscriber and a publisher. It allows creating chains (pipelines) of such processors, so a subscriber can receive an item from a publisher, tweak it, and then pass the result to the next subscriber.

This is the minimal set of interfaces the Reactive Streams initiative has defined (and it is a part of JDK 9 now) in support of the asynchronous data streams with non-blocking back pressure. As you can see, it allows the subscriber and publisher to talk to each other and coordinate, if need be, the rate of incoming data, thus making possible a variety of solutions for the back pressure problem we discussed in the beginning.

There are many ways to implement these interfaces. Currently, in JDK 9, there is only one example of implementation of one of the interfaces--the `SubmissionPublisher` class implements `Flow.Publisher`. But several other libraries already exist that implemented Reactive Streams API: RxJava, Reactor, Akka Streams, and Vert.x are among the most known. We will use RxJava 2.1.3 in our examples. You can find the RxJava 2.x API on `http://reactivex.io` under the name ReactiveX, which stands for Reactive Extension.

While doing that, we would also like to address the difference between the streams of the `java.util.stream` package and Reactive Streams (as implemented in RxJava, for example). It is possible to write very similar code using any of the streams. Let's look at an example. Here is a program that iterates over five integers, selects even numbers only (2 and 4), transforms each of them (takes a square root of each of the selected numbers) and then calculates an average of the two square roots. It is based on the traditional `for` loop.

Let's start with the similarity. It is possible to implement the same functionality using any of the streams. For example, here is a method that iterates over five integers, selects even numbers only (2 and 4, in this case), transforms each of them (takes a square root of each of the even numbers) and then calculates an average of the two square roots. It is based on the traditional `for` loop:

```
void demo_ForLoop(){
    List<Double> r = new ArrayList<>();
    for(int i = 1; i < 6; i++){
        System.out.println(i);
        if(i%2 == 0){
            System.out.println(i);
            r.add(doSomething(i));
```

```
        }
    }
    double sum = 0d;
    for(double d: r){ sum += d; }
    System.out.println(sum / r.size());
}
static double doSomething(int i){
    return Math.sqrt(1.*i);
}
```

If we run this program, the result will be as follows:

```
1
2
2
3
4
4
5
1.7071067811865475
```

The same functionality (with the same output) can be implemented using the package `java.util.stream` as follows:

```
void demo_Stream(){
    double a = IntStream.rangeClosed(1, 5)
        .peek(System.out::println)
        .filter(i -> i%2 == 0)
        .peek(System.out::println)
        .mapToDouble(i -> doSomething(i))
        .average().getAsDouble();
    System.out.println(a);
}
```

The same functionality can be implemented with RxJava:

```
void demo_Observable1(){
    Observable.just(1,2,3,4,5)
        .doOnNext(System.out::println)
        .filter(i -> i%2 == 0)
        .doOnNext(System.out::println)
        .map(i -> doSomething(i))
        .reduce((r, d) -> r + d)
        .map(r -> r / 2)
        .subscribe(System.out::println);
}
```

RxJava is based on the `Observable` object (which plays the role of `Publisher`) and `Observer` that subscribes to the `Observable` and waits for data to be emitted. Each item of the emitted data (on the way from the `Observable` to the `Observer`) can be processed by the operations chained in a fluent style (see the previous code). Each operation takes a lambda expression. The operation functionality is obvious from its name.

Despite being able to behave similarly to the streams, an `Observable` has significantly different capabilities. For example, a stream, once closed, cannot be reopened, while an `Observable` can be reused. Here is an example:

```
void demo_Observable2(){
    Observable<Double> observable = Observable
            .just(1,2,3,4,5)
            .doOnNext(System.out::println)
            .filter(i -> i%2 == 0)
            .doOnNext(System.out::println)
            .map(Demo05Reactive::doSomething);

    observable
            .reduce((r, d) -> r + d)
            .map(r -> r / 2)
            .subscribe(System.out::println);

    observable
            .reduce((r, d) -> r + d)
            .subscribe(System.out::println);
}
```

In the previous code, we use `Observable` twice--for average value calculation and for the summing all the square roots of the even numbers. The output is as shown in the following screenshot:

If we do not want `Observable` to run twice, we can cache its data, by adding the `.cache()` operation:

```
void demo_Observable2(){
    Observable<Double> observable = Observable
            .just(1,2,3,4,5)
            .doOnNext(System.out::println)
            .filter(i -> i%2 == 0)
            .doOnNext(System.out::println)
            .map(Demo05Reactive::doSomething)
            .cache();

    observable
            .reduce((r, d) -> r + d)
            .map(r -> r / 2)
            .subscribe(System.out::println);

    observable
            .reduce((r, d) -> r + d)
            .subscribe(System.out::println);
}
```

The result of the previous code is as follows:

```
1
2
2
3
4
4
5
1.7071067811865475
3.414213562373095
```

You can see that the second usage of the same `Observable` took advantage of the cached data, thus allowing for better performance.

Another `Observable` advantage is that the exception can be caught by `Observer`:

```
subscribe(v -> System.out.println("Result=" + v),
        e -> {
            System.out.println("Error: " + e.getMessage());
            e.printStackTrace();
        },
        () -> System.out.println("All the data processed"));
```

The `subscribe()` method is overloaded and allows to pass in one, two, or three functions:

- The first is to be used in case of success
- The second is to be used in case of an exception
- The third is to be called after all the data is processed

The `Observable` model also allows more control over multithreaded processing. Using `.parallel()` in the streams does not allow you to specify the thread pool to be used. But, in RxJava, you can set the type of pool you prefer using the method `subscribeOn()` in `Observable`:

```
observable.subscribeOn(Schedulers.io())
          .subscribe(System.out::println);
```

The `subscribeOn()` method tells `Observable` on which thread to put the data. The `Schedulers` class has methods that generate thread pools dealing mostly with I/O operations (as in our example), or heavy on computation (method `computation()`), or creating a new thread for each unit of work (method `newThread()`), and several others, including passing in a custom thread pool (method `from(Executor executor)`).

The format of this book does not allow us to describe all the richness of RxJava API and other Reactive Streams implementations. Their main thrust is reflected in Reactive Manifesto (`http://www.reactivemanifesto.org/`) that describes Reactive Systems as a new generation of high performing software solutions. Built on asynchronous message-driven processes and Reactive Streams, such systems are able to demonstrate the qualities declared in the Reactive Manifesto:

- **Elasticity**: This has the ability to expand and contract as needed based on the load
- **Better responsiveness**: Here, the processing can be parallelized using asynchronous calls
- **Resilience**: Here, the system is broken into multiple (loosely coupled via messages) components, thus facilitating flexible replication, containment, and isolation

Writing code for Reactive Systems using Reactive Streams for implementing the previously mentioned qualities constitutes reactive programming. The typical application of such systems today is microservices, which is described in the next chapter.

Summary

In this chapter, we have discussed the ways to improve Java application performance by using multithreading. We described how to decrease an overhead of creating the threads using thread pools and various types of such pools suited for different processing requirements. We also brought up the considerations used for selecting the pool size and how to synchronize threads so that they do not interfere with each other and yield the best performance results. We pointed out that every decision on the performance improvements has to be made and tested through direct monitoring of the application, and we discussed the possible options for such monitoring programmatically and using various external tools. The final step, the JVM tuning, can be done via Java tool flags that we listed and commented in the corresponding section. Yet more gains in Java application performance might be achieved by adopting the concept of reactive programming, which we presented as the strong contender among most effective moves toward highly scalable and highly performing Java applications.

In the next chapter, we will talk about adding more workers by splitting the application into several microservices, each deployed independently and each using multiple threads and reactive programming for better performance, response, scalability, and fault-tolerance.

10
Microservices

As long as we kept talking about the designing, implementation, and tuning of one process, we were able to keep illustrating it with vivid images (albeit in our imagination only) of pyramid building. Multiple thread management, based on the democratic principle of equality between thread pool members, had also a sense of centralized planning and supervision. Different priorities were assigned to threads programmatically, hardcoded (for most cases) after thoughtful consideration by the programmer in accordance with the expected load, and adjusted after monitoring. The upper limits of the available resources were fixed, although they could be increased after, again, a relatively big centralized decision.

Such systems had great success and still constitute the majority of the web applications currently deployed to production. Many of them are monoliths, sealed inside a single `.ear` or `.war` file. This works fine for relatively small applications and a corresponding team size that supports them. They are easy (if the code is well structured) to maintain, build, and if the production load is not very high, they can be easily deployed. If the business does not grow or has little impact on the company's internet presence, they continue to do the job and will do so probably for the foreseeable future. Many service providers are eager to host such websites by charging a small fee and relieving the website owner of the technical worries of production maintenance not directly related to the business. But that is not the case for everybody.

The higher the load, the more difficult and expensive the scaling becomes unless the code and the overall architecture is restructured in order to become more flexible and resilient to the growing load. This chapter describes the solution many leaders of the industry have adopted while addressing the issue and the motivation behind it. The particular aspects of the microservices we are going to discuss in this chapter include the following:

- The motivation for the microservices rising
- The frameworks that were developed recently in support of microservices

- The process of microservices development with practical examples, including the considerations and decision-making process during microservices building
- Pros and cons of the three main deployment methods such as container-less, self-contained, and in-container

Why microservices?

Some businesses have a higher demand for the deployment plan because of the need to keep up with the bigger volume of traffic. The natural answer to this challenge would be and was to add servers with the same `.ear` or `.war` file deployed and join all the servers into a cluster. So, one failed server could be automatically replaced with another one from the cluster, and the site user would never experience disconnect of the service. The database that backed all the clustered servers could be clustered too. A connection to each of the clusters went through a load balancer, making sure that none of the cluster members worked more than the others.

The web server and database clustering help but only to a degree, because as the code base grows, its structure can create one or several bottlenecks unless such and similar issues are addressed with a scalable design. One of the ways to do it is to split the code into tiers: front end (or web tier), middle tier (or app tier) and back end (or backend tier). Then, again, each tier can be deployed independently (if the protocol between tiers has not changed) and in its own cluster of servers, as each tier can grow horizontally as needed independently of other tiers. Such a solution provides more flexibility for scaling up, but makes the deployment plan more complex, especially if the new code introduces breaking changes. One of the approaches is to create a second cluster that will host a new code, then take the servers one by one from the old cluster, deploy the new code, and put them in the new cluster. The new cluster would be turned on as soon as at least one server in each tier has the new code. This approach worked fine for the web and app tiers but was more complex for the backend, which once in a while required data migration and similar joyful exercises. Add to it unexpected outages in the middle of the deployment caused by human errors, defects in the code, pure accidents, or some combination of all the earlier mentioned (one time, for example, an electric power cable was cut by an excavator in the nearby construction site), and it is easy to understand why very few people love a deployment of a major release to production.

Programmers, being by nature problem solvers, tried to prevent the earlier scenario as best as they could by writing defensive code, deprecating instead of changing, testing, and so on. One of the approaches was to break the application into more independently deployable parts with the hope of avoiding deploying everything at the same time. They called these independent units *services*, and **Service-Oriented Architecture (SOA)** was born.

Unfortunately, in many companies, the natural growth of the code base was not adjusted to the new challenges in a timely manner. Like the frog that was eventually boiled in a slowly heated pot of water, they never had time to jump out of the hot spot by changing the design. It was always cheaper to add another feature to the blob of the existing functionality than redesign the whole app. Business metrics of the time-to-market and keeping the bottom line in the black always were and will remain the main criterion for the decision making, until the poorly structured source code eventually stops working, pulling down all the business transactions with it or, if the company is lucky, allows them to weather the storm and shows the importance of the investment in the redesign.

As a result of all that, some lucky companies remained in the business with their monolithic application still running as expected (maybe not for long, but who knows), some went out of business, some learned from their mistakes and progressed into the brave world of the new challenges, and others learned from their mistakes and designed their systems to be SOA upfront.

It is interesting to observe similar tendencies in the social sphere. Society moved from the strong centralized governments to more loosely coupled confederations of semi-independent states tied together by the mutually beneficial economic and cultural exchange.

Unfortunately, maintaining such a loose structure comes with a price. Each participant has to be more responsible in maintaining the contract (social, in the case of a society, and API, in the case of the software) not only formally but also in spirit. Otherwise, for example, the data flowing from a new version of one component, although correct by type, might be unacceptable to another component by value (too big or too small). Maintaining a cross-team understanding and overlapping of responsibility requires constant vigilance in keeping the culture alive and enlightening. Encouraging innovation and risk taking, which can lead to a business breakthrough, contradict the protecting tendencies for stability and risk aversion coming from the same business people.

Moving from monolithic single-team development to multiple teams and an independent components-based system requires an effort on all levels of the enterprise. What do you mean by *No more Quality Assurance Department*? Who then will care about the professional growth of the testers? And what about the IT group? What do you mean by *The developers are going to support production*? Such changes affect human lives and are not easy to implement. That's why SOA architecture is not just a software principle. It affects everybody in the company.

Meanwhile, the industry leaders, who have managed to grow beyond anything we could imagine just a decade ago, were forced to solve even more daunting problems and came back to the software community with their solutions. And that is where our analogy with the pyramid building does not work anymore. Because the new challenge is not just to build something so big that was never built before but also to do it quickly not in a matter of years, but in a few weeks and even days. And the result has to last not for a thousand years but has to be able to evolve constantly and be flexible enough to adapt to new, unexpected requirements in real time. If only one aspect of the functionality has changed, we should be able to redeploy only this one service. If the demand for any service grows, we should be able to scale only along this one service and release resources when the demand drops.

To avoid big deployments with all hands on deck and to come closer to the continuous deployment (which decreases time-to-market and is thus supported by business), the functionality continued to split into smaller chunks of services. In response to the demand, more sophisticated and robust cloud environments, deployment tools (including containers and container orchestration), and monitoring systems supported this move. The reactive streams, described in the previous chapter, started to develop even before the Reactive Manifesto came out and plugged a snag into the stack of modern frameworks.

Splitting an application into independent deployment units brought several not quite expected benefits that have increased the motivation for plowing ahead. The physical isolation of services allows more flexibility in choosing a programming language and platform of implementation. It helps not only to select technology that is the best for the job but also to hire people able to implement it, not being bound by a certain technological stack of the company. It also helped the recruiters to spread the net wider and use smaller cells for bringing in new talent, which is not a small advantage with a limited number of available specialists and the unlimited demand of the fast-growing data processing industry.

Also, such architecture enforced a discussion and explicit definition of the interfaces between smaller parts of the complex system, thus creating a solid foundation for further growth and tuning of the processing sophistication.

And that is how microservices came into the picture and were put to work by giants of traffic such as Netflix, Google, Twitter, eBay, Amazon, and Uber. Now, let's talk about the results of this effort and the lessons learned.

Building microservices

Before diving into the building process, let's revisit the characteristics a chunk of code has to possess in order to be qualified as a microservice. We will do it in no particular order:

- The size of the source code of one microservice should be smaller to that of an SOA, and one development team should be able to support several of them.
- It has to be deployed independently of other services.
- Each has to have its own database (or schema or set of tables), although this statement is still under debate, especially in cases when several services modify the same data set or the inter-dependent data sets; if the same team owns all of the related services, it is easier to accomplish. Otherwise, there are several possible strategies we will discuss later.
- It has to be stateless and idempotent. If one instance of the service has failed, another should be able to accomplish what was expected from the service.
- It should provide a way to check its *health*, meaning that the service is up and running and ready to do the job.

Sharing resources has to be considered during the design, development, and, after deployment, monitored for validation of the assumptions. In the previous chapter, we talked about threads synchronization. You could see that this problem was not easy to solve, and we have presented several possible ways to do it. Similar approaches can be applied toward microservices. Although they are run in different processes, they can communicate to each other if need be, so they can coordinate and synchronize their actions.

Special care has to be taken during modification of the same persistent data whether shared across databases, schemas, or tables within the same schema. If an eventual consistency is acceptable (which is often the case for larger sets of data, used for statistical purposes, for example) then no special measures are necessary. However, the need for transactional integrity poses a more difficult problem.

One way to support a transaction across several microservices is to create a service that would play the role of a **Distributed Transaction Manager** (DTM). Other services that need coordination would pass to it the new modified values. The DTM service could keep the concurrently modified data temporarily in a database table and would move it into the main table(s) in one transaction after all the data is ready (and consistent).

If the time to access the data is an issue or you need to protect the database from an excessive number of concurrent connections, dedicating a database to some services may be an answer. Alternatively, if you would like to try another option, memory cache could be the way to go. Adding a service that provides access to the cache (and updates it as needed) increases isolation from the services that use it, but requires (sometimes difficult) synchronization between the peers that are managing the same cache too.

After considering all the options and possible solutions for data sharing, it is often helpful to revisit the idea of creating its own database (or schema) for each microservice. One may discover that the effort of the data isolation (and subsequent synchronization on the database level) does not look as daunting as before if compared with the effort to synchronize the data dynamically.

That said, let's look over the field of the frameworks for microservices implementation. One can definitely write the microservices from scratch, but before doing that, it is always worth looking at what is out there already, even if to find eventually that nothing fits your particular needs.

There are more than a dozen frameworks that are currently used for building microservices. Two most popular are Spring Boot (`https://projects.spring.io/spring-boot/`) and raw J2EE. The J2EE community founded the initiative MicroProfile (`https://microprofile.io/`) with a declared goal of *Optimizing Enterprise Java* for a microservices architecture. KumuluzEE (`https://ee.kumuluz.com/`) is a lightweight open-source microservice framework coplined with MicroProfile.

The list of some other frameworks include the following (in alphabetical order):

- **Akka**: This is a toolkit for building highly concurrent, distributed, and resilient message-driven applications for Java and Scala (`akka.io`)
- **Bootique**: This is a minimally opinionated framework for runnable Java apps (`bootique.io`)
- **Dropwizard**: This is a Java framework for developing ops-friendly, high-performance, RESTful web services (`www.dropwizard.io`)
- **Jodd**: This is a set of Java microframeworks, tools, and utilities, under 1.7 MB (`jodd.org`)
- **Lightbend Lagom**: This is an opinionated microservice framework built on Akka and Play (`www.lightbend.com`)
- **Ninja**: This is a full stack web framework for Java (`www.ninjaframework.org`)
- **Spotify Apollo**: This is a set of Java libraries used at Spotify for writing microservices (`spotify.github.io/apollo`)
- **Vert.x**: This is a toolkit for building reactive applications on the JVM (`vertx.io`)

All frameworks support HTTP/JSON communication between microservices; some of them also have an additional way to send messages. If not the latter, any lightweight messaging system can be used. We mentioned it here because, as you may recall, message-driven asynchronous processing is a foundation for elasticity, responsiveness, and resilience of a reactive system composed of microservices.

To demonstrate the process of microservices building, we will use Vert.x, an event-driven, non-blocking, lightweight, and polyglot toolkit (components can be written in Java, JavaScript, Groovy, Ruby, Scala, Kotlin, and Ceylon). It supports an asynchronous programming model and a distributed event bus that reaches even into in-browser JavaScript (thus allowing the creation of real-time web applications).

One starts using Vert.x by creating a `Verticle` class that implements the interface `io.vertx.core.Verticle`:

```
package io.vertx.core;
public interface Verticle {
  Vertx getVertx();
  void init(Vertx vertx, Context context);
  void start(Future<Void> future) throws Exception;
  void stop(Future<Void> future) throws Exception;
}
```

The method names previously mentioned are self-explanatory. The method `getVertex()` provides access to the `Vertx` object the entry point into the Vert.x Core API. It provides access to the following functionality necessary for the microservices building:

- Creating TCP and HTTP clients and servers
- Creating DNS clients
- Creating Datagram sockets
- Creating periodic services
- Providing access to the event bus and file system API
- Providing access to the shared data API
- Deploying and undeploying verticles

Using this `Vertx` object, various verticles can be deployed, which talk to each other, receive an external request, and process and store data as any other Java application, thus forming a system of microservices. Using RxJava implementation from the package `io.vertx.rxjava`, we will show how one can create a reactive system of microservices.

A verticle is a building block in Vert.x world. It can easily be created by extending the `io.vertx.rxjava.core.AbstractVerticle` class:

```
package io.vertx.rxjava.core;
import io.vertx.core.Context;
import io.vertx.core.Vertx;
public class AbstractVerticle
                extends io.vertx.core.AbstractVerticle {
  protected io.vertx.rxjava.core.Vertx vertx;
  public void init(Vertx vertx, Context context) {
      super.init(vertx, context);
      this.vertx = new io.vertx.rxjava.core.Vertx(vertx);
  }
}
```

The earlier mentioned class, in turn, extends `io.vertx.core.AbstractVerticle`:

```
package io.vertx.core;
import io.vertx.core.json.JsonObject;
import java.util.List;
public abstract class AbstractVerticle
                                implements Verticle {
    protected Vertx vertx;
    protected Context context;
    public Vertx getVertx() { return vertx; }
    public void init(Vertx vertx, Context context) {
        this.vertx = vertx;
        this.context = context;
    }
    public String deploymentID() {
        return context.deploymentID();
    }
    public JsonObject config() {
        return context.config();
    }
    public List<String> processArgs() {
        return context.processArgs();
    }
    public void start(Future<Void> startFuture)
                                throws Exception {
        start();
        startFuture.complete();
    }
    public void stop(Future<Void> stopFuture)
                                throws Exception {
        stop();
        stopFuture.complete();
    }
```

```
    public void start() throws Exception {}
    public void stop() throws Exception {}

}
```

A verticle can be created by extending the class `io.vertx.core.AbstractVerticle`, too. However, we will write reactive microservices, so we will extend its rx-fied version-- `io.vertx.rxjava.core.AbstractVerticle`.

To use Vert.x and run the provided example, all you need to do is to add the following dependencies:

```
<dependency>
    <groupId>io.vertx</groupId>
    <artifactId>vertx-web</artifactId>
    <version>${vertx.version}</version>
</dependency>

<dependency>
    <groupId>io.vertx</groupId>
    <artifactId>vertx-rx-java</artifactId>
    <version>${vertx.version}</version>
</dependency>
```

Other Vert.x functionality can be added as needed by including other Maven dependencies.

What makes Vert.x `Verticle` reactive is the underlying implementation of an event loop (a thread) that receives an event and delivers it a `Handler` (we will show how to write the code for it). When a `Handler` gets the result, the event loop invokes the callback.

 As you see, it is important not to write a code that blocks the event loop, thus the Vert.x golden rule: don't block the event loop.

If not blocked, the event loop works very quickly and delivers a huge number of events in a short period of time. This is called the reactor pattern (`https://en.wikipedia.org/wiki/ Reactor_pattern`). Such an event-driven non-blocking programming model is a very good fit for reactive microservices. For certain types of code that are blocking by nature (JDBC calls and long computations are good examples) a worker verticle can be executed asynchronously (not by the event loop, but by a separate thread using the method `vertx.executeBlocking()`), which keeps the golden rule intact.

Let's look at a few examples. Here is a `Verticle` class that works as an HTTP server:

```
import io.vertx.rxjava.core.http.HttpServer;
import io.vertx.rxjava.core.AbstractVerticle;

public class Server extends AbstractVerticle{
  private int port;
  public Server(int port) {
    this.port = port;
  }
  public void start() throws Exception {
    HttpServer server = vertx.createHttpServer();
    server.requestStream().toObservable()
        .subscribe(request -> request.response()
        .end("Hello from " +
          Thread.currentThread().getName() +
                    " on port " + port + "!\n\n")
        );
    server.rxListen(port).subscribe();
    System.out.println(Thread.currentThread().getName()
            + " is waiting on port " + port + "...");
  }
}
```

In the previous code, the server is created, and the stream of data from a possible request is wrapped into an `Observable`. We then subscribed to the data coming from the `Observable` and passed in a function (a request handler) that will process the request and generate a necessary response. We also told the server which port to listen. Using this `Verticle`, we can deploy several instances of an HTTP server listening on different ports. Here is an example:

```
import io.vertx.rxjava.core.RxHelper;
import static io.vertx.rxjava.core.Vertx.vertx;
public class Demo01Microservices {
  public static void main(String... args) {
    RxHelper.deployVerticle(vertx(), new Server(8082));
    RxHelper.deployVerticle(vertx(), new Server(8083));
  }
}
```

If we run this application, the output would be as follows:

```
vert.x-eventloop-thread-0 is waiting on port 8082...
vert.x-eventloop-thread-0 is waiting on port 8083...
```

As you can see, the same thread is listening on both ports. If we now place a request to each of the running servers, we will get the response we have hardcoded:

```
demo> curl localhost:8082
Hello from vert.x-eventloop-thread-0 on port 8082!

demo> curl localhost:8083
Hello from vert.x-eventloop-thread-0 on port 8083!
```

We ran our examples from the `main()` method. A plugin `maven-shade-plugin` allows you to specify which verticle you would like to be the starting point of your application. Here is an example from `http://vertx.io/blog/my-first-vert-x-3-application`:

```
<plugin>
  <groupId>org.apache.maven.plugins</groupId>
  <artifactId>maven-shade-plugin</artifactId>
  <version>2.3</version>
  <executions>
    <execution>
      <phase>package</phase>
      <goals>
        <goal>shade</goal>
      </goals>
      <configuration>
        <transformers>
          <transformer
implementation="org.apache.maven.plugins.shade.resource.ManifestResourceTra
nsformer">
            <manifestEntries>
              <Main-Class>io.vertx.core.Starter</Main-Class>
              <Main-Verticle>io.vertx.blog.first.MyFirstVerticle</Main-
Verticle>
            </manifestEntries>
          </transformer>
        </transformers>
        <artifactSet/>
        <outputFile>${project.build.directory}/${project.artifactId}-
${project.version}-fat.jar</outputFile>
      </configuration>
    </execution>
  </executions>
</plugin>
```

Now, run the following command:

```
mvn package
```

It will generate a specified JAR file (called `target/my-first-app-1.0-SNAPSHOT-fat.jar`, in this example). It is called *fat* because it contains all the necessary dependencies. This file will also contain `MANIFEST.MF` with the following entries in it:

```
Main-Class: io.vertx.core.Starter
Main-Verticle: io.vertx.blog.first.MyFirstVerticle
```

You can use any verticle instead of `io.vertx.blog.first.MyFirstVerticle`, used in this example, but `io.vertx.core.Starter` has to be there because that is the name of the `Vert.x` class that knows how to read the manifest and execute the method `start()` of the specified verticle. Now, you can run the following command:

```
java -jar target/my-first-app-1.0-SNAPSHOT-fat.jar
```

This command will execute the `start()` method of the `MyFirstVerticle` class the same way the `main()` method is executed in our example, which we will continue to use for the simplicity of demonstration.

To compliment the HTTP server, we can create an HTTP client too. However, first, we will modify the method `start()` in the `server` verticle to accept the parameter `name`:

```java
public void start() throws Exception {
    HttpServer server = vertx.createHttpServer();
    server.requestStream().toObservable()
        .subscribe(request -> request.response()
        .end("Hi, " + request.getParam("name") +
            "! Hello from " +
            Thread.currentThread().getName() +
                " on port " + port + "!\n\n")
    );
    server.rxListen(port).subscribe();
    System.out.println(Thread.currentThread().getName()
            + " is waiting on port " + port + "...");
}
```

Now, we can create an HTTP `client` verticle that sends a request and prints out the response every second for 3 seconds, then stops:

```
import io.vertx.rxjava.core.AbstractVerticle;
import io.vertx.rxjava.core.http.HttpClient;
import java.time.LocalTime;
import java.time.temporal.ChronoUnit;

public class Client extends AbstractVerticle {
  private int port;
  public Client(int port) {
    this.port = port;
  }
  public void start() throws Exception {
    HttpClient client = vertx.createHttpClient();
    LocalTime start = LocalTime.now();
    vertx.setPeriodic(1000, v -> {
        client.getNow(port, "localhost", "?name=Nick",
          r -> r.bodyHandler(System.out::println));
          if(ChronoUnit.SECONDS.between(start,
                            LocalTime.now()) > 3 ){
            vertx.undeploy(deploymentID());
        }
    });
  }
}
```

Let's assume we deploy both verticles as follows:

```
RxHelper.deployVerticle(vertx(), new Server2(8082));
RxHelper.deployVerticle(vertx(), new Client(8082));
```

The output will be as follows:

```
vert.x-eventloop-thread-0 is waiting on port 8082...
Hi, Nick! Hello from vert.x-eventloop-thread-0 on port 8082!
Hi, Nick! Hello from vert.x-eventloop-thread-0 on port 8082!
Hi, Nick! Hello from vert.x-eventloop-thread-0 on port 8082!
```

In this last example, we demonstrated how to create an HTTP client and periodic service. Now, let's add more functionality to our system. For example, let's add another verticle that will interact with the database and use it via the HTTP server we have already created.

First, we need to add this dependency:

```
<dependency>
    <groupId>io.vertx</groupId>
    <artifactId>vertx-jdbc-client</artifactId>
    <version>${vertx.version}</version>
</dependency>
```

The newly added JAR file allows us to create an in-memory database and a handler to access it:

```
public class DbHandler {
  private JDBCClient dbClient;
  private static String SQL_CREATE_WHO_CALLED =
    "CREATE TABLE IF NOT EXISTS " +
          "who_called ( name VARCHAR(10), " +
          "create_ts TIMESTAMP(6) DEFAULT now() )";
  private static String SQL_CREATE_PROCESSED =
    "CREATE TABLE IF NOT EXISTS " +
          "processed ( name VARCHAR(10), " +
          "length INTEGER, " +
          "create_ts TIMESTAMP(6) DEFAULT now() )";

  public DbHandler(Vertx vertx){
    JsonObject config = new JsonObject()
      .put("driver_class", "org.hsqldb.jdbcDriver")
      .put("url", "jdbc:hsqldb:mem:test?shutdown=true");
    dbClient = JDBCClient.createShared(vertx, config);
    dbClient.rxGetConnection()
      .flatMap(conn ->
                  conn.rxUpdate(SQL_CREATE_WHO_CALLED)
                        .doAfterTerminate(conn::close) )
      .subscribe(r ->
        System.out.println("Table who_called created"),
                            Throwable::printStackTrace);
    dbClient.rxGetConnection()
      .flatMap(conn ->
                  conn.rxUpdate(SQL_CREATE_PROCESSED)
                        .doAfterTerminate(conn::close) )
      .subscribe(r ->
        System.out.println("Table processed created"),
                            Throwable::printStackTrace);

  }
}
```

Those familiar with RxJava can see that Vert.x code closely follows the style and naming convention of RxJava. Nevertheless, we encourage you to go through Vert.x documentation, because it has a very rich API that covers many more cases than just demonstrated. In the previous code, the operation `flatMap()` receives the function that runs the script and then closes the connection. The operation `doAfterTerminate()` in this case acts as if it was placed inside a finally block in a traditional code and closes the connection either in case of success or if an exception is generated. The `subscribe()` method has several overloaded versions. For our code, we have selected the one that takes two functions one is going to be executed in the case of success (we print a message about the table being created) and another in the case of an exception (we just print the stack trace then).

To use the created database, we can add to `DbHandler` methods `insert()`, `process()`, and `readProcessed()` that will allow us to demonstrate how to build a reactive system. The code for the method `insert()` can look like this:

```
private static String SQL_INSERT_WHO_CALLED =
              "INSERT INTO who_called(name) VALUES (?)";
public void insert(String name, Action1<UpdateResult>
              onSuccess, Action1<Throwable> onError){
  printAction("inserts " + name);
  dbClient.rxGetConnection()
    .flatMap(conn ->
       conn.rxUpdateWithParams(SQL_INSERT_WHO_CALLED,
                         new JsonArray().add(name))
                   .doAfterTerminate(conn::close) )
    .subscribe(onSuccess, onError);
}
```

The `insert()` method, as well as other methods we are going to write, takes full advantage of Java functional interfaces. It creates a record in the table `who_called` (using the passed in parameter `name`). Then, the operation `subscribe()` executes one of the two functions passed in by the code that calls this method. We use the method `printAction()` only for better traceability:

```
private void printAction(String action) {
  System.out.println(this.getClass().getSimpleName()
                          + " " + action);
}
```

The method `process()` also accepts two functions but does not need other parameters. It processes all the records from the table `who_called` that are not processed yet (not listed in the table `processed`):

```
private static String SQL_SELECT_TO_PROCESS =
   "SELECT name FROM who_called w where name not in " +
   "(select name from processed) order by w.create_ts " +
   "for update";
private static String SQL_INSERT_PROCESSED =
      "INSERT INTO processed(name, length) values(?, ?)";
public void process(Func1<JsonArray, Observable<JsonArray>>
                    process, Action1<Throwable> onError) {
  printAction("process all records not processed yet");
  dbClient.rxGetConnection()
    .flatMapObservable(conn ->
       conn.rxQueryStream(SQL_SELECT_TO_PROCESS)
          .flatMapObservable(SQLRowStream::toObservable)
          .flatMap(process)
          .flatMap(js ->
             conn.rxUpdateWithParams(SQL_INSERT_PROCESSED, js)
                .flatMapObservable(ur->Observable.just(js)))
          .doAfterTerminate(conn::close))
    .subscribe(js -> printAction("processed " + js), onError);
}
```

If two threads are reading the table `who_called` for the purpose of selecting records not processed yet, the clause `for update` in the SQL query makes sure that only one gets each record, so they are not going to be processed twice. The significant advantage of the method `process()` code is its usage of the `rxQUeryStream()` operation that emits the found records one at a time so that they are processed independently of each other. In the case of a big number of not processed records, such a solution guarantees a smooth delivery of the results without the spiking of the resources consumption. The following `flatMap()` operation does processing using the function passed in. The only requirement for that function is that it must return one integer value (in `JsonArray`) that is going to be used as a parameter for the `SQL_INSERT_PROCESSED` statement. So, it is up to the code that calls this method to decide the nature of the processing. The rest of the code is similar to the method `insert()`. The code indentation helps to follow the nesting of the operations.

The method `readProcessed()` has code that looks very similar to the code of the method `insert()`:

```
private static String SQL_READ_PROCESSED =
  "SELECT name, length, create_ts FROM processed
                    order by create_ts desc limit ?";
public void readProcessed(String count, Action1<ResultSet>
              onSuccess, Action1<Throwable> onError) {
  printAction("reads " + count +
                      " last processed records");
  dbClient.rxGetConnection()
    .flatMap(conn ->
      conn.rxQueryWithParams(SQL_READ_PROCESSED,
                      new JsonArray().add(count))
                  .doAfterTerminate(conn::close) )
    .subscribe(onSuccess, onError);
}
```

The preceding code reads the specified number of the latest processed records. The difference from the method `process()` is that the method `readProcessed()` returns all the read records in one result set, so it is up to the user of this method to decide how to process the result in bulk or one at a time. We show all these possibilities just to demonstrate the variety of the possible options. With the `DbHandler` class in place, we are ready to use it and create the `DbServiceHttp` microservice, which allows a remote access to the `DbHandler` capabilities by wrapping around it an HTTP server. Here is the constructor of the new microservice:

```
public class DbServiceHttp extends AbstractVerticle {
  private int port;
  private DbHandler dbHandler;
  public DbServiceHttp(int port) {
    this.port = port;
  }
  public void start() throws Exception {
    System.out.println(this.getClass().getSimpleName() +
                      "(" + port + ") starts...");
    dbHandler = new DbHandler(vertx);
    Router router = Router.router(vertx);
    router.put("/insert/:name").handler(this::insert);
    router.get("/process").handler(this::process);
    router.get("/readProcessed")
                      .handler(this::readProcessed);
    vertx.createHttpServer()
        .requestHandler(router::accept).listen(port);
  }
}
```

In the earlier mentioned code, you can see how the URL mapping is done in Vert.x. For each possible route, a corresponding `Verticle` method is assigned, each accepting the `RoutingContext` object that contains all the data of HTTP context, including the `HttpServerRequest` and `HttpServerResponse` objects. A variety of convenience methods allows us to easily access the URL parameters and other data necessary to process the request. Here is the method `insert()` referred in the `start()` method:

```
private void insert(RoutingContext routingContext) {
  HttpServerResponse response = routingContext.response();
  String name = routingContext.request().getParam("name");
  printAction("insert " + name);
  Action1<UpdateResult> onSuccess =
    ur -> response.setStatusCode(200).end(ur.getUpdated() +
              " record for " + name + " is inserted");
  Action1<Throwable> onError = ex -> {
    printStackTrace("process", ex);
    response.setStatusCode(400)
        .end("No record inserted due to backend error");
  };
  dbHandler.insert(name, onSuccess, onError);
}
```

All it does is extracts the parameter `name` from the request and constructs the two functions necessary to call method `insert()` of `DbHandler` we discussed earlier. The method `process()` looks similar to the previous method `insert()`:

```
private void process(RoutingContext routingContext) {
  HttpServerResponse response = routingContext.response();
  printAction("process all");
  response.setStatusCode(200).end("Processing...");
  Func1<JsonArray, Observable<JsonArray>> process =
    jsonArray -&gt; {
      String name = jsonArray.getString(0);
      JsonArray js =
          new JsonArray().add(name).add(name.length());
      return Observable.just(js);
  };
  Action1<Throwable> onError = ex -> {
    printStackTrace("process", ex);
    response.setStatusCode(400).end("Backend error");
  };
  dbHandler.process(process, onError);
}
```

The function `process` mentioned earlier defines what should be done with the records coming from the `SQL_SELECT_TO_PROCESS` statement inside the method `process()` in `DbHandler`. In our case, it calculates the length of the caller's name and passes it as a parameter along with the name itself (as a return value) to the next SQL statement that inserts the result into the table `processed`.

Here is the method `readProcessed()`:

```
private void readProcessed(RoutingContext routingContext) {
    HttpServerResponse response = routingContext.response();
    String count = routingContext.request().getParam("count");
    printAction("readProcessed " + count + " entries");
    Action1<ResultSet> onSuccess = rs -> {
        Observable.just(rs.getResults().size() > 0 ?
            rs.getResults().stream().map(Object::toString)
                    .collect(Collectors.joining("\n")) : "")
        .subscribe(s -> response.setStatusCode(200).end(s) );
    };
    Action1<Throwable> onError = ex -> {
        printStackTrace("readProcessed", ex);
        response.setStatusCode(400).end("Backend error");
    };
    dbHandler.readProcessed(count, onSuccess, onError);
}
```

That is where (in the previous code in the function `onSuccess()`) the result set from the query `SQL_READ_PROCESSED` is read and used to construct the response. Notice that we do it by creating an `Observable` first, then subscribing to it and passing the result of the subscription as the response into method `end()`. Otherwise, the response can be returned without waiting for the response to be constructed.

Now, we can launch our reactive system by deploying the `DbServiceHttp` verticle:

```
RxHelper.deployVerticle(vertx(), new DbServiceHttp(8082));
```

If we do that, in the output we will see the following lines of code:

```
DbServiceHttp(8082) starts...
Table processed created
Table who_called created
```

In another window, we can issue the command that generates an HTTP request:

```
demo> curl -XPUT localhost:8082/insert/Bill
1 record for Bill is inserted
demo>
```

If we read the processed records now, there should be none:

```
demo> curl -XPUT localhost:8082/insert/Bill
1 record for Bill is inserted
demo> curl localhost:8082/readProcessed?count=1
```

The log messages show the following:

```
DbServiceHttp.insert Bill
DbHandler inserts Bill
DbServiceHttp.readProcessed 1 entries
DbHandler reads 1 last processed records
```

Now, we can request processing of the existing records and then read the results again:

```
demo> curl -w "\n" localhost:8082/process
Processing...
demo> curl -w "\n" localhost:8082/readProcessed?count=1
["Bill",4,"2017-09-20T02:49:17.623-06:00"]
demo>
```

In principle, it is enough already to build a reactive system. We can deploy many `DbServiceHttp` microservices on different ports or cluster them to increase processing capacity, resilience, and responsiveness. We can wrap other services inside an HTTP client or an HTTP server and let them talk to each other, processing the input and passing the results along the processing pipeline.

However, Vert.x also has a feature that even better suits the message-driven architecture (without using HTTP). It is called an event bus. Any verticle has access to the event bus and can send any message to any address (which is just a string) using either method `send()` (`rxSend()` in the case of reactive programming) or method `publish()`. One or many verticles can register themselves as a consumer for a certain address.

If many verticles are consumers for the same address, then the method `send()` (`rxSend()`) delivers the message only to one of them (using a round-robin algorithm to pick the next consumer). The method `publish()`, as you would expect, delivers the message to all consumers with the same address. Let's see an example, using the already familiar `DbHandler` as the main working horse.

A microservice, based on an event bus, looks very similar to the one based on the HTTP protocol we discussed already:

```
public class DbServiceBus extends AbstractVerticle {
   private int id;
   private String instanceId;
   private DbHandler dbHandler;
   public static final String INSERT = "INSERT";
   public static final String PROCESS = "PROCESS";
   public static final String READ_PROCESSED
                             = "READ_PROCESSED";
   public DbServiceBus(int id) { this.id = id; }
   public void start() throws Exception {
      this.instanceId = this.getClass().getSimpleName()
                                  + "(" + id + ")";
      System.out.println(instanceId + " starts...");
      this.dbHandler = new DbHandler(vertx);
      vertx.eventBus().consumer(INSERT).toObservable()
        .subscribe(msg -> {
            printRequest(INSERT, msg.body().toString());
            Action1<UpdateResult> onSuccess
                              = ur -> msg.reply(...);
            Action1<Throwable> onError
                    = ex -> msg.reply("Backend error");
            dbHandler.insert(msg.body().toString(),
                              onSuccess, onError);
      });

      vertx.eventBus().consumer(PROCESS).toObservable()
        .subscribe(msg -> {
              .....
              dbHandler.process(process, onError);
      });

      vertx.eventBus().consumer(READ_PROCESSED).toObservable()
        .subscribe(msg -> {
            ...
          dbHandler.readProcessed(msg.body().toString(),
                              onSuccess, onError);
      });
   }
```

We simplified the preceding code by skipping some sections (that are very similar to the `DbServiceHttp` class) and trying to highlight the code structure. For demo purposes, we will deploy two instances of this class and send three messages to each of the addresses `INSERT`, `PROCESS`, and `READ_PROCESSED`:

```
void demo_DbServiceBusSend() {
  Vertx vertx = vertx();
  RxHelper.deployVerticle(vertx, new DbServiceBus(1));
  RxHelper.deployVerticle(vertx, new DbServiceBus(2));
  delayMs(200);
  String[] msg1 = {"Mayur", "Rohit", "Nick" };
  RxHelper.deployVerticle(vertx,
    new PeriodicServiceBusSend(DbServiceBus.INSERT, msg1, 1));
  String[] msg2 = {"all", "all", "all" };
  RxHelper.deployVerticle(vertx,
    new PeriodicServiceBusSend(DbServiceBus.PROCESS, msg2, 1));
  String[] msg3 = {"1", "1", "2", "3" };
  RxHelper.deployVerticle(vertx,
    new PeriodicServiceBusSend(DbServiceBus.READ_PROCESSED,
                                              msg3, 1));
}
```

Notice the delay for 200 ms we inserted using the method `delayMs()`:

```
void delayMs(int ms){
    try {
        TimeUnit.MILLISECONDS.sleep(ms);
    } catch (InterruptedException e) {}
}
```

The delay is necessary to let the `DbServiceBus` verticle to be deployed and started (and the consumers registered with the address). Otherwise, an attempt to send a message may fail because the consumer is not registered with the address yet. The `PeriodicServiceBusSend()` verticle code is as follows:

```
public class PeriodicServiceBusSend
                            extends AbstractVerticle {
  private EventBus eb;
  private LocalTime start;
  private String address;
  private String[] caller;
  private int delaySec;
  public PeriodicServiceBusSend(String address,
                    String[] caller, int delaySec) {
      this.address = address;
      this.caller = caller;
      this.delaySec = delaySec;
```

```
  }
  public void start() throws Exception {
    System.out.println(this.getClass().getSimpleName()
      + "(" + address + ", " + delaySec + ") starts...");
    this.eb = vertx.eventBus();
    this.start  = LocalTime.now();
    vertx.setPeriodic(delaySec * 1000, v -> {
      int i = (int)ChronoUnit.SECONDS.between(start,
                                LocalTime.now()) - 1;
      System.out.println(this.getClass().getSimpleName()
        + " to address " + address + ": " + caller[i]);
      eb.rxSend(address, caller[i]).subscribe(reply -> {
        System.out.println(this.getClass().getSimpleName()
                + " got reply from address " + address
                            + ":\n    " + reply.body());
        if(i + 1 >= caller.length ){
            vertx.undeploy(deploymentID());
        }
      }, Throwable::printStackTrace);
    });
  }
}
```

The previous code sends a message to an address every `delaySec` seconds as many times as the length of the array `caller[]`, and then undeploys the verticle (itself). If we run the demo, the beginning of the output will be as follows:

```
PeriodicServiceBusSend to address PROCESS: all
PeriodicServiceBusSend to address READ_PROCESSED: 1
PeriodicServiceBusSend to address INSERT: Mayur
DbServiceBus(1).PROCESS got request: all
PeriodicServiceBusSend got reply from address PROCESS:
    DbServiceBus(1).PROCESS: Processing all...
DbHandler process all records not processed yet
DbServiceBus(1).READ_PROCESSED got request: 1
DbHandler reads 1 last processed records
DbServiceBus(1).INSERT got request: Mayur
DbHandler inserts Mayur
PeriodicServiceBusSend got reply from address READ_PROCESSED:
    DbServiceBus(1).READ_PROCESSED:

PeriodicServiceBusSend got reply from address INSERT:
    DbServiceBus(1).INSERT: 1 record for Mayur is inserted
PeriodicServiceBusSend to address READ_PROCESSED: 1
PeriodicServiceBusSend to address INSERT: Rohit
PeriodicServiceBusSend to address PROCESS: all
DbServiceBus(2).READ_PROCESSED got request: 1
DbHandler reads 1 last processed records
DbServiceBus(2).INSERT got request: Rohit
DbHandler inserts Rohit
DbServiceBus(2).PROCESS got request: all
```

As you can see, for each address, only `DbServiceBus(1)` was a receiver of the first message. The second message to the same address was received by `DbServiceBus(2)`. That was the round-robin algorithm (which we mentioned earlier) in action. The final section of the output looks like this:

```
DbHandler inserts Nick
DbServiceBus(1).READ_PROCESSED got request: 2
DbHandler reads 2 last processed records
DbServiceBus(1).PROCESS got request: all
DbHandler process all records not processed yet
PeriodicServiceBusSend got reply from address PROCESS:
    DbServiceBus(1).PROCESS: Processing all...
PeriodicServiceBusSend got reply from address INSERT:
    DbServiceBus(1).INSERT: 1 record for Nick is inserted
DbHandler processed ["Nick",4]
PeriodicServiceBusSend got reply from address READ_PROCESSED:
    DbServiceBus(1).READ_PROCESSED:
        ["Rohit",5,"2017-09-21T02:52:43.270-06:00"]
["Mayur",5,"2017-09-21T02:52:43.258-06:00"]
PeriodicServiceBusSend to address READ_PROCESSED: 3
DbServiceBus(2).READ_PROCESSED got request: 3
DbHandler reads 3 last processed records
PeriodicServiceBusSend got reply from address READ_PROCESSED:
    DbServiceBus(2).READ_PROCESSED:
        ["Nick",4,"2017-09-21T02:52:44.118-06:00"]
["Rohit",5,"2017-09-21T02:52:43.270-06:00"]
["Mayur",5,"2017-09-21T02:52:43.258-06:00"]
```

We can deploy as many verticles of the same type as needed. For example, let's deploy four verticles that send messages to the address `INSERT`:

```
String[] msg1 = {"Mayur", "Rohit", "Nick" };
RxHelper.deployVerticle(vertx,
  new PeriodicServiceBusSend(DbServiceBus.INSERT, msg1, 1));
RxHelper.deployVerticle(vertx,
  new PeriodicServiceBusSend(DbServiceBus.INSERT, msg1, 1));
RxHelper.deployVerticle(vertx,
  new PeriodicServiceBusSend(DbServiceBus.INSERT, msg1, 1));
RxHelper.deployVerticle(vertx,
  new PeriodicServiceBusSend(DbServiceBus.INSERT, msg1, 1));
```

To see the results, we will also ask the reading `Verticle` to read the last eight records:

```
String[] msg3 = {"1", "1", "2", "8" };
RxHelper.deployVerticle(vertx,
  new PeriodicServiceBusSend(DbServiceBus.READ_PROCESSED,
                                        msg3, 1));
```

The result (the final section of the output) then will be as expected:

```
PeriodicServiceBusSend to address READ_PROCESSED: 8
DbServiceBus(2).READ_PROCESSED got request: 8
DbHandler reads 8 last processed records
PeriodicServiceBusSend got reply from address READ_PROCESSED:
    DbServiceBus(2).READ_PROCESSED:
        ["Nick",4,"2017-09-22T02:18:45.591-06:00"]
["Nick",4,"2017-09-22T02:18:45.579-06:00"]
["Nick",4,"2017-09-22T02:18:45.568-06:00"]
["Nick",4,"2017-09-22T02:18:45.558-06:00"]
["Rohit",5,"2017-09-22T02:18:44.591-06:00"]
["Rohit",5,"2017-09-22T02:18:44.580-06:00"]
["Rohit",5,"2017-09-22T02:18:44.570-06:00"]
["Rohit",5,"2017-09-22T02:18:44.558-06:00"]
```

Four verticles have sent the same messages, so each name was sent four times and processed that is what we see in the previous output.

We will now return to one inserting periodic verticle but will change it from using the method `rxSend()` to the method `publish()`:

```
PeriodicServiceBusPublish(String address, String[] caller, int delaySec) {
   ...
   vertx.setPeriodic(delaySec * 1000, v -> {
     int i = (int)ChronoUnit.SECONDS.between(start,
                                   LocalTime.now()) - 1;
     System.out.println(this.getClass().getSimpleName()
           + " to address " + address + ": " + caller[i]);
     eb.publish(address, caller[i]);
     if(i + 1 == caller.length ){
         vertx.undeploy(deploymentID());
     }
   });
}
```

This change would mean that the message has to be sent to all verticles that are registered as the consumers at that address. Now, let's run the following code:

```
Vertx vertx = vertx();
RxHelper.deployVerticle(vertx, new DbServiceBus(1));
RxHelper.deployVerticle(vertx, new DbServiceBus(2));
delayMs(200);
String[] msg1 = {"Mayur", "Rohit", "Nick" };
RxHelper.deployVerticle(vertx,
   new PeriodicServiceBusPublish(DbServiceBus.INSERT,
```

```
                                                        msg1, 1));
    delayMs(200);
    String[] msg2 = {"all", "all", "all" };
    RxHelper.deployVerticle(vertx,
        new PeriodicServiceBusSend(DbServiceBus.PROCESS,
                                                        msg2, 1));
    String[] msg3 = {"1", "1", "2", "8" };
    RxHelper.deployVerticle(vertx,
        new PeriodicServiceBusSend(DbServiceBus.READ_PROCESSED,
                                                        msg3, 1));
```

We have included another delay for 200 ms to give the publishing verticle time to send the message. The output (in the final section) now shows that each message was processed twice:

```
PeriodicServiceBusSend to address READ_PROCESSED: 8
DbServiceBus(2).READ_PROCESSED got request: 8
DbHandler reads 8 last processed records
PeriodicServiceBusSend got reply from address READ_PROCESSED:
    DbServiceBus(2).READ_PROCESSED:
        ["Nick",4,"2017-09-22T02:31:21.275-06:00"]
["Nick",4,"2017-09-22T02:31:21.264-06:00"]
["Rohit",5,"2017-09-22T02:31:20.276-06:00"]
["Rohit",5,"2017-09-22T02:31:20.265-06:00"]
["Mayur",5,"2017-09-22T02:31:19.406-06:00"]
["Mayur",5,"2017-09-22T02:31:19.394-06:00"]
```

That is because two consumers DbServiceBus(1) and DbServiceBus(2) were deployed, and each received a message to the address INSERT and inserted it in the table who_called.

All the previous examples we have run in one JVM process. If necessary, Vert.x instances can be deployed in different JVM processes and clustered by adding the -cluster option to the run command. Therefore, they share the event bus and the addresses are visible to all Vert.x instances. This way, the resources can be added to each address as needed. For example, we can increase the number of processing microservices only and compensate the load's increase.

Other frameworks we mentioned earlier have similar capabilities. They make microservices creation easy and may encourage breaking the application into tiny single-method operations with an expectation of assembling a very resilient and responsive system. However, these are not the only criteria of good quality. System decomposition increases the complexity of its deployment. Also, if one development team is responsible for many microservices, the complexity of versioning so many pieces in different stages (development, test, integration test, certification, staging, production) may lead to confusion and a very challenging deployment process, which, in turn, may slow down the rate of changes necessary to keep the system in sync with the market requirements.

In addition to the developing of the microservices, many other aspects have to be addressed to support the reactive system:

- A monitoring system has to be designed to provide an insight into the state of the application, but it should not be so complex as to pull the development resources away from the main application.
- Alerts have to be installed to warn the team about possible and actual issues in a timely manner, so they can be addressed before affecting the business.
- If possible, self-correcting automated processes have to be implemented. For example, the system should be able to add and release resources in accordance with the current load; the retry logic has to be implemented with a reasonable upper limit of a attempts before declaring the failure.
- A layer of circuit breakers has to protect the system from the domino effect when failure of one component deprives other components of the necessary resources.
- An embedded testing system should be able to introduce disruptions and simulate processing load to ensure that the application resilience and responsiveness do not degrade over time. For example, the Netflix team has introduced a *chaos monkey* a system that is able to shut down various parts of the production system to test the ability to recover. They use it even in production because a production environment has a specific configuration, and no test in another environment can guarantee that all possible issues are found.

One of the main considerations of a reactive system design is the selection of the deployment methodology that can be either container-less, self-contained, or in-container. We will look into the pros and cons of each of these approaches in the following sections of this chapter.

Container-less deployment

People use the term *container* to refer to very different things. In the original usage, a container was something that carried its content from one location to another without changing anything inside. However, when servers were introduced, only one aspect was emphasized the ability to hold an application to contain it. Also, another meaning was added to provide life-supportive infrastructure so that the container's content (an application) can not only survive but also be active and respond to the external requests. Such a redefined notion of a container was applied to web servers (servlet container), application servers (an application container with or without an EJB container), and other software facilities that provided the supportive environment for applications. Sometimes, even the JVM itself was called a container, but this association did not survive, probably, because the ability to actively engage (execute) the content does not align well with the original meaning of a container.

That is why, later, when people started talking about container-less deployment, they typically meant the ability to deploy an application into a JVM directly, without first installing WebSphere, WebLogic, JBoss, or any other mediating software that provides the runtime environment for the application.

In the previous sections, we described many frameworks that allow us to build and deploy an application (or rather a reactive system of microservices) without the need for any other container beyond the JVM itself. All you need to do is to build a fat JAR file that includes all the dependencies (except those that come from the JVM itself) and then run it as a standalone Java process:

```
$ java -jar myfatjar.jar
```

Well, you also need to make sure that MANIFEST.MF in your JAR file has an entry main class that points to the fully qualified class name that has the main() method and will be run at the startup. We have described how to do it in the previous section, *Building Microservices*.

That is the promised compile-once-run-everywhere of Java, everywhere meaning everywhere where JVM of a certain version or higher is installed. There are several advantages and disadvantages of this approach. We will discuss them not relative to the traditional deployment in a server container. The advantages of deployment without using the traditional containers are quite obvious, starting with much fewer (if any) licensing costs and ending up with much a lighter deployment and scalability process, not even mentioning much less consumption of resources. Instead, we will compare container-less deployment not with the traditional one, but with a self-contained and an in-container in a new generation of containers that have been developed a few years ago.

They allow the ability not only to contain and execute the contained code, which the traditional containers did too, but also to move it to a different location without any change to the contained code. From now on, by a container, we are going to mean only the new ones.

The advantages of container-less deployment are as follows:

- It is easy to add more Java processes either inside the same physical (or virtual or in the cloud) machine or on new hardware
- An isolation level between processes is high, which is especially important in the shared environment when you have no control over other co-deployed applications, and it is possible that a rogue application would try to penetrate the neighboring execution environment
- It has a small footprint since it does not include anything else beyond the application itself or a group of microservices

The disadvantages of container-less deployment are as follows:

- Each JAR file requires the JVM of a certain version or higher, which may force you to bring up a new physical or virtual machine just for this reason, to deploy one particular JAR file
- In the case of an environment you do not control, your code might be deployed with a wrong version of JVM, which could lead to unpredictable results
- Processes in the same JVM compete for resources, which are especially hard to manage in the case of the environments shared by different teams or different companies
- When several microservices are bundled into the same JAR file, they might require different versions of a third-party library or even incompatible libraries

Microservices can be deployed one per JAR or bundled together by a team, by related services, by the unit of scale, or using another criterion. Not the least important consideration is the total number of such JAR files. As this number grows (Google today deals with hundreds of thousands of deployment units at a time), it may become impossible to handle deployment via simple bash script and require a complex process that allows account ability for possible incompatibilities. If that is the case, then it is reasonable to consider using virtual machines or containers (in their new incarnation, see the following section) for better isolation and management.

Self-contained microservices

Self-contained microservices look much similar to container-less. The only difference is that the JVM (or JRE, actually) or any other external frameworks and servers necessary for the application to run are included in the fat JAR file too. There are many ways to build such an all-inclusive JAR file.

Spring Boot, for example, provides a convenient GUI with checkbox list that allows you to select which parts of your Spring Boot application and the external tools you would like to package. Similarly, WildFly Swarm allows you to choose which parts of the Java EE components you would like to bundle along with your application. Alternatively, you can do it yourself using the `javapackager` tool. It compiles and packages the application and JRE in the same JAR file (it can also be `.exe` or `.dmg`) for distribution. You can read about the tool on the Oracle website `https://docs.oracle.com/javase/9/tools/javapackager.htm` or you can just run the command `javapackager` on a computer where JDK is installed (it comes with Java 8 too) you will get the list of tool options and their brief description.

Basically, to use the `javapackager` tool, all you need to do is to prepare a project with everything you would like to package together, including all the dependencies (packaged in JAR files), and run the `javapackager` command with the necessary options that allow you to specify the type of output you would like to have (`.exe` or `.dmg`, for example), the JRE location you would like to bundle together, the icon to use, the `main` class entry for `MANIFEST.MF`, and so on. There are also Maven plugins that make the packaging command simpler because much of the setup has to be configured in `pom.xml`.

The advantages of self-contained deployment are as follows:

- It is one file (with all the microservices that compose the reactive system or some part of it) to handle, which is simpler for a user and for a distributor
- There is no need to pre-install JRE and no risk of mismatching the required version
- The isolation level is high because your application has a dedicated JRE, so the risk of an intrusion from a co-deployed application is minimal
- You have full control over the dependencies included in the bundle

The disadvantages are as follows:

- The size of the file is bigger, which might be an impediment if it has to be downloaded
- The configuration is more complex than in the case of a container-less JAR file
- The bundle has to be generated on a platform that matches the target one, which might lead to mismatch if you have no control over the installation process
- Other processes deployed on the same hardware or virtual machine can hog the resources critical for your application needs, which are especially hard to manage if your application is downloaded and run not by the team that has developed it

In-container deployment

Those who are familiar with **Virtual Machine** (**VM**) and not familiar with modern containers (such as Docker, Rocket by CoreOS, VMware Photon, or similar) could get the impression that we were talking about VM while saying that a container could not only contain and execute the contained code, but also to move it to a different location without any change to the contained code. If so, that would be quite an apt assumption. VM does allow all of that, and a modern container can be considered a lightweight VM as it also allows the allocation of resources and provides the feeling of a separate machine. Yet, a container is not a full-blown isolated virtual computer.

The key difference is that the bundle that can be passed around as a VM includes an entire operating system (with the application deployed). So, it is quite possible that a physical server running two VMs would have two different operating systems running on it. By contrast, a physical server (or a VM) running three containerized applications has only one operating system running, and the two containers share (read-only) the operating system kernel, each having its own access (mount) for writing to the resources they do not share. This means, for example, a much shorter start time, because starting a container does not require us to boot the operating system (as in the case of a VM).

For an example, let's take a closer look at Docker the community leader in container. In 2015, an initiative called *Open Container Project* was announced, later renamed the **Open Container Initiative** (**OCI**), which was supported by Google, IBM, Amazon, Microsoft, Red Hat, Oracle, VMware, HP, Twitter, and many other companies. Its purpose was to develop industry standards for a container format and container runtime software for all platforms. Docker has donated about 5 percent of its code base to the project because its solution was chosen as the starting point.

There is an extensive Docker documentation at: `https://docs.docker.com`. Using Docker, one can include in the package all the Java EE Container and the application as a Docker image, achieving essentially the same result as with a self-contained deployment. Then, you can launch your application by starting the Docker image in the Docker engine using this command:

```
$ docker run mygreatapplication
```

It starts a process that looks like running an OS on a physical computer, although it can also be happening in a cloud inside a VM that is running on the physical Linux server shared by many different companies and individuals. That is why an isolation level (which, in the case of containers, is almost as high as in a VM) may be critical in choosing between different deployment models.

A typical recommendation would be to put one microservice in each container, but nothing prevents you from putting several microservices in one Docker image (or any other container for that matter). However, there are already mature systems of container management (in the world of containers called *orchestration*) that can help you with deployment, so the complexity of having many containers, although a valid consideration, should not be a big obstacle if resilience and responsiveness are at stake. One of the popular orchestrations called *Kubernetes* supports microservice registry, discovery, and load balancing. Kubernetes can be used in any cloud or in a private infrastructure.

Containers allow a fast, reliable, and consistent deployment in practically any of the current deployment environments, whether it is your own infrastructure or a cloud at Amazon, Google, or Microsoft. They also allow the easy movement of an application through the development, testing, and production stages. Such infrastructure independence allows you, if necessary, to use a public cloud for development and testing and your own computers for production.

Once a base operating image is created, each development team can then build their application on top, thus avoiding the complexities of environment configuration. The versions of a container can also be tracked in a version control system.

The advantages of using containers are as follows:

- The level of isolation is the highest if compared with container-less and self-contained deployment. In addition, more efforts were put recently into adding security to containers.
- Each container is managed, distributed, deployed, started, and stopped by the same set of commands.
- There is no need to pre-install JRE and risk of mismatching the required version.

- You have full control over the dependencies included in the container.
- It is straightforward to scale up/down each microservice by adding/removing container instances.

The disadvantages of using containers are as follows:

- You and your team have to learn a whole new set of tools and become involved more heavily in the production stage. On the other hand, that seems to be the general tendency in recent years.

Summary

Microservices is a new architectural and design solution for highly loaded processing systems that became popular after being successfully used in production by such giants as Amazon, Google, Twitter, Microsoft, IBM, and others. It does not mean though that you must adopt it too, but you can consider the new approach and see if some or any of it can help your applications to be more resilient and responsive.

Using microservices can provide a substantial value, but it is not free. It comes with increased complexity of the need to manage many more units through all the lifecycle from requirements and development through testing to production. Before committing to the full-scale microservice architecture, give it a shot by implementing just a few microservices and move them all the way to production. Then, let it run for some time and gauge the experience. It will be very specific to your organization. Any successful solution must not be blindly copied but adopted as fit for your particular needs and abilities.

Better performance and overall efficiency often can be achieved by gradual improvements of what is already in place than by radical redesign and re-architecture.

In the next chapter, we will discuss and demonstrate new API that can improve your code by making it more readable and faster performing.

11
Making Use of New APIs to Improve Your Code

In the previous chapters, we talked about possible ways to improve the performance of your Java application--from using the new command and monitoring tools to adding multithreading and introducing reactive programming and even to radically re-architecting your current solution into an unruly and flexible bunch of small independent deployment units and microservices. Without knowing your particular situation, there is no way for us to guess which of the provided recommendations can be helpful to you. That's why, in this chapter, we will describe a few recent additions to the JDK that can be helpful to you too. As we mentioned in the previous chapter, the gain in performance and overall code improvement does not always require us to radically redesign it. Small incremental changes can sometimes bring more significant improvements than we could have expected.

To bring back our analogy of a pyramid building, instead of trying to change the logistics of the delivery of the stones to the final destination--in order to shorten the construction time-- it is often prudent to look closer at the tools the builders are using first. If each operation can be completed in half the time, the overall time of the project's delivery can be shortened accordingly, even if each of the stone blocks travels the same, if not a larger, distance.

These are the improvements of the programming tools we will discuss in this chapter:

- Using filters on streams as a way to find what you need and to decrease workload
- A new stack-walking API as the way analyze the stack trace programmatically in order to apply an automatic correction
- New convenient static factory methods that create compact, unmodifiable collection instances

- The new `CompletableFuture` class as a way to access the results of asynchronous processing
- The JDK 9 stream API improvements that can speed up processing while making your code more readable

Filtering streams

The `java.util.streams.Stream` interface was introduced in Java 8. It emits elements and supports a variety of operations that perform computations based on these elements. A stream can be finite or infinite, slow or fast emitting. Naturally, there is always a concern that the rate of the newly emitted elements may be higher than the rate of the processing. Besides, the ability to keep up with the input reflects the application's performance. The `Stream` implementations address the backpressure (when the rate of the element processing is lower than their emitting rate) by adjusting the emitting and processing rates using a buffer and various other techniques. In addition, it is always helpful if an application developer makes sure that the decision about processing or skipping each particular element is made as early as possible so that the processing resources are not wasted. Depending on the situation, different operations can be used for filtering the data.

Basic filtering

The first and the most straightforward way to do filtering is using the `filter()` operation. To demonstrate all the following capabilities, we will use the `Senator` class:

```
public class Senator {
    private int[] voteYes, voteNo;
    private String name, party;
    public Senator(String name, String party,
                   int[] voteYes, int[] voteNo) {
        this.voteYes = voteYes;
        this.voteNo = voteNo;
        this.name = name;
        this.party = party;
    }
    public int[] getVoteYes() { return voteYes; }
    public int[] getVoteNo() { return voteNo; }
    public String getName() { return name; }
    public String getParty() { return party; }
    public String toString() {
        return getName() + ", P" +
            getParty().substring(getParty().length() - 1);
```

```
        }
    }
```

As you can see, this class captures a senator's name, party, and how they voted for each of the issues (0 means No and 1 means Yes). If for a particular issue i, voteYes[i]=0, and voteNo[i]=0, it means that the senator was not present. It is not possible to have voteYes[i]=1 and voteNo[i]=1 for the same issue.

Let's assume that there are 100 senators, each belonging to one of the two parties--Party1 or Party2. We can use these objects to collect statistics of how senators voted for the last 10 issues using the Senate class:

```
public class Senate {
    public static List<Senator> getSenateVotingStats(){
        List<Senator> results = new ArrayList<>();
        results.add(new Senator("Senator1", "Party1",
                        new int[]{1,0,0,0,0,0,1,0,0,1},
                        new int[]{0,1,0,1,0,0,0,1,0}));
        results.add(new Senator("Senator2", "Party2",
                        new int[]{0,1,0,1,0,1,0,1,0,0},
                        new int[]{1,0,1,0,1,0,0,0,0,1}));
        results.add(new Senator("Senator3", "Party1",
                        new int[]{1,0,0,0,0,0,1,0,0,1},
                        new int[]{0,1,0,1,0,0,0,0,1,0}));
        results.add(new Senator("Senator4", "Party2",
                        new int[]{1,0,1,0,1,0,1,0,0,1},
                        new int[]{0,1,0,1,0,0,0,0,1,0}));
        results.add(new Senator("Senator5", "Party1",
                        new int[]{1,0,0,1,0,0,0,0,0,1},
                        new int[]{0,1,0,0,0,0,1,0,1,0}));
        IntStream.rangeClosed(6, 98).forEach(i -> {
            double r1 = Math.random();
            String name = "Senator" + i;
            String party = r1 > 0.5 ? "Party1" : "Party2";
            int[] voteNo = new int[10];
            int[] voteYes = new int[10];
            IntStream.rangeClosed(0, 9).forEach(j -> {
                double r2 = Math.random();
                voteNo[j] = r2 > 0.4 ? 0 : 1;
                voteYes[j] = r2 < 0.6 ? 0 : 1;
            });
            results.add(new Senator(name,party,voteYes,voteNo));
        });
        results.add(new Senator("Senator99", "Party1",
                        new int[]{0,0,0,0,0,0,0,0,0,0},
                        new int[]{1,1,1,1,1,1,1,1,1,1}));
          results.add(new Senator("Senator100", "Party2",
```

```
                            new int[]{1,1,1,1,1,1,1,1,1,1},
                            new int[]{0,0,0,0,0,0,0,0,0,0}));
        return results;
    }
    public static int timesVotedYes(Senator senator){
        return Arrays.stream(senator.getVoteYes()).sum();
    }
}
```

We hardcoded statistics for the first five senators so we can get predictable results while testing our filters and verify that the filters work. We also hardcoded voting statistics for the last two senators so we can have a predictable count while looking for senators who voted only `Yes` or only `No` for each of the ten issues. And we added the `timesVotedYes()` method, which provides the count of how many times the given `senator` voted `Yes`.

Now we can collect some data from the `Senate` class. For example, let's see how many members of each party comprise the `Senate` class:

```
List<Senator> senators = Senate.getSenateVotingStats();
long c1 = senators.stream()
    .filter(s -> s.getParty() == "Party1").count();
System.out.println("Members of Party1: " + c1);

long c2 = senators.stream()
    .filter(s -> s.getParty() == "Party2").count();
System.out.println("Members of Party2: " + c2);
System.out.println("Members of the senate: " + (c1 + c2));
```

The result of the preceding code differs from run to run because of the random value generator we used in the `Senate` class, so do not expect to see exactly the same numbers if you try to run the examples. What is important is that the total of the two party members should be equal 100--the total number of the senators in the `Senate` class:

```
Members of Party1: 58
Members of Party2: 42
Members of the senate: 100
```

The expression `s -> s.getParty()=="Party1"` is the predicate that filters out only those senators who are members of `Party1`. So, the elements (`Senator` objects) of `Party2` do not get through and are not included in the count. That was pretty straightforward.

Now let's look at a more complex example of filtering. Let's count how many senators of each party voted on `issue 3`:

```
int issue = 3;
c1 = senators.stream()
   .filter(s -> s.getParty() == "Party1")
   .filter(s -> s.getVoteNo()[issue] != s.getVoteYes()[issue])
   .count();
System.out.println("Members of Party1 who voted on Issue" +
                                    issue + ": " + c1);

c2 = senators.stream()
   .filter(s -> s.getParty() == "Party2" &&
              s.getVoteNo()[issue] != s.getVoteYes()[issue])
   .count();
System.out.println("Members of Party2 who voted on Issue" +
                                    issue + ": " + c2);
System.out.println("Members of the senate who voted on Issue"
                            + issue + ": " + (c1 + c2));
```

For `Party1`, we used two filters. For `Party2`, we combined them just to show another possible solution. The important point here is to use the filter by a party (`s -> s.getParty() == "Party1"`) first before the filter that selects only those who voted. This way, the second filter is used only for approximately half of the elements. Otherwise, if the filter that selects only those who voted were placed first, it would be applied to all 100 of `Senate` members.

The result looks like this:

```
Members of Party1 who voted on Issue3: 46
Members of Party2 who voted on Issue3: 36
Members of the senate who voted on Issue3: 82
```

Similarly, we can calculate how many members of each party voted `Yes` on `issue 3`:

```
c1 = senators.stream()
        .filter(s -> s.getParty() == "Party1" &&
                 s.getVoteYes()[issue] == 1)
        .count();
System.out.println("Members of Party1 who voted Yes on Issue"
                                    + issue + ": " + c1);

c2 = senators.stream()
        .filter(s -> s.getParty() == "Party2" &&
                 s.getVoteYes()[issue] == 1)
```

```
            .count();
System.out.println("Members of Party2 who voted Yes on Issue"
                                    + issue + ": " + c2);
System.out.println("Members of the senate voted Yes on Issue"
                            + issue + ": " + (c1 + c2));
```

The result of the preceding code is as follows:

```
Members of Party1 who voted Yes on Issue3: 19
Members of Party2 who voted Yes on Issue3: 19
Members of the senate voted Yes on Issue3: 38
```

We can refactor the preceding examples by taking advantage of the Java functional programming capability (using lambda expressions) and creating the countAndPrint() method:

```
long countAndPrint(List<Senator> senators,
    Predicate<Senator> pred1, Predicate<Senator> pred2,
                                    String prefix) {
    long c = senators.stream().filter(pred1::test)
                        .filter(pred2::test).count();
    System.out.println(prefix + c);
    return c;
}
```

Now all the earlier code can be expressed in a more compact way:

```
int issue = 3;

Predicate<Senator> party1 = s -> s.getParty() == "Party1";
Predicate<Senator> party2 = s -> s.getParty() == "Party2";
Predicate<Senator> voted3 =
        s -> s.getVoteNo()[issue] != s.getVoteYes()[issue];
Predicate<Senator> yes3 = s -> s.getVoteYes()[issue] == 1;

long c1 = countAndPrint(senators, party1, s -> true,
                            "Members of Party1: ");
long c2 = countAndPrint(senators, party2, s -> true,
                            "Members of Party2: ");
System.out.println("Members of the senate: " + (c1 + c2));

c1 = countAndPrint(senators, party1, voted3,
    "Members of Party1 who voted on Issue" + issue + ": ");
c2 = countAndPrint(senators, party2, voted3,
    "Members of Party2 who voted on Issue" + issue + ": ");
System.out.println("Members of the senate who voted on Issue"
```

```
                                      + issue + ": " + (c1 + c2));

c1 = countAndPrint(senators, party1, yes3,
   "Members of Party1 who voted Yes on Issue" + issue + ": ");
c2 = countAndPrint(senators, party2, yes3,
   "Members of Party2 who voted Yes on Issue" + issue + ": ");
System.out.println("Members of the senate voted Yes on Issue"
                                      + issue + ": " + (c1 + c2));
```

We created four predicates, `party1`, `party2`, `voted3`, and `yes3`, and we used each of them several times as parameters of the `countAndPrint()` method. The output of this code is the same as that of the earlier examples:

```
Members of Party1: 58
Members of Party2: 42
Members of the senate: 100
Members of Party1 who voted on Issue3: 46
Members of Party2 who voted on Issue3: 36
Members of the senate who voted on Issue3: 82
Members of Party1 who voted Yes on Issue3: 19
Members of Party2 who voted Yes on Issue3: 19
Members of the senate voted Yes on Issue3: 38
```

Using the `filter()` method of the `Stream` interface is the most popular way of filtering. But it is possible to use other `Stream` methods to accomplish the same effect.

Using other stream operations for filtering

Alternatively, or in addition to the basic filtering described in the previous section, other operations (methods of the `Stream` interface) can be used for selection and filtering emitted stream elements.

For example, let's use the `flatMap()` method to filter out the members of the Senate by their party membership:

```
long c1 = senators.stream()
        .flatMap(s -> s.getParty() == "Party1" ?
                    Stream.of(s) : Stream.empty())
        .count();
System.out.println("Members of Party1: " + c1);
```

This method takes advantage of the `Stream.of()` (produces a stream of one element) and `Stream.empty()` factory methods (it produces a stream without elements, so nothing is emitted further downstream). Alternatively, the same effect can be achieved using a new factory method (introduced in Java 9) called `Stream.ofNullable()`:

```
c1 = senators.stream().flatMap(s ->
  Stream.ofNullable(s.getParty() == "Party1" ? s : null))
                                           .count();
System.out.println("Members of Party1: " + c1);
```

The `Stream.ofNullable()` method creates a stream of one element if not `null`; otherwise, it creates an empty stream, as in the previous example. Both the preceding code snippets-- produce the same output if we run them for the same senate composition:

```
Members of Party1: 58
Members of Party1: 58
```

However, the same result can be achieved using a `java.uti.Optional` class that may or may not contain a value. If a value is present (and not `null`), its `isPresent()` method returns `true` and the `get()` method returns the value. Here is how we can use it to filter out the members of one party:

```
long c2 = senators.stream()
  .map(s -> s.getParty() == "Party2" ?
                     Optional.of(s) : Optional.empty())
  .flatMap(o -> o.map(Stream::of).orElseGet(Stream::empty))
  .count();
System.out.println("Members of Party2: " + c2);
```

First, we map (transform) an element (the `Senator` object) to an `Optional` object with or without the value. Next, we use the `flatMap()` method to either generate a stream of a single element or else an empty stream, and then we count the elements that made it through. In Java 9, the `Optional` class acquired a new factory `stream()` method that produces a stream of one element if the `Optional` object carries a non-null value; otherwise, it produces an empty stream. Using this new method, we can rewrite the previous code as follows:

```
long c2 = senators.stream()
  .map(s -> s.getParty() == "Party2" ?
                     Optional.of(s) : Optional.empty())
  .flatMap(Optional::stream)
  .count();
System.out.println("Members of Party2: " + c2);
```

Both the previous examples produce the same output if we run them for the same senate composition:

```
Members of Party2: 42
Members of Party2: 42
```

We can apply another kind of filtering when we need to capture the first element emitted by the stream. This means that we terminate the stream after the first element is emitted. For example, let's find the first senator of `Party1` who voted `Yes` on `issue 3`:

```
senators.stream()
    .filter(s -> s.getParty() == "Party1" &&
                             s.getVoteYes()[3] == 1)
    .findFirst()
    .ifPresent(s -> System.out.println("First senator "
            "of Party1 found who voted Yes on issue 3: "
                             + s.getName())));
```

In the preceding code snippet, we highlighted the `findFirst()` method, which does the described job. It returns the `Optional` object, so we have added another `ifPresent()` operator that is invoked only if the `Optional` object contains a non-null value. The resulting output is as follows:

```
First senator of Party1 found who voted Yes on issue 3: Senator5
```

This was exactly what we expected when we seeded data in the `Senate` class.

Similarly, we can use the `findAny()` method to find any `senator` who voted `Yes` on `issue 3`:

```
senators.stream().filter(s -> s.getVoteYes()[3] == 1)
        .findAny()
        .ifPresent(s -> System.out.println("A senator " +
                "found who voted Yes on issue 3: " + s));
```

The result is also as we expected:

```
A senator found who voted Yes on issue 3: Senator2, P2
```

It is typically (but not necessarily) the first element of the stream. But one should not rely on this assumption, especially in the case of parallel processing.

The `Stream` interface also has three `match` methods that, although they return a Boolean value, can be used for filtering too if the specific object is not required and we only need to establish the fact that such an object exists or not. The names of these methods are `anyMatch()`, `allMatch()`, and `noneMatch()`. Each of them takes a predicate and returns a Boolean. Let's start by demonstrating the `anyMatch()` method. We will use it to find out if there is at least one `senator` of `Party1` who voted `Yes` on `issue 3`:

```
boolean found = senators.stream()
        .anyMatch(s -> (s.getParty() == "Party1" &&
                           s.getVoteYes()[3] == 1));
String res = found ?
    "At least one senator of Party1 voted Yes on issue 3"
    : "Nobody of Party1 voted Yes on issue 3";
System.out.println(res);
```

The result of running the previous code should look like the following:

```
At least one senator of Party1 voted Yes on issue 3
```

To demonstrate the `allMatch()` method, we will use it to find out if all the members of `Party1` in the `Senate` class have voted `Yes` on `issue 3`:

```
boolean yes = senators.stream()
        .allMatch(s -> (s.getParty() == "Party1" &&
                           s.getVoteYes()[3] == 1));
String res = yes ?
    "All senators of Party1 voted Yes on issue 3"
    : "Not all senators of Party1 voted Yes on issue 3";
System.out.println(res);
```

The result of the previous code may look like this:

```
Not all senators of Party1 voted Yes on issue 3
```

And the last of the three `match` methods--the `noneMatch()` method--will be used to figure out if some senators of `Party1` have voted `Yes` on `issue 3`:

```
boolean yes = senators.stream()
    .noneMatch(s -> (s.getParty() == "Party1" &&
                        s.getVoteYes()[3] == 1));
String res = yes ?
    "None of the senators of Party1 voted Yes on issue 3"
    : "Some of senators of Party1 voted Yes on issue 3";
```

```
System.out.println(res);
```

The result of the earlier example is as follows:

```
Some of senators of Party1 voted Yes on issue 3
```

However, in real life, it could be very different because quite a few issues in the `Senate` class are voted for along party lines.

Yet another type of filtering is required when we need to skip all the duplicate elements in a stream and select only unique ones. The `distinct()` method is designed for the purpose. We will use it to find the names of the parties that have their members in the `Senate` class:

```
senators.stream().map(s -> s.getParty())
        .distinct().forEach(System.out::println);
```

The result, as expected, is as follows:

```
Party1
Party2
```

Well, no surprise there?

We can also filter out all the elements of the `stream` except the certain count of the first ones, using the `limit()` method:

```
System.out.println("These are the first 3 senators "
                    + "of Party1 in the list:");
senators.stream()
        .filter(s -> s.getParty() == "Party1")
        .limit(3)
        .forEach(System.out::println);

System.out.println("These are the first 2 senators "
                    + "of Party2 in the list:");
senators.stream().filter(s -> s.getParty() == "Party2")
        .limit(2)
        .forEach(System.out::println);
```

If you remember how we have set up the first five senators in the list, you could predict that the result will be as follows:

```
These are the first 3 senators of Party1 in the list:
Senator1, P1
Senator3, P1
Senator5, P1
These are the first 2 senators of Party2 in the list:
Senator2, P2
Senator4, P2
```

Now let's find only one element in a stream--the biggest one. To do this, we can use the `max()` method of the `Stream` interface and the `Senate.timeVotedYes()` method (we will apply it on each senator):

```
senators.stream()
    .max(Comparator.comparing(Senate::timesVotedYes))
    .ifPresent(s -> System.out.println("A senator voted "
        + "Yes most of times (" + Senate.timesVotedYes(s)
                                    + "): " + s));
```

In the preceding snippet, we use the result of the `timesVotedYes()` method to select the senator who voted `Yes` most often. You might remember, we have assigned all instances of `Yes` to `Senator100`. Let's see if that would be the result:

```
A senator voted Yes most of times (10): Senator100, P2
```

Yes, we got `Senator100` filtered as the one who voted `Yes` on all 10 issues.

Similarly, we can find the senator who voted `No` on all 10 issues:

```
senators.stream()
    .min(Comparator.comparing(Senate::timesVotedYes))
    .ifPresent(s -> System.out.println("A senator voted "
        + "Yes least of times (" + Senate.timesVotedYes(s)
                                    + "): " + s));
```

We expect it to be `Senator99`, and here is the result:

```
A senator voted Yes least of times (0): Senator99, P1
```

That's why we hardcoded several stats in the `Senate` class, so we can verify that our queries work correctly.

As the last two methods can help us with filtering, we will demonstrate the `takeWhile()` and `dropWhile()` methods introduced in JDK 9. We will first print the data of all the first five senators and then use the `takeWhile()` method to print the first senators until we encounter the one who voted `Yes` more than four times, and then stop printing:

```
System.out.println("Here is count of times the first "
                            + "5 senators voted Yes:");
senators.stream().limit(5)
  .forEach(s -> System.out.println(s + ": "
                            + Senate.timesVotedYes(s)));
System.out.println("Stop printing at a senator who "
                        + "voted Yes more than 4 times:");
senators.stream().limit(5)
        .takeWhile(s -> Senate.timesVotedYes(s) < 5)
        .forEach(s -> System.out.println(s + ": "
                            + Senate.timesVotedYes(s)));
```

The result for the previous code is as follows :

```
Here is count of times the first 5 senators voted Yes:
Senator1, P1: 3
Senator2, P2: 4
Senator3, P1: 3
Senator4, P2: 5
Senator5, P1: 3
Stop printing at a senator who voted Yes more than 4 times:
Senator1, P1: 3
Senator2, P2: 4
Senator3, P1: 3
```

The `dropWhile()` method can be used for the opposite effect, that is, to filter away, to skip the first senators until we encounter the one who voted `Yes` more than four times, then continue printing all the rest of the senators:

```
System.out.println("Here is count of times the first "
                            + "5 senators voted Yes:");
senators.stream().limit(5)
        .forEach(s -> System.out.println(s + ": "
                            + Senate.timesVotedYes(s)));
System.out.println("Start printing at a senator who "
                        + "voted Yes more than 4 times:");
senators.stream().limit(5)
        .dropWhile(s -> Senate.timesVotedYes(s) < 5)
        .forEach(s -> System.out.println(s + ": "
```

```
                                        + Senate.timesVotedYes(s)));
        System.out.println("...");
```

The result will be as follows:

```
Here is count of times the first 5 senators voted Yes:
Senator1, P1: 3
Senator2, P2: 4
Senator3, P1: 3
Senator4, P2: 5
Senator5, P1: 3
Start printing at a senator who voted Yes more than 4 times:
Senator4, P2: 5
Senator5, P1: 3
...
```

This concludes our demonstration of the ways in which a stream of elements can be filtered. We hope you have learned enough to be able to find a solution for any of your filtering needs. Nevertheless, we encourage you to study and experiment with the Stream API on your own, so you can retain what you have learned so far and acquire your own view on the rich APIs of Java 9.

Stack-walking APIs

Exceptions do happen, especially during development or the period of software stabilization. But in a big complex system, the chance of getting an exception is possible even in production, especially when several third-party systems are brought together and the need arises to analyze the stack trace programmatically in order to apply an automatic correction. In this section, we will discuss how it can be done.

Stack analysis before Java 9

The traditional reading of the stack trace, using objects of the java.lang.Thread and java.lang.Throwable classes, was accomplished by capturing it from the standard output. For example, we can include this line in any section of the code:

```
Thread.currentThread().dumpStack();
```

The previous line will produce the following output:

```
java.lang.Exception: Stack trace
    at java.base/java.lang.Thread.dumpStack(Thread.java:1435)
    at com.packt.java9hp.ch11_newapis.Demo02StackWalking.demo_standard_output(Demo02Stack
    at com.packt.java9hp.ch11_newapis.Demo02StackWalking.main(Demo02StackWalking.java:15)
```

Similarly, we can include this line in the code:

```
new Throwable().printStackTrace();
```

The output will then look like this:

```
java.lang.Throwable
    at com.packt.java9hp.ch11_newapis.Demo02StackWalking.demo_standard_output2(Demo02Stack
    at com.packt.java9hp.ch11_newapis.Demo02StackWalking.main(Demo02StackWalking.java:16)
```

This output can be captured, read, and analyzed programmatically, but requires quite a bit of custom code writing.

JDK 8 made this easier via the usage of streams. Here is the code that allows reading the stack trace from the stream:

```
Arrays.stream(Thread.currentThread().getStackTrace())
        .forEach(System.out::println);
```

The previous line produces the following output:

```
java.base/java.lang.Thread.getStackTrace(Thread.java:1654)
com.packt.java9hp.ch11_newapis.Demo02StackWalking.demo_reading_stream1(Demo02Stack
com.packt.java9hp.ch11_newapis.Demo02StackWalking.main(Demo02StackWalking.java:18)
```

Alternatively, we could use this code:

```
Arrays.stream(new Throwable().getStackTrace())
        .forEach(System.out::println);
```

The output of the previous code shows the stack trace in a similar way:

```
com.packt.java9hp.ch11_newapis.Demo02StackWalking.demo_reading_stream2(Demo02Stack
com.packt.java9hp.ch11_newapis.Demo02StackWalking.main(Demo02StackWalking.java:19)
```

If, for example, you would like to find the fully qualified name of the caller class, you can use one of these approaches:

```
new Throwable().getStackTrace()[1].getClassName();

Thread.currentThread().getStackTrace()[2].getClassName();
```

Such coding is possible because the `getStackTrace()` method returns an array of objects of the `java.lang.StackTraceElement` class, each representing a stack frame in a stack trace. Each object carries stack trace information accessible by the `getFileName()`, `getClassName()`, `getMethodName()`, and `getLineNumber()` methods.

To demonstrate how it works, we have created three classes, `Clazz01`, `Clazz02`, and `Clazz03`, that call each other:

```
public class Clazz01 {
   public void method(){ new Clazz02().method();  }
}
public class Clazz02 {
   public void method(){ new Clazz03().method();  }
}
public class Clazz03 {
   public void method(){
     Arrays.stream(Thread.currentThread()
                        .getStackTrace()).forEach(ste -> {
       System.out.println();
       System.out.println("ste=" + ste);
       System.out.println("ste.getFileName()=" +
                                      ste.getFileName());
       System.out.println("ste.getClassName()=" +
                                      ste.getClassName());
       System.out.println("ste.getMethodName()=" +
                                      ste.getMethodName());
       System.out.println("ste.getLineNumber()=" +
                                      ste.getLineNumber());
     });
   }
}
```

Now, let's call the `method()` method of `Clazz01`:

```
public class Demo02StackWalking {
    public static void main(String... args) {
        demo_walking();
    }
    private static void demo_walking(){
        new Clazz01().method();
```

```
      }
   }
```

Here are two (the second and the third) of the six stack trace frames printed out by the preceding code:

```
ste=com.packt.java9hp.ch11_newapis.walk.Clazz03.method(Clazz03.java:12)
ste.getFileName()=Clazz03.java
ste.getClassName()=com.packt.java9hp.ch11_newapis.walk.Clazz03
ste.getMethodName()=method
ste.getLineNumber()=12

ste=com.packt.java9hp.ch11_newapis.walk.Clazz02.method(Clazz02.java:9)
ste.getFileName()=Clazz02.java
ste.getClassName()=com.packt.java9hp.ch11_newapis.walk.Clazz02
ste.getMethodName()=method
ste.getLineNumber()=9
```

In principle, every called class has access to this information. But to find out which class called the current class may not be so easy because you need to figure out which frame represents the caller. Also, in order to provide this info, JVM captures the entire stack (except for the hidden stack frames), and it may affect performance.

That was the motivation for introducing the `java.lang.StackWalker` class, its nested `Option` class, and the `StackWalker.StackFrame` interface in JDK 9.

New better way to walk the stack

The `StackWalker` class has four `getInstance()` static factory methods:

- `getInstance()`: This returns a `StackWalker` class instance configured to skip all hidden frames and the caller class reference

- `getInstance(StackWalker.Option option)`: This creates a `StackWalker` class instance with the given option specifying the stack frame information it can access

- `getInstance(Set<StackWalker.Option> options)`: This creates a `StackWalker` class instance with the given set of options

- `getInstance(Set<StackWalker.Option> options, int estimatedDepth)`: This allows you to pass in the `estimatedDepth` parameter that specifies the estimated number of stack frames this instance will traverse so that the Java machine can allocate the appropriate buffer size it might need

The value passed as an option can be one of the following:

- `StackWalker.Option.RETAIN_CLASS_REFERENCE`
- `StackWalker.Option.SHOW_HIDDEN_FRAMES`
- `StackWalker.Option.SHOW_REFLECT_FRAMES`

The other three methods of the `StackWalker` class are as follows:

- `T walk(Function<Stream<StackWalker.StackFrame>, T> function)`: This applies the passed in function to the stream of stack frames, the first frame representing the method that called this `walk()` method
- `void forEach(Consumer<StackWalker.StackFrame> action)`: This performs the passed in action on each element (of the `StalkWalker.StackFrame` interface type) of the stream of the current thread
- `Class<?> getCallerClass()`: This gets objects of the `Class` class of the caller class

As you can see, it allows much more straightforward stack trace analysis. Let's modify our demo classes using the following code and access the caller name in one line:

```java
public class Clazz01 {
  public void method(){
    System.out.println("Clazz01 was called by " +
      StackWalker.getInstance(StackWalker
        .Option.RETAIN_CLASS_REFERENCE)
        .getCallerClass().getSimpleName());
    new Clazz02().method();
  }
}
public class Clazz02 {
  public void method(){
    System.out.println("Clazz02 was called by " +
      StackWalker.getInstance(StackWalker
        .Option.RETAIN_CLASS_REFERENCE)
        .getCallerClass().getSimpleName());
    new Clazz03().method();
  }
}
public class Clazz03 {
  public void method(){
    System.out.println("Clazz01 was called by " +
      StackWalker.getInstance(StackWalker
        .Option.RETAIN_CLASS_REFERENCE)
        .getCallerClass().getSimpleName());
  }
```

```
}
```

The previous code will produce this output:

```
Clazz01 was called by Demo02StackWalking
Clazz02 was called by Clazz01
Clazz03 was called by Clazz02
```

You can appreciate the simplicity of the solution. If we need to see the entire stack trace, we can add the following line to the code in Clazz03:

```
StackWalker.getInstance().forEach(System.out::println);
```

The resulting output will be as follows:

```
Clazz01 was called by Demo02StackWalking
Clazz02 was called by Clazz01
Clazz03 was called by Clazz02
com.packt.java9hp.ch11_newapis.walk.Clazz03.method(Clazz03.java:33)
com.packt.java9hp.ch11_newapis.walk.Clazz02.method(Clazz02.java:9)
com.packt.java9hp.ch11_newapis.walk.Clazz01.method(Clazz01.java:10)
com.packt.java9hp.ch11_newapis.Demo02StackWalking.demo_walking(Demo02StackWalking.java:13)
com.packt.java9hp.ch11_newapis.Demo02StackWalking.main(Demo02StackWalking.java:10)
```

Again, with only one line of code, we have achieved much more readable output. We could achieve the same result by using the walk() method:

```
StackWalker.getInstance().walk(sf -> {
  sf.forEach(System.out::println); return null;
});
```

Instead of just printing StackWalker.StackFrame, we also could run a deeper analysis on it, if need be, using its API, which is more extensive than the API of java.lang.StackTraceElement. Let's run the code example that prints every stack frame and its information:

```
StackWalker stackWalker =
    StackWalker.getInstance(Set.of(StackWalker
                    .Option.RETAIN_CLASS_REFERENCE), 10);
stackWalker.forEach(sf -> {
    System.out.println();
    System.out.println("sf="+sf);
    System.out.println("sf.getFileName()=" +
                                    sf.getFileName());
```

```
              System.out.println("sf.getClass()=" + sf.getClass());
              System.out.println("sf.getMethodName()=" +
                                              sf.getMethodName());
              System.out.println("sf.getLineNumber()=" +
                                              sf.getLineNumber());
              System.out.println("sf.getByteCodeIndex()=" +
                                              sf.getByteCodeIndex());
              System.out.println("sf.getClassName()=" +
                                              sf.getClassName());
              System.out.println("sf.getDeclaringClass()=" +
                                              sf.getDeclaringClass());
              System.out.println("sf.toStackTraceElement()=" +
                                              sf.toStackTraceElement());
      });
```

The output of the previous code is as follows:

```
sf=com.packt.java9hp.ch11_newapis.walk.Clazz03.method(Clazz03.java:63)
sf.getFileName()=Clazz03.java
sf.getClass()=class java.lang.StackFrameInfo
sf.getMethodName()=method
sf.getLineNumber()=63
sf.getByteCodeIndex()=78
sf.getClassName()=com.packt.java9hp.ch11_newapis.walk.Clazz03
sf.getDeclaringClass()=class com.packt.java9hp.ch11_newapis.walk.Clazz03
sf.toStackTraceElement()=com.packt.java9hp.ch11_newapis.walk.Clazz03.method(Clazz03.java:63)
```

Note the `StackFrameInfo` class that implements the `StackWalker.StackFrame` interface and actually does the job. The API also allows converting back to the familiar `StackTraceElement` object for backward compatibility and for the enjoyment of those who are used to it and do not want to change their code and habits.

In contrast, with the full stack trace generated and stored in the array in the memory (like in the case of the traditional stack trace implementation), the `StackWalker` class brings only the requested elements. This is another motivation for its introduction in addition to the demonstrated simplicity of use. More details about the `StackWalker` class API and its usage can be found at `https://docs.oracle.com/javase/9/docs/api/java/lang/StackWalker.html`.

Convenience factory methods for collections

With the introduction of functional programming in Java, the interest in and need for immutable objects increased. The functions passed into the methods may be executed in substantially different contexts than the one they were created in, so the need to decrease the chances of unexpected side effects made the case for immutability stronger. Besides, the Java way of creating an unmodifiable collection was quite verbose anyway, so the issue was addressed in Java 9. Here is an example of the code that creates an immutable collection of the Set interface in Java 8:

```
Set<String> set = new HashSet<>();
set.add("Life");
set.add("is");
set.add("good!");
set = Collections.unmodifiableSet(set);
```

After one does it several times, the need for a convenience method comes up naturally as the basic refactoring consideration that always lingers in the background thinking of any software professional. In Java 8, the previous code could be changed to the following:

```
Set<String> immutableSet =
  Collections.unmodifiableSet(new HashSet<>(Arrays
                      .asList("Life", "is", "good!")));
```

Alternatively, if streams are your friends, you could write the following:

```
Set<String> immutableSet = Stream.of("Life","is","good!")
  .collect(Collectors.collectingAndThen(Collectors.toSet(),
                      Collections::unmodifiableSet));
```

Another version of the previous code is as follows:

```
Set<String> immutableSet =
  Collections.unmodifiableSet(Stream.of("Life","is","good!")
                      .collect(Collectors.toSet()));
```

However, it has more boilerplate code than the values you are trying to encapsulate. So, in Java 9, a shorter version of the previous code became possible:

```
Set<String> immutableSet = Set.of("Life","is","good!");
```

Similar factories were introduced to generate immutable collections of `List` interfaces and `Map` interfaces:

```
List<String> immutableList = List.of("Life","is","good!");

Map<Integer,String> immutableMap1 =
                Map.of(1, "Life", 2, "is", 3, "good!");

Map<Integer,String> immutableMap2 =
        Map.ofEntries(entry(1, "Life "), entry(2, "is"),
                                    entry(3, "good!");

Map.Entry<Integer,String> entry1 = Map.entry(1,"Life");
Map.Entry<Integer,String> entry2 = Map.entry(2,"is");
Map.Entry<Integer,String> entry3 = Map.entry(3,"good!");
Map<Integer,String> immutableMap3 =
                Map.ofEntries(entry1, entry2, entry3);
```

Why new factory methods?

The ability to express the same functionality in more compact manner is very helpful, but it would probably not be enough motivation to introduce these new factories. It was much more important to address the weakness of the existing implementation of `Collections.unmodifiableList()`, `Collections.unmodifiableSet()`, and `Collections.unmodifiableMap()`. Although the collections created using these methods throw an `UnsupportedOperationException` class when you try to modify or add/remove their elements, they are just wrappers around the traditional modifiable collections and can thus be susceptible to modifications, depending on the way you construct them. Let's walk through examples to illustrate the point. By the way, another weakness of the existing unmodifiable implementation is that it does not change how the source collection is constructed, so the difference between `List`, `Set`, and `Map`--the ways in which they can be constructed--remains in place, which may be a source of bugs or even frustration when a programmer uses them. The new factory methods address this issue too, providing a more unified approach using the `of()` factory method (and the additional `ofEntries()` method for `Map`) only. Having said that, let's get back to the examples. Look at the following code snippet:

```
List<String> list = new ArrayList<>();
list.add("unmodifiableList1: Life");
list.add(" is");
list.add(" good! ");
list.add(null);
list.add("\n\n");
```

```
List<String> unmodifiableList1 =
                    Collections.unmodifiableList(list);
//unmodifiableList1.add(" Well..."); //throws exception
//unmodifiableList1.set(2, " sad."); //throws exception
unmodifiableList1.stream().forEach(System.out::print);

list.set(2, " sad. ");
list.set(4, " ");
list.add("Well...\n\n");
unmodifiableList1.stream().forEach(System.out::print);
```

Attempts of direct modification of the elements of `unmodifiableList1` lead to `UnsupportedOperationException`. Nevertheless, we can modify them via the underlying `list` object. If we run the previous example, the output will be as follows:

```
unmodifiableList1: Life is good! null

unmodifiableList1: Life is sad. null Well...
```

Even if we use `Arrays.asList()` for the source list creation, it will only protect the created collection from adding a new element, but not from modifying the existing one. Here is a code example:

```
List<String> list2 =
        Arrays.asList("unmodifiableList2: Life",
                    " is", " good! ", null, "\n\n");
List<String> unmodifiableList2 =
                    Collections.unmodifiableList(list2);
//unmodifiableList2.add(" Well..."); //throws exception
//unmodifiableList2.set(2, " sad."); //throws exception
unmodifiableList2.stream().forEach(System.out::print);

list2.set(2, " sad. ");
//list2.add("Well...\n\n");  //throws exception
unmodifiableList2.stream().forEach(System.out::print);
```

If we run the previous code, the output will be as follows:

```
unmodifiableList2: Life is good! null

unmodifiableList2: Life is sad. null
```

We also included a `null` element to demonstrate how the existing implementation treats them, because, by contrast, the new factories of immutable collections do not allow `null` to be included. By the way, they do not allow duplicate elements in `Set` either (while the existing implementation just ignores them), but we will demonstrate this aspect later while using the new factory methods in code examples.

To be fair, there is a way to create a truly immutable collection of `List` interfaces with the existing implementation too. Look at the following code:

```
List<String> immutableList1 =
        Collections.unmodifiableList(new ArrayList<>() {{
            add("immutableList1: Life");
            add(" is");
            add(" good! ");
            add(null);
            add("\n\n");
        }});
//immutableList1.set(2, " sad.");      //throws exception
//immutableList1.add("Well...\n\n");   //throws exception
immutableList1.stream().forEach(System.out::print);
```

Another way to create an immutable list is as follows:

```
List<String> immutableList2 =
  Collections.unmodifiableList(Stream
    .of("immutableList2: Life"," is"," good! ",null,"\n\n")
    .collect(Collectors.toList()));
//immutableList2.set(2, " sad.");      //throws exception
//immutableList2.add("Well...\n\n");   //throws exception
immutableList2.stream().forEach(System.out::print);
```

The following is a variation of the earlier code:

```
List<String> immutableList3 =
  Stream.of("immutableList3: Life",
                        " is"," good! ",null,"\n\n")
    .collect(Collectors.collectingAndThen(Collectors.toList(),
                        Collections::unmodifiableList));
//immutableList3.set(2, " sad.");      //throws exception
//immutableList3.add("Well...\n\n");   //throws exception
immutableList3.stream().forEach(System.out::print);
```

If we run the previous three examples, we will see the following output:

```
immutableList1: Life is good! null

immutableList2: Life is good! null

immutableList3: Life is good! null
```

Note that although we cannot modify the content of these lists, we can put `null` in them.

The situation with `Set` is quite similar to what we have seen with the lists earlier. Here is the code that shows how an unmodifiable collection of `Set` interfaces can be modified:

```
Set<String> set = new HashSet<>();
set.add("unmodifiableSet1: Life");
set.add(" is");
set.add(" good! ");
set.add(null);
Set<String> unmodifiableSet1 =
                    Collections.unmodifiableSet(set);
//unmodifiableSet1.remove(" good! "); //throws exception
//unmodifiableSet1.add("...Well..."); //throws exception
unmodifiableSet1.stream().forEach(System.out::print);
System.out.println("\n");

set.remove(" good! ");
set.add("...Well...");
unmodifiableSet1.stream().forEach(System.out::print);
System.out.println("\n");
```

The resulting collection of `Set` interfaces can be modified even if we convert the original collection from an array to a list and then to a set, as follows:

```
Set<String> set2 =
   new HashSet<>(Arrays.asList("unmodifiableSet2: Life",
                               " is", " good! ", null));
Set<String> unmodifiableSet2 =
                    Collections.unmodifiableSet(set2);
//unmodifiableSet2.remove(" good! "); //throws exception
//unmodifiableSet2.add("...Well..."); //throws exception
unmodifiableSet2.stream().forEach(System.out::print);
System.out.println("\n");

set2.remove(" good! ");
set2.add("...Well...");
unmodifiableSet2.stream().forEach(System.out::print);
System.out.println("\n");
```

Here is the output of running the previous two examples:

```
nullunmodifiableSet1: Life good!  is

nullunmodifiableSet1: Life is...Well...

null good!  isunmodifiableSet2: Life

null isunmodifiableSet2: Life...Well...
```

If you have not worked with sets in Java 9, you may be surprised to see the unusually messed up order of the set elements in the output. In fact, it is another new feature of set and maps introduced in JDK 9. In the past, `Set` and `Map` implementations did not guarantee to preserve the elements' order. But more often than not, the order was preserved and some programmers wrote code that relied on it, thus introducing an annoyingly inconsistent and not easily reproducible defect into an application. The new `Set` and `Map` implementations change the order more often, if not at every new run of the code. This way, it exposes potential defects early in development and decreases the chance of its propagation into production.

Similar to the lists, we can create immutable sets even without using Java 9's new immutable set factory. One way to do it is as follows:

```java
Set<String> immutableSet1 =
    Collections.unmodifiableSet(new HashSet<>() {{
            add("immutableSet1: Life");
            add(" is");
            add(" good! ");
            add(null);
        }});
//immutableSet1.remove(" good! "); //throws exception
//immutableSet1.add("...Well..."); //throws exception
immutableSet1.stream().forEach(System.out::print);
System.out.println("\n");
```

Also, as in the case with lists, here is another way to do it:

```java
Set<String> immutableSet2 =
    Collections.unmodifiableSet(Stream
        .of("immutableSet2: Life"," is"," good! ", null)
                        .collect(Collectors.toSet()));
//immutableSet2.remove(" good!"); //throws exception
//immutableSet2.add("...Well..."); //throws exception
immutableSet2.stream().forEach(System.out::print);
```

```
System.out.println("\n");
```

Another variant of the previous code is as follows:

```
Set<String> immutableSet3 =
  Stream.of("immutableSet3: Life"," is"," good! ", null)
   .collect(Collectors.collectingAndThen(Collectors.toSet(),
                      Collections::unmodifiableSet));
//immutableList5.set(2, "sad.");   //throws exception
//immutableList5.add("Well...");   //throws exception
immutableSet3.stream().forEach(System.out::print);
System.out.println("\n");
```

f we run all three examples of creating an immutable collection of iSet interfaces that we have just introduced, the result would be as follows:

```
nullimmutableSet1: Life good!  is

nullimmutableSet2: Life good!  is

null good! immutableSet3: Life is
```

With Map interfaces, we were able to come up with only one way to modify the unmodifiableMap object:

```
Map<Integer, String> map = new HashMap<>();
map.put(1, "unmodifiableleMap: Life");
map.put(2, " is");
map.put(3, " good! ");
map.put(4, null);
map.put(5, "\n\n");
Map<Integer, String> unmodifiableleMap =
                    Collections.unmodifiableMap(map);
//unmodifiableleMap.put(3, " sad.");    //throws exception
//unmodifiableleMap.put(6, "Well...");  //throws exception
unmodifiableleMap.values().stream()
                       .forEach(System.out::print);
map.put(3, " sad. ");
map.put(4, "");
map.put(5, "");
map.put(6, "Well...\n\n");
unmodifiableleMap.values().stream()
                       .forEach(System.out::print);
```

The output of the previous code is as follows:

```
unmodifiableleMap: Life is good! null

unmodifiableleMap: Life is sad. Well...
```

We found four ways to create an immutable collection of Map interfaces without using Java 9 enhancements. Here is the first example:

```
Map<Integer, String> immutableMap1 =
        Collections.unmodifiableMap(new HashMap<>() {{
            put(1, "immutableMap1: Life");
            put(2, " is");
            put(3, " good! ");
            put(4, null);
            put(5, "\n\n");
        }});
//immutableMap1.put(3, " sad. ");    //throws exception
//immutableMap1.put(6, "Well...");   //throws exception
immutableMap1.values().stream().forEach(System.out::print);
```

The second example has a bit of a complication:

```
String[][] mapping =
        new String[][] {{"1", "immutableMap2: Life"},
                        {"2", " is"}, {"3", " good! "},
                        {"4", null}, {"5", "\n\n"}};

Map<Integer, String> immutableMap2 =
   Collections.unmodifiableMap(Arrays.stream(mapping)
     .collect(Collectors.toMap(a -> Integer.valueOf(a[0]),
                         a -> a[1] == null? "" : a[1])));
immutableMap2.values().stream().forEach(System.out::print);
```

We tried first to use `Collectors.toMap(a -> Integer.valueOf(a[0]), a -> a[1])`, but the `toMap()` method uses the `merge()` functions which does not allow `null` as a value. So, we had to add a check for `null` and replace it with an empty `String` value. This, in effect, brought us to the next version of the previous code snippet--without a `null` value in the source array:

```
String[][] mapping =
    new String[][]{{"1", "immutableMap3: Life"},
        {"2", " is"}, {"3", " good! "}, {"4", "\n\n"}};
Map<Integer, String> immutableMap3 =
    Collections.unmodifiableMap(Arrays.stream(mapping)
      .collect(Collectors.toMap(a -> Integer.valueOf(a[0]),
```

```
    a -> a[1])));
//immutableMap3.put(3, " sad.");    //throws Exception
//immutableMap3.put(6, "Well...");  //throws exception
immutableMap3.values().stream().forEach(System.out::print);
```

A variant of the previous code is as follows:

```
mapping[0][1] = "immutableMap4: Life";
Map<Integer, String> immutableMap4 = Arrays.stream(mapping)
            .collect(Collectors.collectingAndThen(Collectors
             .toMap(a -> Integer.valueOf(a[0]), a -> a[1]),
                          Collections::unmodifiableMap));
//immutableMap4.put(3, " sad.");     //throws exception
//immutableMap4.put(6, "Well...");   //throws exception
immutableMap4.values().stream().forEach(System.out::print);
```

After we run all the four last examples, the output is as follows:

```
immutableMap1: Life is good! null

immutableMap2: Life is good!

immutableMap3: Life is good!

immutableMap4: Life is good!
```

With that revision of the existing collections implementations, we can now discuss and appreciate the new factory methods of collections in Java 9.

The new factory methods in action

After revisiting the existing methods of collection creation, we can now review and enjoy the related API introduced in Java 9. As in a previous section, we start with the `List` interface. Here is how simple and consistent the immutable list creation can be using the new `List.of()` factory method:

```
List<String> immutableList =
  List.of("immutableList: Life",
      " is", " is", " good!\n\n"); //, null);
//immutableList.set(2, "sad.");    //throws exception
//immutableList.add("Well...");    //throws exception
immutableList.stream().forEach(System.out::print);
```

As you can see from the previous code comments, the new factory method does not allow including `null` as the list value.

The `immutableSet` creation looks similar to this:

```
Set<String> immutableSet =
    Set.of("immutableSet: Life", " is", " good!");
                                //, " is" , null);
//immutableSet.remove(" good!\n\n");  //throws exception
//immutableSet.add("...Well...\n\n"); //throws exception
immutableSet.stream().forEach(System.out::print);
System.out.println("\n");
```

As you can see from the previous code comments, the `Set.of()` factory method does not allow adding `null` or a duplicate element when creating an immutable collection of `Set` interfaces.

The immutable collection of `Map` interfaces has similar format too:

```
Map<Integer, String> immutableMap =
    Map.of(1</span>, "immutableMap: Life", 2, " is", 3, " good!");
                                //, 4, null);
//immutableMap.put(3, " sad.");     //throws exception
//immutableMap.put(4, "Well...");   //throws exception
immutableMap.values().stream().forEach(System.out::print);
System.out.println("\n");
```

The `Map.of()` method does not allow `null` as a value either. Another feature of the `Map.of()` method is that it allows a compile-time check of the element type, which decreases the chances of a runtime problem.

For those who prefer more compact code, here is another way to express the same functionality:

```
Map<Integer, String> immutableMap3 =
            Map.ofEntries(entry(1, "immutableMap3: Life"),
                    entry(2, " is"), entry(3, " good!"));
immutableMap3.values().stream().forEach(System.out::print);
System.out.println("\n");
```

And here is the output if we run all the previous examples of the usage of the new factory methods:

```
immutableList: Life is is good!

immutableSet: Life is good!

 good! isimmutableMap: Life

 good! isimmutableMap2: Life

 good! isimmutableMap3: Life
```

As we mentioned already, the ability to have immutable collections, including empty ones, is very helpful for functional programming as this feature makes sure that such a collection cannot be modified as a side effect and cannot introduce unexpected and difficult to trace defects. The full variety of the new factories methods includes up to 10 explicit entries plus one with an arbitrary number of elements. Here's how it looks for List interface:

```
static <E> List<E> of()
static <E> List<E> of(E e1)
static <E> List<E> of(E e1, E e2)
static <E> List<E> of(E e1, E e2, E e3)
static <E> List<E> of(E e1, E e2, E e3, E e4)
static <E> List<E> of(E e1, E e2, E e3, E e4, E e5)
static <E> List<E> of(E e1, E e2, E e3, E e4, E e5, E e6)
static <E> List<E> of(E e1, E e2, E e3, E e4, E e5, E e6, E e7)
static <E> List<E> of(E e1, E e2, E e3, E e4, E e5, E e6, E e7, E e8)
static <E> List<E> of(E e1, E e2, E e3, E e4, E e5, E e6, E e7, E e8, E e9)
static <E> List<E> of(E e1, E e2, E e3, E e4, E e5, E e6, E e7, E e8, E e9,
E e10)
static <E> List<E> of(E... elements)
```

The Set factory methods look similar:

```
static <E> Set<E> of()
static <E> Set<E> of(E e1)
static <E> Set<E> of(E e1, E e2)
static <E> Set<E> of(E e1, E e2, E e3)
static <E> Set<E> of(E e1, E e2, E e3, E e4)
static <E> Set<E> of(E e1, E e2, E e3, E e4, E e5)
static <E> Set<E> of(E e1, E e2, E e3, E e4, E e5, E e6)
static <E> Set<E> of(E e1, E e2, E e3, E e4, E e5, E e6, E e7)
static <E> Set<E> of(E e1, E e2, E e3, E e4, E e5, E e6, E e7, E e8)
static <E> Set<E> of(E e1, E e2, E e3, E e4, E e5, E e6, E e7, E e8, E e9)
static <E> Set<E> of(E e1, E e2, E e3, E e4, E e5, E e6, E e7, E e8, E e9,
E e10)
```

```
static <E> Set<E> of(E... elements)
```

Also, the `Map` factory methods follow suit:

```
static <K,V> Map<K,V> of()
static <K,V> Map<K,V> of(K k1, V v1)
static <K,V> Map<K,V> of(K k1, V v1, K k2, V v2)
static <K,V> Map<K,V> of(K k1, V v1, K k2, V v2, K k3, V v3)
static <K,V> Map<K,V> of(K k1, V v1, K k2, V v2, K k3, V v3, K k4, V v4)
static <K,V> Map<K,V> of(K k1, V v1, K k2, V v2, K k3, V v3, K k4, V v4, K
k5, V   v5
static <K,V> Map<K,V> of(K k1, V v1, K k2, V v2, K k3, V v3, K k4, V v4, K
k5, V v5, K k6, V v6)
static <K,V> Map<K,V> of(K k1, V v1, K k2, V v2, K k3, V v3, K k4, V v4, K
k5, V v5, K k6, V v6, K k7, V v7
static <K,V> Map<K,V> of(K k1, V v1, K k2, V v2, K k3, V v3, K k4, V v4, K
k5, V v5, K k6, V v6, K k7, V v7,
K k8, V v8)
static <K,V> Map<K,V> of(K k1, V v1, K k2, V v2, K k3, V v3, K k4, V v4, K
k5, V v5, K k6, V v6, K k7, V v7,
K k8, V v8, K k9, V v9)
static <K,V> Map<K,V> of(K k1, V v1, K k2, V v2, K k3, V v3, K k4, V v4, K
k5, V v5, K k6, V v6, K k7, V v7,
K k8, V v8, K k9, V v9, K k10, V v10)
static <K,V> Map<K,V> ofEntries(Map.Entry<? extends K,? extends V>...
entries
```

The decision not to add new interfaces for immutable collections left them susceptible to causing occasional confusion when programmers assumed they could call `add()` or `put()` on them. Such an assumption, if not tested, will cause a runtime error that throws an `UnsupportedOperationException`. Despite this potential pitfall, the new factory methods for immutable collection creation are very useful additions to Java.

CompletableFuture in support of asynchronous processing

The `java.util.concurrent.CompletableFuture<T>` class was first introduced in Java 8. It is the next level of asynchronous call control over `java.util.concurrent.Future<T>` interface. It actually implements `Future`, as well as `java.util.concurrent.CompletionStage<T>`. In Java 9, `CompletableFuture` was enhanced by adding new factory methods, support for delays and timeouts, and improved subclassing--we will discuss these features in more details in the sections to follow. But first, let's have an overview of the `CompletableFuture` API.

The CompletableFuture API overview

The CompletableFuture API consists of more than 70 methods, 38 of which are implementations of the CompletionStage interface, and five are the implementations of Future. Because the CompletableFuture class implements the Future interface, it can be treated as Future and will not break the existing functionality based on the Future API.

So, the bulk of the API comes from CompletionStage. Most of the methods return CompletableFuture (in the CompletionStage interface, they return CompletionStage, but they are converted to CompletableFuture when implemented in CompletableFuture class), which means that they allow chaining the operations similar to how the Stream methods do when only one element goes through a pipe. Each method has a signature that accepts a function. Some methods accept Function<T,U>, which is going to be applied to the passed-in value T and return the result U. Other methods accept Consumer<T>, which takes the passed-in value and returns void. Yet other methods accept Runnable, which does not take any input and returns void. Here is one group of these methods:

```
thenRun(Runnable action)
thenApply(Function<T,U> fn)
thenAccept(Consumer<T> action)
```

They all return CompletableFuture, which carries the result of the function or void (in the case of Runnable and Consumer). Each of them has two companion methods that perform the same function asynchronously. For example, let's take the thenRun(Runnable action) method. The following are its companions:

- The thenRunAsync(Runnable action) method, which runs the action in another thread from the default ForkJoinPool.commonPool() pool
- The thenRun(Runnable action, Executor executor) method, which runs the action in another thread from the pool passed in as the parameter executor

With that, we have covered nine methods of the CompletionStage interface.

Another group of methods consists of the following:

```
thenCompose(Function<T,CompletionStage<U>> fn)
applyToEither(CompletionStage other, Function fn)
acceptEither(CompletionStage other, Consumer action)
runAfterBoth(CompletionStage other, Runnable action)
runAfterEither(CompletionStage other, Runnable action)
thenCombine(CompletionStage<U> other, BiFunction<T,U,V> fn)
thenAcceptBoth(CompletionStage other, BiConsumer<T,U> action)
```

These methods execute the passed in action after one or both the `CompletableFuture` (or `CompletionStage`) objects produce a result that is used as an input to the action. By both, we mean the `CompletableFuture` that provides the method and the one that is passed in as a parameter of the method. From the name of these methods, you can quite reliably guess what their intent is. We will demonstrate some of them in the following examples. Each of these seven methods has two companions for asynchronous processing, too. This means that we have already described 30 (out of 38) methods of the `CompletionStage` interface.

There is a group of two methods that are typically used as terminal operations because they can handle either the result of the previous method (passed in as `T`) or an exception (passed in as `Throwable`):

```
handle(BiFunction<T,Throwable,U> fn)
whenComplete(BiConsumer<T,Throwable> action)
```

We will see an example of the use of these methods later. When an exception is thrown by a method in the chain, all the rest of the chained methods are skipped until the first `handle()` method or `whenComplete()` is encountered. If neither of these two methods are present in the chain, then the exception will bubble up as any other Java exception. These two also have asynchronous companions, which means that we talked about 36 (out of 38) methods of `CompletionStage` interface already.

There is also a method that handles exceptions only (similar to a catch block in the traditional programming):

```
exceptionally(Function<Throwable,T> fn)
```

This method does not have asynchronous companions, just like the last remaining method:

```
toCompletableFuture()
```

It just returns a `CompletableFuture` object with the same properties as this stage. With that, we have described all 38 methods of the `CompletionStage` interface.

There are also some 30 methods in the `CompletableFuture` class that do not belong to any of the implemented interfaces. Some of them return the `CompletableFuture` object after asynchronously executing the provided function:

```
runAsync(Runnable runnable)
runAsync(Runnable runnable, Executor executor)
supplyAsync(Supplier<U> supplier)
supplyAsync(Supplier<U> supplier, Executor executor)
```

Others execute several objects of `CompletableFuture` in parallel:

```
allOf(CompletableFuture<?>... cfs)
anyOf(CompletableFuture<?>... cfs)
```

There is also a group of the methods that generate completed futures, so the `get()` method on the returned `CompletableFuture` object will not block any more:

```
complete(T value)
completedStage(U value)
completedFuture(U value)
failedStage(Throwable ex)
failedFuture(Throwable ex)
completeAsync(Supplier<T> supplier)
completeExceptionally(Throwable ex)
completeAsync(Supplier<T> supplier, Executor executor)
completeOnTimeout(T value, long timeout, TimeUnit unit)
```

The rest of the methods perform various other functions that can be helpful:

```
join()
defaultExecutor()
newIncompleteFuture()
getNow(T valueIfAbsent)
getNumberOfDependents()
minimalCompletionStage()
isCompletedExceptionally()
obtrudeValue(T value)
obtrudeException(Throwable ex)
orTimeout(long timeout, TimeUnit unit)
delayedExecutor(long delay, TimeUnit unit)
```

Refer to the official Oracle documentation, which describes these and other methods of the `CompletableFuture` API at `http://download.java.net/java/jdk9/docs/api/index.html?java/util/concurrent/CompletableFuture.html`.

The CompletableFuture API enhancements in Java 9

Java 9 introduces several enhancements to `CompletableFuture`:

- The `CompletionStage<U> failedStage(Throwable ex)` factory method returns the `CompletionStage` object completed with the given exception

- The `CompletableFuture<U> failedFuture(Throwable ex)` factory method returns the `CompletableFuture` object completed with the given exception
- The new `CompletionStage<U> completedStage(U value)` factory method returns the `CompletionStage` object completed with the given `U` value
- `CompletableFuture<T> completeOnTimeout(T value, long timeout, TimeUnit unit)` completes `CompletableFuture` task with the given `T` value if not otherwise completed before the given timeout
- `CompletableFuture<T> orTimeout(long timeout, TimeUnit unit)` completes `CompletableFuture` with `java.util.concurrent.TimeoutException` if not completed before the given timeout
- It is possible now to override the `defaultExecutor()` method to support another default executor
- A new method, `newIncompleteFuture()`, makes it easier to subclass the `CompletableFuture` class.

The problem and the solution using Future

To demonstrate and appreciate the power of `CompletableFuture`, let's start with a problem implemented using just `Future` and then see how much more effectively it can be solved with `CompletableFuture`. Let's imagine that we are tasked with modeling a building that consists of four stages:

- Collecting materials for the foundation, walls, and roof
- Installing the foundation
- Raising up the walls
- Constructing and finishing the roof

In the traditional sequential programming for the single thread, the model would look like this:

```
StopWatch stopWatch = new StopWatch();
Stage failedStage;
String SUCCESS = "Success";

stopWatch.start();
String result11 = doStage(Stage.FoundationMaterials);
String result12 = doStage(Stage.Foundation, result11);
String result21 = doStage(Stage.WallsMaterials);
String result22 = doStage(Stage.Walls,
```

```
                        getResult(result21, result12));
String result31 = doStage(Stage.RoofMaterials);
String result32 = doStage(Stage.Roof,
                        getResult(result31, result22));
System.out.println("House was" +
        (isSuccess(result32)?"":" not") + " built in "
                + stopWatch.getTime()/1000. + " sec");
```

Here, `Stage` is an enumeration:

```
enum Stage {
    FoundationMaterials,
    WallsMaterials,
    RoofMaterials,
    Foundation,
    Walls,
    Roof
}
```

The `doStage()` method has two overloaded versions. Here is the first one:

```
String doStage(Stage stage) {
    String result = SUCCESS;
    boolean failed = stage.equals(failedStage);
    if (failed) {
        sleepSec(2);
        result = stage + " were not collected";
        System.out.println(result);
    } else {
        sleepSec(1);
        System.out.println(stage + " are ready");
    }
    return result;
}
```

The second version is as follows:

```
String doStage(Stage stage, String previousStageResult) {
  String result = SUCCESS;
  boolean failed = stage.equals(failedStage);
  if (isSuccess(previousStageResult)) {
    if (failed) {
      sleepSec(2);
      result = stage + " stage was not completed";
      System.out.println(result);
    } else {
      sleepSec(1);
      System.out.println(stage + " stage is completed");
```

```
        }
    } else {
        result = stage + " stage was not started because: "
                                    + previousStageResult;
        System.out.println(result);
    }
    return result;
}
```

The `sleepSec()`, `isSuccess()`, and `getResult()` methods look like this:

```
private static void sleepSec(int sec) {
    try {
        TimeUnit.SECONDS.sleep(sec);
    } catch (InterruptedException e) {
    }
}
boolean isSuccess(String result) {
    return SUCCESS.equals(result);
}
String getResult(String result1, String result2) {
    if (isSuccess(result1)) {
        if (isSuccess(result2)) {
            return SUCCESS;
        } else {
            return result2;
        }
    } else {
        return result1;
    }
}
```

The successful house construction (if we run the previous code without assigning any value to the `failedStage` variable) looks like this:

If we set `failedStage=Stage.Walls`, the result will be as follows:

```
FoundationMaterials are ready
Foundation stage is completed
WallsMaterials are ready
Walls stage was not completed
RoofMaterials are ready
Roof stage was not started because: Walls stage was not completed
House was not built in 6.069 sec
```

Using `Future`, we can shorten the time it takes to build the house:

```
ExecutorService execService = Executors.newCachedThreadPool();
Callable<String> t11 =
                      () -> doStage(Stage.FoundationMaterials);
Future<String> f11 = execService.submit(t11);
List<Future<String>> futures = new ArrayList<>();
futures.add(f11);

Callable<String> t21 = () -> doStage(Stage.WallsMaterials);
Future<String> f21 = execService.submit(t21);
futures.add(f21);

Callable<String> t31 = () -> doStage(Stage.RoofMaterials);
Future<String> f31 = execService.submit(t31);
futures.add(f31);

String result1 = getSuccessOrFirstFailure(futures);

String result2 = doStage(Stage.Foundation, result1);
String result3 =
      doStage(Stage.Walls, getResult(result1, result2));
String result4 =
      doStage(Stage.Roof, getResult(result1, result3));
```

Here, the `getSuccessOrFirstFailure()` method looks like this:

```
String getSuccessOrFirstFailure(
                      List<Future<String>> futures) {
    String result = "";
    int count = 0;
    try {
        while (count < futures.size()) {
            for (Future<String> future : futures) {
                if (future.isDone()) {
                    result = getResult(future);
```

```
                        if (!isSuccess(result)) {
                            break;
                        }
                        count++;
                    } else {
                        sleepSec(1);
                    }
                }
                if (!isSuccess(result)) {
                    break;
                }
            }
        } catch (Exception ex) {
            ex.printStackTrace();
        }
        return result;
    }
```

The successful building of the house now is faster because material collection happens in parallel:

```
RoofMaterials are ready
WallsMaterials are ready
FoundationMaterials are ready
Foundation stage is completed
Walls stage is completed
Roof stage is completed
House was built in 5.039 sec
```

By taking advantage of Java functional programming, we can change the second half of our implementation to the following:

```
Supplier<String> supplier1 =
                () -> doStage(Stage.Foundation, result1);
Supplier<String> supplier2 =
                () -> getResult(result1, supplier1.get());
Supplier<String> supplier3 =
                () -> doStage(Stage.Walls, supplier2.get());
Supplier<String> supplier4 =
                () -> getResult(result1, supplier3.get());
Supplier<String> supplier5 =
                () -> doStage(Stage.Roof, supplier4.get());
System.out.println("House was" +
                (isSuccess(supplier5.get()) ? "" : " not") +
        " built in " + stopWatch.getTime() / 1000. + " sec");
```

The chain of the previous nested functions is triggered by `supplier5.get()` in the last line. It blocks until all the functions are completed sequentially, so there is no performance improvement:

```
Out!!!!!
FoundationMaterials stage is completed
WallsMaterials stage is completed
RoofMaterials stage is completed
Foundation stage is completed
Walls stage is completed
Roof stage is completed
House was built in 4.056 sec
```

And that is as far as we can go with `Future`. Now let's see if we can improve the previous code using `CompletableFuture`.

The solution with CompletableFuture

Here's how we can chain the same operations using the `CompletableFuture` API:

```
stopWatch.start();
ExecutorService pool = Executors.newCachedThreadPool();
CompletableFuture<String> cf1 =
   CompletableFuture.supplyAsync(() ->
         doStageEx(Stage.FoundationMaterials), pool);
CompletableFuture<String> cf2 =
   CompletableFuture.supplyAsync(() ->
               doStageEx(Stage.WallsMaterials), pool);
CompletableFuture<String> cf3 =
   CompletableFuture.supplyAsync(() ->
               doStageEx(Stage.RoofMaterials), pool);
CompletableFuture.allOf(cf1, cf2, cf3)
  .thenComposeAsync(result ->
      CompletableFuture.supplyAsync(() -> SUCCESS), pool)
  .thenApplyAsync(result ->
               doStage(Stage.Foundation, result), pool)
  .thenApplyAsync(result ->
               doStage(Stage.Walls, result), pool)
  .thenApplyAsync(result ->
               doStage(Stage.Roof, result), pool)
  .handleAsync((result, ex) -> {
     System.out.println("House was" +
        (isSuccess(result) ? "" : " not") + " built in "
              + stopWatch.getTime() / 1000. + " sec");
```

```
               if (result == null) {
                 System.out.println("Because: " + ex.getMessage());
                 return ex.getMessage();
               } else {
                 return result;
               }
         }, pool);
      System.out.println("Out!!!!!");
```

To make it work, we had to change the implementation of one of the `doStage()` to `doStageEx()` methods:

```
String doStageEx(Stage stage) {
  boolean failed = stage.equals(failedStage);
  if (failed) {
    sleepSec(2);
    throw new RuntimeException(stage +
                      " stage was not completed");
  } else {
    sleepSec(1);
    System.out.println(stage + " stage is completed");
  }
  return SUCCESS;
}
```

The reason we do this is because the `CompletableFuture.allOf()` method returns `CompletableFuture<Void>`, while we need to communicate to the further stages the result of the first three stages of collecting materials. The result looks now as follows:

```
Out!!!!!
FoundationMaterials stage is completed
WallsMaterials stage is completed
RoofMaterials stage is completed
Foundation stage is completed
Walls stage is completed
Roof stage is completed
House was built in 4.056 sec
```

There are two points to note:

- We used a dedicated pool of threads to run all the operations asynchronously; if there were several CPUs or some operations use IO while others do not, the result could be even better

- The last line of the code snippet (Out!!!!!) came out first, which means that all the chains of the operations related to building the house were executed asynchronously

Now, let's see how the system behaves if one of the first stages of collecting materials fails (`failedStage = Stage.WallsMaterials`):

```
Out!!!!!
RoofMaterials stage is completed
FoundationMaterials stage is completed
House was not built in 2.033 sec
Because: java.lang.RuntimeException: WallsMaterials stage was not completed
```

The exception was thrown by the `WallsMaterials` stage and caught by the `handleAsync()` method, as expected. And, again, the processing was done asynchronously after the Out!!!!! message was printed.

Other useful features of CompletableFuture

One of the great advantages of `CompletableFuture` is that it can be passed around as an object and used several times to start different chains of operations. To demonstrate this capability, let's create several new operations:

```java
String getData() {
  System.out.println("Getting data from some source...");
  sleepSec(1);
  return "Some input";
}
SomeClass doSomething(String input) {
  System.out.println(
    "Doing something and returning SomeClass object...");
  sleepSec(1);
  return new SomeClass();
}
AnotherClass doMore(SomeClass input) {
  System.out.println("Doing more of something and " +
                     "returning AnotherClass object...");
  sleepSec(1);
  return new AnotherClass();
}
YetAnotherClass doSomethingElse(AnotherClass input) {
  System.out.println("Doing something else and " +
```

```
                    "returning YetAnotherClass object...");
    sleepSec(1);
    return new YetAnotherClass();
}
int doFinalProcessing(YetAnotherClass input) {
    System.out.println("Processing and finally " +
                               "returning result...");
    sleepSec(1);
    return 42;
}
AnotherType doSomethingAlternative(SomeClass input) {
    System.out.println("Doing something alternative " +
                  "and returning AnotherType object...");
    sleepSec(1);
    return new AnotherType();
}
YetAnotherType doMoreAltProcessing(AnotherType input) {
    System.out.println("Doing more alternative and " +
                    "returning YetAnotherType object...");
    sleepSec(1);
    return new YetAnotherType();
}
int doFinalAltProcessing(YetAnotherType input) {
    System.out.println("Alternative processing and " +
                          "finally returning result...");
    sleepSec(1);
    return 43;
}
```

The results of these operations are going to be handled by the myHandler() method:

```
int myHandler(Integer result, Throwable ex) {
    System.out.println("And the answer is " + result);
    if (result == null) {
        System.out.println("Because: " + ex.getMessage());
        return -1;
    } else {
        return result;
    }
}
```

Note all the different types returned by the operations. Now we can build a chain that forks in two at some point:

```
ExecutorService pool = Executors.newCachedThreadPool();
CompletableFuture<SomeClass> completableFuture =
    CompletableFuture.supplyAsync(() -> getData(), pool)
       .thenApplyAsync(result -> doSomething(result), pool);
```

```
completableFuture
    .thenApplyAsync(result -> doMore(result), pool)
    .thenApplyAsync(result -> doSomethingElse(result), pool)
    .thenApplyAsync(result -> doFinalProcessing(result), pool)
    .handleAsync((result, ex) -> myHandler(result, ex), pool);

completableFuture
    .thenApplyAsync(result -> doSomethingAlternative(result), pool)
    .thenApplyAsync(result -> doMoreAltProcessing(result), pool)
    .thenApplyAsync(result -> doFinalAltProcessing(result), pool)
    .handleAsync((result, ex) -> myHandler(result, ex), pool);

System.out.println("Out!!!!!");
```

The result of this example is as follows:

```
Getting data from some source...
Out!!!!!
Doing something and returning SomeClass object...
Doing something alternative and returning AnotherType object...
Doing more of something and returning AnotherClass object...
Doing more alternative and returning YetAnotherType object...
Doing something else and returning YetAnotherClass object...
Alternative processing and finally returning result...
Processing and finally returning result...
And the answer is 43
And the answer is 42
```

The CompletableFuture API provides a very rich and well-thought-through API that supports, among other things, the latest trends in reactive microservices because it allows processing data fully asynchronously as it comes in, splitting the flow if needed, and scaling to accommodate the increase of the input. We encourage you to study the examples (many more are provided in the code that accompanies this book) and look at the API at http://download.java.net/java/jdk9/docs/api/index.html?java/util/concurrent/CompletableFuture.html.

Stream API improvements

Most of the new `Stream` API features in Java 9 have already been demonstrated in the section that describes `Stream` filtering. To remind you, here are the examples we have demonstrated based on the `Stream` API improvements in JDK 9:

```
long c1 = senators.stream()
        .flatMap(s -> Stream.ofNullable(s.getParty()
                            == "Party1" ? s : null))
        .count();
System.out.println("OfNullable: Members of Party1: " + c1);

long c2 = senators.stream()
        .map(s -> s.getParty() == "Party2" ? Optional.of(s)
                            : Optional.empty())
        .flatMap(Optional::stream)
        .count();
System.out.println("Optional.stream(): Members of Party2: "
                            + c2);


senators.stream().limit(5)
        .takeWhile(s -> Senate.timesVotedYes(s) < 5)
        .forEach(s -> System.out.println("takeWhile(<5): "
                + s + ": " + Senate.timesVotedYes(s)));

senators.stream().limit(5)
        .dropWhile(s -> Senate.timesVotedYes(s) < 5)
        .forEach(s -> System.out.println("dropWhile(<5): "
                + s + ": " + Senate.timesVotedYes(s)));
```

The only one we have not mentioned yet is the new overloaded `iterate()` method:

```
static <T> Stream<T> iterate(T seed, UnaryOperator<T> f)
```

An example of its usage is as follows:

```
String result =
    IntStream.iterate(1, i -> i + 2)
            .limit(5)
            .mapToObj(i -> String.valueOf(i))
            .collect(Collectors.joining(", "));
System.out.println("Iterate: " + result);
```

We had to add `limit(5)` because this version of the `iterate()` method creates an unlimited stream of integer numbers. The result of the previous code is as follows:

```
Iterate: 1, 3, 5, 7, 9
```

In Java 9, an overloaded `iterate()` method was added:

```
static <T> Stream<T> iterate(T seed,
     Predicate<? super T> hasNext, UnaryOperator<T> next)
```

As you see, it has now a `Predicate` functional interface as a parameter that allows limiting the stream as needed. For example, the following code produces exactly the same result as the previous example with `limit(5)`:

```
String result =
    IntStream.iterate(1, i -> i < 11, i -> i + 2)
             .mapToObj(i -> String.valueOf(i))
             .collect(Collectors.joining(", "));
System.out.println("Iterate: " + result);
```

Note that the type of the stream element does not need to be an integer. It can be any type produced by the source. So, the new `iterate()` method can be used to provide criteria for the termination of the stream of any type of data.

Summary

In this chapter, we covered a lot of ground in the area of the new features introduced with Java 9. First, we looked at many ways to stream filtering, starting with the basic `filter()` method and ending up using the `Stream` API additions of JDK 9. Then, you learned a better way to analyze the stack trace using the new `StackWalker` class. The discussion was illustrated by specific examples that help you to see the real working code.

We used the same approach while presenting new convenient factory methods for creating immutable collections and new capabilities for asynchronous processing that came with the `CompletableFuture` class and its enhancements in JDK 9.

We ended this chapter by enumerating the improvements to the `Stream` API--those we have demonstrated in the filtering code examples and the new `iterate()` method.

Overall, we have shown the richness of Java APIs that has substantially expanded in Java 8 and has continued to improve in Java 9. You can now try and apply the tips and techniques you have learned to your project or, if it is not suitable for that, to build your own Java project for high performance. While doing that, try to solve real problems. That will force you to learn new skills and frameworks instead of just applying the knowledge you have already, although the latter is helpful too--it keeps your knowledge fresh and practical.

The best way to learn is to do it yourself. This is why we included as many examples in the book as we could; try and run them in your environment. There are quite a few other examples included in the companion code for which there was no space in the book. We encourage you to experiment and modify them and take ownership of the solutions that could become the foundation of your new application or framework.

As Java continues to improve and expand, watch out for new editions of this and similar books by Packt.

Index

Printed in Great Britain
by Amazon

56132097R00220